The Strange

of

Dr John

BODKIN ADAMS

and the views of those who knew him

John Surtees

In Eastbourne it is healthy
And the residents are wealthy:
It's a miracle that anybody dies.
Yet this pearl of English lidos
Is a slaughterhouse of widows -
If their bankrolls are above the normal size.

S. B. Publications

By the same author

The House Physician's Handbook
Barracks, workhouse and hospital, St Mary's Eastbourne
The Princess Alice and other Eastbourne hospitals
St Wilfrid's, the Eastbourne and district hospice
Chaseley, a Home from Home
Beachy Head

First published in 2000

District General Hospital
Eastbourne BN21 2UD

A catalogue record for this book is available from the British Library.

ISBN 1 85770 108 9

Front cover illustration by Nick Taylor
Back cover: Dr Bodkin Adams at Lewes Assizes in 1957 {Topham Picturepoint}

Printed by Adland Print Group Ltd
Unit 11 Bellingham Trading Estate, Franthorne Way, London SE6 3BX
Tel (020) 8695 6262

CONTENTS

Acknowledgements

My thanks are especially due to my wife, Sheila, and Vivien Ackroyd, Hugh Alexander, Frank D Alford, JF Allchorn, Mary Alston, Dr DAL Ashforth, Jane Backhouse, Dr FBS Barkworth, Nat Barnardiston, Dr JJ Bending, Steve Benz, Jane Booth-Clibborn, Mr PL Brooks, Dr Ian M Brown, A Caffyn, R Caffyn, Bridget Chapman, Nancy Chapman, Philip G Cheal, John W Cheesborough, Gordon Clark, Michael Clark, Sarah Clarke, Dr Anthony Churcher, JVC Claremont, Eileen R Comer, Dr PL Cook, Mr & Mrs LH Cooper, Doris Cruttenden, Marlene Davey, Roger Davey, D Deamer, Maureen Devlin, Richard Diplock, James Donne, Robert A Elliston, Jill Emslie, Dr Michael J Emslie, TB Entwistle, Supt Clive Evans, David Farmer, Rosie Fern, Jean Fuller, E George, Harry Gibson, Dr Tim Gietzen, Mrs S Gordon, Dr Valerie Gurney, Ray Haine, Jill & Adrian Hamilton, Paul Harris, Dr Vincent Harris, Michael Harding, Brian Harral, Jennifer Herbert, Mrs FM Hobden, Vera Hodsoll, John & Joan Hughes, Barbara Hutchison, Mr & Mrs RC James, Derek G Keay, Lorna Kenward, Yvonne King, Margaret Kinman, William Lawrence and family, Margaret & Nigel Lees, Jessie Leybourne, Dr Keith Liddell, Dr DA McGill, Douglas Martin, Kenneth E Miles, Bruce Money, Dr Colin Morley, MA Morley, Dr MJ Mynott, AG Newman, Dr JD O'Connor, M O'Donnell, Emma Olivari, Liz Oliver-Taylor, Emilio G Orduna, Jo Osbourne, Dr Gordon Ostlere, Olive Pack, AP Page, Ronald Parsons, RE Patching, Dr FR Philps, Patricia Piper, Martha Plant, John D Porter, Ron Price, Hilary Pringle, Mrs G Reynolds, Fiona Robertson, MD Rolfe, Tom Searle, John Seath, Barbara Selby, Doris B Sellens, M Shera, Dr Mary Simpson, Joseph Slater, Duncan Smart, Peter Smith, Adèle Snashall, Mr LAH Snowball, Ron & Joy Spicer, W Stapley, D Stead, Dawn Stebbings, Anthony J Stevens, John Stevens, Dr IT Stuttaford, Donna Taberer, Dr DC Taylor, Edith & Maurice Taylor, Nick Taylor, May Thorne, Louisa Tomasetti, John Underhill, Graham & Jan Upton, Dr KOA Vickery, Eileen Vine, Morris Walker, Ray Ward, Derek Wilkinson, Mr T Henry & Mrs Valerie Wilson, and Pamela Young, and the many others who have contributed.

Associated Newspapers, Arnold Desser, Beckett Newspapers, The British Library Newspaper Library Colindale, Central Library Eastbourne, Clay Pigeon Shooting Association Ltd, Eastbourne Local History Society, Eastbourne Registration District, East Sussex Record Office Lewes, *Daily Express, Daily Herald, Daily Mail, Daily Mirror, Daily Sketch, Daily Telegraph, Eastbourne Herald/Chronicle, Gazette and Advertiser, Evening Argus, Evening Standard, The Guardian*, Solo Syndication, Ian Kemp, *The Independent,* Medical Defence Union, Public Record Office Image Library Kew, Popperfoto, Press Association, *Pulse, News Chronicle, The Times,* Topham Picturepoint, Towner Art Gallery & Local History Museum. See also the selected Bibliography.

Whilst every effort has been made to contact all the relevant people and organisations, it is regretted that at the time of going to press it has not been possible to publish all the names. Those concerned are asked to accept apologies.

John Bodkin Adams

1899 Born 21 January.
1921 Qualifies in medicine.
1922 Comes to Eastbourne as a general practitioner.
1926 Awarded MD, and becomes a partner in the practice.
1930 Buys *Kent Lodge*, Trinity Trees, for £3 000.
1934 Appointed part-time anaesthetist at the Princess Alice Hospital, Eastbourne.
1935 Visits Mayo Clinic, USA.
1936 Becomes senior partner in the practice. Breaks off engagement to Miss Norah O'Hara. A patient, Mrs Matilda Whitton, leaves him over £7 000, contested by the family, judgement given to Dr Adams.
1940 One of the few doctors left in Eastbourne during the war. Works under difficult conditions, and with no private patients.
1941 Takes his Diploma in Anaesthetics.
1943 Mother dies.
1948 Mrs Edith Morrell, 79, has a stroke at her son's home in Cheshire on 25 June. Moves to an Eastbourne nursing home on 5 July. First prescription of morphine by Dr Adams on 9 July.
1949 Mrs Morrell moved to her home *Marden Ash* in Meads, Eastbourne, on 30 March. Dr Adams informs solicitor, Mr H Sogno, that Mrs Morrell wishes to alter her will. Nurses' notebooks date from 21 June.
1950 On 8 March Dr Adams informs solicitor that Mrs Morrell wants to make a new will. Dr Adams goes on holiday to Scotland on 12 September. On 15 September Mrs Morrell cuts Dr Adams out of her will with a codicil. Codicil torn up 23 October. Mrs Morrell dies 13 November.
1955 In November Dr Adams diagnoses cancer of bowel in Mr Jack Hullett. Top surgeon, Sir Arthur Porritt, operates at the Esperance Nursing Home.
1956 Mr Hullett dies on 14 March, leaving £500 to Dr Adams. Mrs Hullett very depressed. On 14 July makes out will leaving Rolls-Royce and £100 to Dr Adams. Mrs Hullett dies at her home *Holywell Mount* of barbiturate overdosage, 23 July. On 21 August, inquest verdict of suicide. The Police search *Kent Lodge* for dangerous drugs on 24 November. Dr Adams charged with murder of Mrs Morrell on 19 December, and later of Mr and Mrs Hullett.
1957 Committal proceedings at Eastbourne Magistrates' Court, 14-23 January, in public. Old Bailey trial starts 18 March. Struck off Medical Register in November.
1961 Restored to the Medical Register.
1983 4 July, dies after falling and breaking his hip.

John Bodkin Adams MD (Belfast) 1926, MB BCh BAO 1921, DPH (Bristol) 1922, DA (Eng) 1941. In May 1957 {Popperfoto}

1. THE SCENE

'A Bodkin, used to do up swaddling clothes, had an ear scoop at one end'

When people who have never been to the town learn that you are from Eastbourne, there are two responses, either "Ah, Beachy Head", or just as likely, "Ah, Bodkin Adams".

If we accept that the chalk cliffs have been there for 80 million years, we must assume that the 20th century event of Eastbourne was 'Dr John', and that his 1957 Old Bailey trial on charges of murdering patients put Eastbourne on the map.

This is despite the inclusion in Eastbourne's story of the Summerdown Camp of 1915-20, where some 150 000 soldiers recovered from 1914-18 war wounds, the largest such camp in Europe. Continuing the military theme there was also the town's heroism in the 1939-45 war, when it was the most bombed town on the south coast. Again, what about the scandal of the 1960s development of South Cliff Tower on land sold by a Mayor of Eastbourne; or the 1992 shame of the local solicitor whose deliberately fraudulent activities led to the biggest claim yet, some £9 million, on the Law Society's Compensation Fund? Yet none have made the impact of Dr John Bodkin Adams.

Clearly, suffering, heroism, infamy and dishonourable conduct do not have the punch to justify the front pages in the press, compared with the tale of a respectable doctor who does away with rich old ladies in a select holiday town.

If you talk to people of a certain age in countries from Australia to Belgium, and from Finland to the Netherlands, they confirm that their local newspapers carried columns of report and comment on the case. In Britain, with the *Daily Mail's* front page headlines of ***The great mystery of Eastbourne,*** and ***Yard study wills of 300 women in £1m probe,*** there was saturation coverage, so much that the judiciary doubted whether Dr Adams could receive a fair trial.

There are many examples of the international coverage, long before the Doctor was charged. *Paris-Match* was in the van, and Vera Hodsoll says that the first foreign periodical she saw with an account was *Time* of the USA, on 24 September 1956. Eugenio Lopez says that Spanish magazines carried the story, and in Munich, the *Revue,* an illustrated magazine, carried articles under titles such as *Kein Platz für reiche Witwen* and *Das tödliche Rezept* in its issues of 22 and 29 September, and 6 and 13 October 1956.

John Underhill recalls that about the time of the trial his son was travelling in France and stopped at a garage in Lyons. When the staff heard he was from Eastbourne they exclaimed, "You must tell us about Bodkin Adams".

Kenneth Miles and his wife were in Southern Rhodesia (now Zimbabwe) during the 1950s. "The local newspaper carried whole pages of reports of the trial each day. To earn an extra bob or two I was even tempted to offer the editor an article on 'I knew Dr Bodkin Adams', but never got round to it".

Whether you consider Bodkin Adams famous or infamous, or whether you consider him guilty or innocent of murdering patients, you have to admit that curiosity about this pudgy, provincial general practitioner will not fade away.

When Lord Devlin, former Lord of Appeal, died a few years ago the national papers were quite definite about his place in the scheme of things. They paid scant attention to the many committees he had competently chaired; failed to highlight the reports he had skilfully produced, and hardly mentioned the many trials over which he had presided. No, their screaming headlines showed they knew where he lay in the hall of fame – ***BODKIN ADAMS' JUDGE DIES.***

Eastbourne: Kein Platz für reiche Witwen

Das tödliche Rezept

Mordverdacht gegen Dr. Adams verstärkt / Scotland Yard will Leichen exhumieren lassen / Patientin zwischen Todesangst und Vertrauen zum Arzt

In dem englischen Luxusbad Eastbourne hat die Untersuchung über Massenmorde an reichen Witwen einen Höhepunkt erreicht: Scotland Yard will die Leiche der 1952 unter verdächtigen Umständen gestorbenen Frau Julia Bradnum exhumieren lassen. Man vermutet, daß durch die Untersuchung der einbalsamierten sterblichen Überreste der im Alter von 85 Jahren gestorbenen Greisin Giftreste festgestellt werden — was den seit vier Wochen unter Mordverdacht stehenden Dr. John Bodkin Adams schwerer belasten würde als alle bisherigen Indizien. Inzwischen gehen die Ermittlungen des Mordspezialisten Kriminalrat Hannam weiter: Testamentsüberprüfungen, Zeugenvernehmungen und chemische Untersuchungen von Erdproben aus den Gräbern der reichen Witwen, die Dr. Adams Patientinnen waren und ihm Geld und Sachwerte hinterließen. In der Coroner-Verhandlung, einem Laiengerichtsverfahren nach dem Tode der Frau Hullet, wurde Hannam gefragt, ob er öffentlich Zeugen vernehmen wolle.

Atemlose Spannung liegt über dem Raum, als der „Graf von Scotland Yard" einen Augenblick nachdenklich mit der gepflegten Hand über sein wohlrasiertes Kinn streicht.

„Nein", sagt er dann und wischt ein Stäubchen von seinem Revers, „ich habe keine Fragen zu stellen."

Der Coroner blickt ihn unverwandt an: „Aber Sie haben vielleicht den Wunsch, eine Vertagung dieser Verhandlung zu beantragen, bis . . ."

„Nein", erwidert Hannam höflich, „auch das ist nicht nötig."

Er wird aus dem Zeugenstand entlassen. Sorgfältig zieht er die Bügelfalten seiner grauen Nadelstreifenhose hoch, als er sich hinsetzt. Dann wirft er einen kurzen Blick hinüber zur Zeugenbank, wo Dr. Adams uninteressiert zwischen seinen gespreizten Knien hindurch den Boden fixiert, beugt sich zu seinem Nebenmann und flüstert ihm etwas zu. Dieser Nebenmann ist Detektiv-Sergeant Charles Hewitt von der Mordabteilung Scotland Yards, Hannams unentbehrlicher Assistent.

Während der Coroner die erste Zeugin aufruft, Miß Evelyn Patricia Tomlinson, die Tochter der verstorbenen Mrs. Hullet aus erster Ehe, lassen die beiden Kriminalbeamten das bisherige Ergebnis ihrer Ermittlungen noch einmal vor ihrem inneren Auge Revue passieren:

In Somerset House, dem britischen Staatsarchiv für die Familiendokumente jedes britischen Staatsbürgers werden in diesen Tagen von einem Dutzend Kriminalbeamten über 400 Testamente überprüft — Testamente von Witwen und alten Jungfern, die in den vergangenen zwanzig Jahren in Eastbourne starben, und von einigen alten Junggesellen, deren merkwürdiger Tod zwar nicht recht ins Konzept von dem „Witwenmörder" paßt.

Fortsetzung übernächste Seite

German magazine "Revue" of 29 September 1956

Yet surely the most incredible example of the Doctor's fame is recounted by a civil engineer, who lived in Eastbourne, but in the course of his work travelled the world erecting bridges and harbours. About 1980 he was sent by an international agency to Albania to build a road. This was before the East-West thaw and, as was the custom, he was assigned a minder. In his description, "A dour young woman, with a purse-string for a mouth, who had never been outside Albania, had learnt her English there, and whose sole knowledge of Britain appeared to be, 'They have Kings and Queens who exploit the workers'. Until, that is, I mentioned that I came from Eastbourne, when immediately her face altered, her eyes lit up, and a smile spread from ear to ear, as she declared, 'Eaastboourne, Budkin Adoms' country'."

It is neither here nor there that that she had been told of the Doctor as an example of the degenerate West, held up by her mentors as a typical example of bourgeois excesses and decadence – never mind that, his fame had spread to isolated Albania. Dr Bodkin Adams, *alias* Budkin Adoms, had penetrated the inner fastnesses of that closed book society. Surely, you can't be much better known than that, can you?

And his trial for murder in 1957 was a remarkable event. At the time it was the longest murder trial of the century.

It was the first English trial in the 20th century of a doctor accused of murdering a patient, and it was possibly a unique case of a doctor charged with murdering a patient in the course of treatment. No one, not even his worst enemies, suggested that Bodkin Adams strangled his ladies with old lace, and they certainly didn't suggest any use of arsenic. Essentially, the rumours were that sometimes he gave too much treatment, or on occasions too little treatment, with the result that his old and infirm patients died sooner than expected, all to his financial benefit.

Among the important consequences of the trial were the introduction of restrictions on the reporting of proceedings in Magistrates' Courts, and changes in the recording and handling of dangerous drugs.

The trial also established a case law that if a doctor administered a drug to a patient with the intention of shortening their life, no matter how ill the patient was, or how slight the shortening, that was murder. On the other hand, if a doctor gave treatment to a seriously ill patient with the aim of relieving or easing pain or distress, and as a result that patient's life was inadvertently shortened, the doctor was not guilty of murder; the doctrine of 'double effect'.

So the Bodkin Adams' trial had far-reaching effects, but the trial also possessed a more immediate *frisson*. In March 1957 the sentence for those found guilty of murder remained hanging by the neck until dead; the last executions in Britain being seven years ahead. The Doctor faced a finality of sentence guaranteed to concentrate the mind of the court, the participants, onlookers, the press and its readers.

It obviously had an effect on Dr Adams too, for he was known to say, 'You know, if they find me guilty, they'll string me up like that', completing his words by flourishing an arm over his head.

Yes, the Doctor had the gift of the gab, and was very likely to come out with an ambiguous remark, if given the chance. You can hear him saying, "I'm sure it was all for the best", "Her time had come", or "I tried to make everything go easy to help the family". He was always helpful, but was it to the patient, the nurses, the family, or himself? You could say he was just the sort who, under cross-examination in court, might helpfully tighten the rope around his own neck. So, what was he like, how did it all come about, who were the heroes and villains, and how did the murder trial go of Doctor Bodkin Adams?

2. THE PATIENT'S FRIEND

John Bodkin Adams was born at the turn of a century, 21 January 1899, in Randalstown, County Antrim, which had a population of some 1000 in the 1890s.

Bodkin was his mother's maiden name. He thought the world of her, but he preferred to be known as John Adams. Perhaps this was because 'Bodkin' became so associated with his newspaper image that he came to dislike it. In spite of his wishes, Bodkin was the name that everyone called him at some time or other.

It is said that the family were not rich. His father, Samuel, a JP, and variously described as a watchmaker and jeweller, in the linen trade, and an engineer, was said to be 'popular and a good man'. Samuel, with his wife Ellen, and their two sons moved to Coleraine to be near John's school, the Academical Institution.

His father died when John was 15, and his younger brother, William, died in his teens during the 1918 influenza pandemic. John missed some schooling with fluid on his lung so, understandably, his mother became very close to him. He does not appear to have been a bright student; determined might better express his approach.

It is alleged that Bodkin Adams was tight with money as a medical student; a situation not unknown amongst undergraduates.

He obtained the degrees of Bachelor of Medicine, Bachelor of Surgery and Bachelor of the Art of Obstetrics [Midwifery] in 1921, to become a medical doctor.

After qualification he met Professor Arthur Rendle Short, a surgeon, at a missionary conference in Belfast and was invited to join his staff in Bristol.

In Dr Adams' words, "I came from Belfast to Bristol to work with Rendle Short, an evangelical doctor. My intention was to go back to Belfast to look after my mother and I asked for six months to get my DPH [Diploma in Public Health], and took a job as the Casualty Officer at Bristol Royal Infirmary". These posts had regular hours and were often used to swot for higher exams.

"When I was working for my DPH the pathologist gave me the key to the fire escape door of the laboratory, so that I could go there out of hours and get the experience needed on the plating and culturing of bacteria. Pneumococci were important then because the organism killed lots of people. I know that they had the smallpox virus in the lab, without any of the fuss which came later. When my colleagues went out of an evening I worked at the books and obtained my DPH.

"Rendle Short asked why not try a practice in England, and there was a colleague working with me who was also thinking of practising in England so I was encouraged.

"I saw an advert for a Christian practice assistant in a fashionable South Coast resort, with a view to partnership, and applied. I heard the post was filled, then two weeks later I received a letter asking me to go for an interview. It was my weekend off - Providence again, you see - and so I came to Eastbourne on a blustery day. I was successful at the interview, and joined the Emerson, Gurney, and Rainey practice in College Road."

This practice, started in 1901 by Dr AC Gurney, was sometimes known as the *Red House* to distinguish it from its rival, the nearby *White House* practice in South Street. The partners started the day with prayers.

The new general practitioner had to buy into the practice for £2000, which he raised by a bank overdraft covered by life insurance. "I was happy to come to Eastbourne because I could make a home for my mother. She was a good sort."

The doctor he replaced, Dr DNB Emerson, was a wealthy man whose family owned estates in the Argentine. He retired to Switzerland shortly afterwards to start up a home for retired missionaries.

The "Red House" practice, College Road, Eastbourne

From 1922 Dr Adams rented Dr Emerson's old home, 12 Upperton Road, near the station. Dr Leslie Muir-Smith, 'Physician and Surgeon', and EH Muir-Smith, dentist, were at number 10 so it was a mini-Wimpole Street, and handy for the Maternity Home on the opposite side of the road. Nurses there say that he seldom drew the curtains and they had a view of him going to bed at night, "Not that we particularly watched", observes Mrs Doris Bates (née Clarke), a student nurse in the 1920s. It is doubtful if there was much to see for, having been joined by his mother and a cousin Florence, the main features of the household were the strongly religious routines of prayer. Even at the surgery the Bible was his main reading, and he went to bed under a wall text of 'Rest in the Lord'.

In a small town of the time a doctor had a standing in society, because he held a close and special relationship with his patients. Surprisingly little could be done to cure in the way of tablets, possibly why surgery was held in such high esteem. Antibiotics had not been discovered, and effective treatments for Pernicious

Anaemia, many cancers, high blood pressure, and the prevention of diphtheria and polio were in the future. It was said the best treatment for pneumonia was a Bart's nurse and morphia. Sudden death from infection in a young, previously healthy person was expected, and months of convalescence after pneumonia or injuries were taken for granted. Yet patients required their suffering to be ameliorated, and relatives needed to be comforted in their distress, and so the doctor's support at such times was vital, marked by the assiduity of his visiting.

Advances were being made, for example, insulin was isolated in 1922. Beforehand if a doctor diagnosed diabetes, and the family was wealthy enough, they were advised to take the patient to the Riviera, where he could enjoy his last few days. If tuberculosis was diagnosed, there was a desperate attempt to obtain one of the few places available in the local sanatorium. Not that much could be done, the mortality in such places was over 50%, but at least the infection was kept away from the family, hence visiting by children was discouraged. Sanatoria practised open-air treatment and perhaps helped to reduce the spread of infection. Elizabeth Brockhurst, a patient at Gildredge Hospital, the local sanatorium, mentions that one day she woke up to find snow on her bed sheets as the windows were kept open all the year. These situations were hard on the patient and family who welcomed any encouragement their doctor, and friend, could provide.

Medical practice had not entirely shed desperate measures. Dr Adams recalled that he used leeches in 1922, for an old lady with pneumonia. "She did very well and made a full recovery. It was the only time I used leeches in Eastbourne."

They were supplied by HR Browne's the main dispensing chemist [pharmacist] which he patronised throughout his professional life. He made occasional sorties when convenient to Harmer's, of South Street, and other pharmacists such as Bessie Temple from Meads, Searle's of Willingdon, and J Senior's of Compton Street. All were later caught up in his 'little problem'.

John Seath, a pharmacist, says, "In those days things were very different, pharmacists made up so many medicines that are now bought in. I would make up ampoules of morphia for Dr Adams and sterilise them in my kitchen at home."

Times were different for the Doctor too. Norman Portis, a patient, said that he remembered Bodkin arriving in Eastbourne with little more than a couple of suitcases, and Douglas Wilson says that in his early months in Eastbourne Dr Adams did his rounds on a bicycle.

For the first few years he rode a motor cycle, a 2½ hp Velocette. Dr Ian M Brown writes of a rumour that Dr Adams had taken part in the Isle of Man Tourist Trophy races, confirming in some minds that he must have been 'mad'. John Waite looked into the records and could find no evidence that the Doctor competed in the official TT, or in the races which follow. He might have ridden over the course in a run for enthusiastic, inexperienced riders, but records are not kept of these. Dr Brown adds that with Bodkin's bulk he was sometimes known as 'Bull' Adams.

Douglas Wilson recalls,"Bodkin Adams was my doctor and my parents' doctor. They ran *Downsmeade* School in Upperton Road and he was the school doctor. They wouldn't hear any ill of the doctor.

"As a child I remember him as a gruff man. He would say, 'What's the matter with you now?' Throughout my childhood I had recurrent attacks of tonsillitis and he was on at my mother to have them out, but mother would say, 'No they have a purpose and he'll keep them'. I continued with attacks until I was about 40."

Nurse Doris Bates says that Dr Bodkin Adams was one of four doctors who gave basic lectures in anatomy, physiology and nursing care at the Maternity Home's baby care unit in the 1920s. "On Twelfth Night there was always a Christmas Dinner and Dance. One year, about 1925, I danced with Dr Bodkin Adams. All I remember was that his dinner jacket smelt strongly of moth balls".

Dr Adams was establishing himself in the town and joined the Eastbourne Medical Society. The first record of him at a meeting was on 26 February 1924 at the Technical Institute, 'JB Adams showed a case of a male baby aged 3 weeks with congenital malformations of both arms. Only four fingers on one hand and no thumb, on the other hand four fingers and a rudimentary thumb. An X-ray photograph showed absence of both radii. Child was fourth in family - the others quite healthy. Dr Adams was thanked for showing the case and asked to show it again in a year's time.' It has to be said that he did not attend consistently.

Richard C James, later a local solicitor says, "From the time Bodkin Adams came to Eastbourne in 1922 my father, Herbert Victor James, was his solicitor. Adams arrived in Eastbourne about the same time as the dentist Norman Gray, and both were connected with the Plymouth Brethren."[1]

It was with Norman Gray that Dr Adams organised Young Crusaders' Bible Classes, at Upperton Road. Kenneth Miles confirms, "He was a supporter of Holy Trinity Church and of the Crusaders Union,[2] a church group helping children."

He was working long hours in the practice too. A nurse said he worked from seven in the morning to nine at night, and a Nursing Home nurse commented that he often visited after nine at night and would never allow a nurse in the room. She added darkly, "The lady visited always had a disturbed night afterwards."

The start of a fruitful relationship began when he was called to *Ratton Place,* the mansion of William E Mawhood, a wealthy steel merchant. Edith, his wife, had injured her leg and although Dr Adams' attempts to treat it did not appear successful and eventually the leg had to be operated on by a London surgeon, the Mawhoods took to him. William Mawhood kept a large establishment, including a gamekeeper for his estate, and the Doctor joined their pheasant shoots.

Dr Adams was a champion shot all his life and so he was welcome to the county set. The Mawhoods introduced him to their friends, and his undoubted energy sealed his success. Over time he added many of the Sussex shootin' and fishin' fraternity to his list of patients.

The practice of Gurney, Rainey and Adams, prospered so they took on another assistant, Dr HCV Joy, who had worked as a missionary in Africa.

Drs Gurney and Rainey decided that Adams should have a car. The College Road surgery had a lucrative clientele, with some patients living permanently in private suites at the *Grand Hotel* where Gurney (of Barts) and Rainey (of The London) would call in their cars. When he stood in for them, and turned up on his bike, he rather let the side down. Adams argued that cycling was good for him, and in view of his love of sweets and rich puddings, kept his weight down. He added, in a typical Bodkinism, that if they insisted on him having a car, the practice should pay for it. Perhaps, but not the response designed to endear him to his partners.

James Donne, a Sussex journalist wrote, "Adams could be very persuasive. He had a way with people that is very difficult to explain. He was an Irish doctor among doctors of mainly Scottish descent, and his Irish charm more than made up for his few years of medical experience, and it worked like magic".

So within two years of joining the practice Dr Adams bought his first car, a Renault two-seater coupé. Already keen on photography with his own dark room, he was delighted with the car and soon became an enthusiastic motorist as well.

Once smitten, he never lost his zest for the motor car. Each year he had a new and better one; a 9hp Belsize, a Humber 15, a Hillman followed by an Austin. Never a good driver, there is little doubt that cars gave him the feeling of having arrived; after all it was successful doctors who had modern motor carriages, smelling richly of leather, with a pleasant oily tang, instead of hay and manure.

Those were the days when, if you happened to change your mind, you simply turned the car round in the middle of any road, and 'Going for a Drive' meant a gentle pootling about in the car, just for the pleasure of driving. Days when there were few cars on the road (250 000 in 1921, compared with 22 million in 1996) and when petrol cost one shilling a gallon [1p a litre].

By 1926, in the light of his progress up the medical ladder, he was able to engage his first chauffeur, Mr Jenkins.

Dr Adams explained, "Both Rainey and Gurney had postgraduate qualifications. Rainey had an FRCS, a top surgical diploma, hence he was labelled 'Mr', and Gurney had an MD. They said I could have a partnership if I obtained an MD: one of the rules of the practice being that a doctor could not become a full partner without an appropriate higher qualification."

Dr Adams went on, "In those days the practices vied with each other for patients. I sometimes wondered whether there was not some competition between the practices on the grounds of qualifications as well. You see, Rainey had a London FRCS and the firm that had it in for me later was Mr Wilson Hall and the *White House* practice, and he had an Edinburgh FRCS.

"I worked hard for four years. I took my holidays going round the London hospitals and read all the journals to keep up to date, and finally obtained my MD by thesis, after failing the first time, specialising in Public Health."

As a result of his efforts he became a partner in 1926, which further improved his financial status, and hence the chauffeur.

A doctor in a rich town in the 1920s could expect to be on an annual £1000 or more. Theoretically, that is about £35 000 at the end of the century, but with the much greater disparity of salaries and wages in the 20s than today, it was nearer £50 000. Dr Rex Binning, of Brighton, said that he never lived so well as on £1000 in 1934, and when in 1935 Mr Tom Henry Wilson was offered £1651 [a one-sixth share in an Eastbourne three-doctor practice] he thought it "extremely good".

Dr Adams remained committed to his patients. Kenneth E Miles, who was born in Eastbourne, says, "Our family doctor had previously been Dr Emerson, so Dr Adams took over when he joined the College Road practice. About 1928 my younger brother developed a cancer, a sarcoma. In spite of radium treatment the disease developed rapidly and he died in September 1929, aged 9½ years. Throughout the illness and death, Dr Adams was most attentive and sympathetic. My mother, in particular, thought very highly of him as a fine, upstanding Christian gentleman, of great compassion. In giving his full attention and always being ready to come out, he was clearly not after our money because although we were not poor, we were not well off, and lived in a terrace house in Birling Street."

Richard James says, "When I was six years old I was admitted to *Southfields* Nursing Home to have my tonsils out and Dr Adams gave the anaesthetic. I have never forgotten that he gave me a book on pirates; I was most impressed because the piratical cry was, 'Odds Boddikins and Split my Tonsils'."

The next year, 1929, was eventful. Miss Elizabeth Hood who lived at *Kent Lodge,* 6 Seaside Road (now Trinity Trees), had to put her fine house up for sale. It seems that she had been hard hit by the 1929 Wall Street stock market crash.

Driving by one day the Doctor saw this large detached, double-fronted, greystone house, looked over it and was impressed.

The house was advertised as, '... a four-square superior Victorian villa, with adequate front lawn and spacious back garden ...' with 'Some work required'. It stood near to the stylish residential area of Chiswick Place, and was close to Grand Parade on the sea front, with its expensive hotels. Across the road was Eastbourne's main private hospital, the Esperance Nursing Home, opened by nuns for wounded troops in 1917, which boasted an operating theatre and X-ray room.

He discussed it with his mother, then aged 63. She was classic middle class, astute in financial matters, and he was a mother's son.

The house had been a doctor's surgery in the 1880s, but Mrs Adams declared that they could never afford to buy it, and it would need servants; hardly a problem for there was no shortage of them at 12/6d [62½p] a week, live in, and charwomen were keen to work three hours for half-a-crown [12½p]. By 1930 the house was still unsold due to the market slump, and Miss Hood was living at Ocklynge. She said she was willing to let it for three years, pending a sale.

Dr Adams seemed determined to have the house and tried to persuade his partners to rent it. They thought it too close to the College Road surgery, but in the end he had his way, and it is said that he borrowed most of the £3000 price from William Mawhood, who had just received £8000 when the town bought his Downland. So the street directory for 1931 shows 'Drs AC Gurney EH Rainey, JB Adams and V Williams with surgeries at College Road and Seaside Road'. Dr Victor Williams had replaced Dr Joy who had settled in Bridport.

The Doctor spent £2000, his own savings plus some borrowings, to convert the house to his requirements and around Christmas 1930 he moved in with his mother, his cousin, a servant, and chauffeur. Over the semi-basement, the ground floor had a lounge, dining room, waiting room, and adequate surgery (16½ by 13½ feet or 5.5x4.5m). There were four bedrooms on the next floor, and the top, or second, floor had another four, partly used to store his possessions. The electoral roll for 1932 shows that Mrs Adams was ensconced with her son at *Kent Lodge.*

He helped to found the Bisley Rifle Club, became a member of André Simon's Wine and Food Society and attended their dinners. In 1936 he formed a local Camera Club.

About this time Dr Adams was introduced to Lt Colonel Roland V Gwynne of Folkington Manor, Polegate: a man of some peculiarities, but of great wealth and one of the most powerful men in Sussex. He had studied law at Cambridge, was called to the Bar in 1910, and was a member of the Tory Carlton Club in London. He won a *DSO* in the 1914-18 war. A former High Sheriff for Sussex, he was chairman of the Board of Guardians for its last years, Mayor of Eastbourne for two years from 1929, was at times chairman of East Sussex County Council, chairman of Hailsham Rural District Council, and chairman of Hailsham magistrates.

He was renowned for the parties he gave at Folkington, which were fully reported in the county newspapers and high-class magazines. It is alleged they were on such a scale that, although the Colonel was teetotal, every week a lorry from the Star Brewery made a special delivery to the manor to stock up the cellars.

To be in with the Colonel was to be in with the jet set of the county, men of great riches and influence with many contacts.

If Dr Adams was attracted by the high life, he did not forget his patients. He prospered and was popular with both his 'panel' patients and private patients. He never refused to visit and his patients found he always had time to listen.

Mrs Maureen Devlin writes, "My father, Fred Sivers, had polio when an infant and had over forty operations on his legs. He didn't have a lot of time for doctors, but he was treated several times by Dr Bodkin Adams and said that the Doctor was one of the kindest of men.

"He lived in Dennis Road [now Dursley Road] and it was regarded as one of the poorer parts of Eastbourne, but the Doctor was well thought of in the neighbourhood."

The 6 College Road practice opened a branch surgery in 1930 at the neighbouring village of East Dean. This was an extra five-mile drive from the centre of Eastbourne, but Dr Adams was noted for always being willing to attend any call.

Mrs Grace Taylor, of East Dean, says, "In the 1930s my husband, Rupert, went down with double pneumonia. Dr Adams came out to see him, prescribed M&B[3] and said that he was extremely ill and he feared for his life. At 6.30 the next morning he was ringing the doorbell having come out to see his patient. I wouldn't hear a word against him."

Philip Clear says he isn't sure, but thinks that he was delivered by Dr Adams. He does remember going to have a boil behind his knee lanced, "Which he did without anaesthetic and did it hurt, but the family thought he was a good doctor".

He gave Mrs Moyra Malam an anaesthetic, "I can remember him well. He anaesthetised me at our home in Eastbourne when I had my tonsils and adenoids out. One of my memories was that he had chubby hands. It was in 1934, and I had a trained nurse from Great Ormond Street Hospital to look after me."

Along with building up his practice, he became involved in good works, was on the town's YMCA committee, and maintained his association with Bible Classes.

Michael TH Clark (who became a local pharmacist) confirms that Dr Adams was a leading light in the Crusaders and that the classes, divided by age, were held at *Kent Lodge,* "Although Bodkin didn't take my class he was an active teacher".

Joseph Slater says, "Dr Bodkin Adams was the doctor to my parents before the war and both had a high regard for him. He would come out in the middle of the night for a modest fee and without any extra charge. I attended Bible Classes before the war which were held in the semi-basement of *Kent Lodge.* Dr Adams didn't take the class, but he presented prizes and I got a book from him."

Cousin Florence, Dr Adams and his mother in the 1930s {Associated Press}

Dr Adams gave lifts to boys of the Eastbourne Crusader Bible Class to and from picnics at Horseshoe plantation near Beachy Head. A class member recalls, "He drove wildly, he was a terrible driver, but I recall one of the boys in the front seat yelling, with a sense of great achievement, 'We're going at over 60 mph'."

His good deeds rather than his bad driving were receiving recognition. On Thursday, 22 November 1934, HRH Princess Helena Victoria visited Eastbourne to receive purses as a result of a YMCA appeal for funds for its local and national work. Her Royal Highness was met at the railway station by Lt Col Roland

Gwynne DL, Dr J Bodkin Adams and the Town Clerk, Mr HW Fovargue. The ceremony took place at a civic reception at the Town Hall in the afternoon when 74 purses containing £2204 were received.

Dr Adams not only expressed his religious convictions in his home and on ecclesiastical occasions, but also in the course of his medical practice. He would leave religious tracts and Biblical quotations in the sickroom, and it was not unknown for him to fall on his knees to pray before entering a patient's bedroom. Some believe that this evoked the first whisperings about him, questioning his genuineness. While his actions may have attracted some criticism, it is likely that his patients welcomed the sureness of his beliefs, and he was merely drawing the usual envy and malice that at a certain stage assails any successful person. One satisfied patient went as far as providing him with a kneeler on the landing.

Kingsley Amis mentions Dr Adams in his memoirs; of the time when he slipped in a hallway as he knelt to pray and issued an impious expletive.

Even in the 1930s there were always those for and against him. Ken Miles says, "My family thought him a wonderful doctor. On the other hand my mother-in-law told me that when she mentioned Dr Adams to Nurse Holman, a friend of the family, this was greeted with a snort, 'Oh! Dr Adams and his old ladies'."

An Eastbourne YWCA member said that while her mother did have him as her doctor she changed because she couldn't stand his unctuous manner.

Joyce Donkin who lived at East Dean for many years says, "Dr Bodkin Adams was our family doctor and my mother thought highly of him. He was go-ahead in that he went to America to improve his practice. He was a typical Irishman, however, very forgetful. I recall he ordered some flooring for the YMCA and then forgot all about it".

In the spring of 1935 he did visit the USA, studying at the Rockefeller Institute, Chicago, and the Mayo Clinic, Minnesota. Such a BTA ('Been To America') qualification was unusual for the average doctor in a moderate-sized English town of the 1930s. Very commendable would be the first thought, but as always with Dr Adams there were other interpretations. He admitted that he had special lenses ground for him by Bausch & Lomb, "large, rimless and corrected for all astigmatism", but implied that he truly went there to attend the Mayo Clinic.

Aided, or otherwise, by his ocular state, Dr Adams kept up his shooting expertise. According to Colin Huggett, "There was a shoot at Westham near the Pantiles behind the railway station. It closed with the war".

Dr Adams said, "In the 1930s I shot all over Europe, including the Monte Carlo live bird shoots and later the Z shoot.

"For ordinary straight clay pigeon shooting I would expect to get 25 out of 25 every time, using the British method of having the gun ready and calling. The Continental is not so easy, you call and it can come any time within three seconds and from a variety of directions. I also did the Olympic type of shoot".

Dr Adams involved himself in research as well, again unusual for a provincial GP in the 1930s. He worked with Dr Geoffrey Shera, an Eastbourne pathologist, who was interested in intestinal disorders and had isolated *Salmonella eastbourne.* Dr Adams described their work; "Shera and I worked together a lot and did our own variety of gastric function in which we examined the urine for pepsins and the motions for fat and remnants of muscle fibres. It was amateurish, but ahead of its time. I had seen the procedure described by a German doctor".

In 1934 he was appointed part-time anaesthetist at the Princess Alice Memorial Hospital, the local Voluntary Hospital, although he had no special qualifications in the subject. The adequate reason being that none were on offer in 1934.

Before the NHS most GPs in Eastbourne had some hospital appointment, usually unpaid, but providing kudos that went down well with their private patients. Along with Dr Francis Gillette, another general practitioner, Dr Adams was the first specialist anaesthetist appointment in Eastbourne. Beforehand, as in most hospitals, anaesthetics were administered either by a partner in the surgeon's GP practice, or by the most junior doctor, or at times by any doctor who could be prevailed upon to give "just a whiff of gas".

The status of anaesthetists was low, and they were the butt of surgical jokes; 'I don't know what he's like at your end; but he appears to be dead at mine'. An anaesthetic appointment, therefore, did not have the aura of a surgical or medical specialist, but it was being recognised that patients could die just as much from their 'gassing' as from their 'cutting'.

Anaesthesia had hardly moved since 1846, ether and chloroform and nitrous oxide [laughing gas] were the mainstays, all vapours or gases, which had to be inhaled through a facemask. With the anaesthetic agents available it was almost impossible to have the patient at the correct level of unconsciousness; too deep and they developed chest complications, too light and they became violent. A patient suddenly going berserk was such a fact of anaesthetic life that it was customary to have two or three strong porters handy to restrain them.

Changes were about. The first Professor of Anaesthetics, Robert Macintosh, was appointed at Oxford in 1935; new products were appearing, anaesthesia by injection was coming in, and specialist anaesthetists were another way ahead.

Lowly though Dr Adams' first step on the hospital ladder might be, it provided opportunities for advancement. He considered himself "a progressive anaesthetist", and in some ways he was for he later introduced cyclopropane to Eastbourne.

Not everyone agreed he was a leading anaesthetist, and there are numerous tales of him going asleep in the middle of operations. Mr Henry Wilson, an Eastbourne surgeon 1935-69, recalls saying as he completed an operation, "Well, Bodkin, the patient's awake, isn't it time you woke up too?" Mrs Jessie Leybourne, a retired nurse said, "He did go asleep during operations and Mr Wilson would yell down the table 'Would you kindly wake up Bodkin', he got very exasperated with Dr Adams, but he was always the gentleman". Ex-nurse Mrs Ruth Tucker (née Saunders) can hear Mr Snowball saying at the end of an operation, 'Wake up Bodkin, we've finished', and Mrs Doris Kingsford (née West) says that in the 1940s a tiny pillow was kept in the PA operating theatre for him to rest his head.

The news spread; pharmacist, Michael Clark, says, "I heard that Bodkin Adams went asleep during anaesthetics". Another Eastbourne pharmacist recounts, "One-day Bodkin Adams was leaving the shop when the surgeon, Mr Wilson Hall, entered and greeted him, 'Good morning, Adams'. Bodkin mumbled something and left, hurriedly. 'Some years ago', declared Wilson Hall, 'That man was my anaesthetist at the PA hospital. My patient appeared unhappy, so I looked at Adams and damn me, if he wasn't asleep'. What transpired was left to my imagination."

No doubt some routine operations could be boring at 'his end', and as Dr Adams worked long hours, and all anaesthetists inevitably inhaled some of their gases he might become dozy, but actually going asleep sounds hazardous. Coming from so many sources there must be some basis to the stories: perhaps some of them received embellishment as part of the 'other end' banters?

Mr Henry Wilson, says "Bodkin gassed for me over 20 years. One Thursday afternoon at the Princess Alice Hospital, Bodkin was anaesthetising and half an hour after we were due to start the patient had still not been brought into the theatre from the anaesthetic room. I asked a nurse to open the door, as I was 'scrubbed up' and could touch only the patient, to find the patient was blue but not anaesthetised. JBA and I decided to send her back to the ward. The same thing happened to the next patient. By now it was after 1530h and I had to go at 1630, so I did a few small cases under local anaesthetic. It was only the following day that the next anaesthetist discovered that the lines to the nitrous oxide anaesthetic and the oxygen cylinders had been transposed and JBA had not noticed."

It has to be said that he later learnt to intubate patients [pass a tube into the lungs], which most 1940s anaesthetists could not do, but which was essential if the new relaxant agents were to be used. He could put a needle in a vein, important when intravenous agents were used for the induction of anaesthesia, also more than one Eastbourne anaesthetist of the 1940s could do. He wasn't perfect for Mr Wilson goes on, "It wouldn't be the first time that I had to put the needle in the vein for the *Pentothal* induction injection, as well as do the surgery."

Dr Adams points out, "I gave the first nasal dental anaesthetic, and used the first closed-circuit machine in Eastbourne, knowing Macintosh who had made it. I gave the anaesthetic for the first total hysterectomy [removal of womb] in Eastbourne. For that I had King's College make up a machine with a mask to fit round the head. It had a no-return valve on one side and the other side was connected to a Wolff's Bottle. You controlled the chloroform by turning a valve.

"I often used it for maternity cases. There were only two midwives on the district and any difficult cases were moved to 9 Upperton Road [the Maternity Home]. Most doctors had a 'Handy Lady' to assist at deliveries – some were terrible – but I had one called Mrs Barber who was very good and knew when and what to call me for. I remember being called out to find the baby's hand protruding and the legs extended. I managed to deliver the baby, stillborn, but without rupturing the mother's womb, which would have meant certain death at that time."

Dr Adams continued, "I often sat up all night with the mothers. You got two guineas for the delivery and for care over the following two weeks.

"During all my practice I only lost two babies and never had an anaesthetic death. This was because I never took risks and always examined the patient beforehand, yet I often had the more difficult ones. I have heard MacQueen [a surgeon] say, 'We'll leave it until Tuesday when JB Adams will do it'."

As far as can be ascertained, he did not lose a patient over 22 years of administering anaesthetics in hospitals. Whatever he says, it is possible that he wasn't given the risky cases, but the record is amazing.

Mr Desmond O'Connor Cuffey, ENT surgeon at the Princess Alice Hospital, said he always liked Bodkin Adams giving his anaesthetics because, "He gets them deep so I can get on with the operation". In the days before tubes into the lungs, and injections into a vein, ENT surgery often meant that the facemask had to be taken off for the surgeon to get to work, and then replaced if the patient seemed to be coming round before the operation was complete. Of course, the comment could be just a case of two Irishmen getting on well together.

There is little doubt that Dr Adams would like doing ENT cases because, whereas for most private operations anaesthetists were paid less than 10% of the surgeon's fee, in ENT it was always about 15%.

Mr EH Rainey FRCS, twice mentioned in dispatches during the 1914-18 war, and who used to throw scalpels round the operating theatre

Doris Cruttenden (née Gross) did three years, 1934-7, of nurse training at the Princess Alice Hospital followed by one year as a Staff Nurse. "In those days you were put straight into the wards, even so I enjoyed my days in Eastbourne. The Matron, Miss Flora MacDonald was austere, frightening in a way, but very understanding. I recall the first use of *Prontosil* at the PA. It was given to a desperately ill man on Gurney ward, and the new drug brought his temperature down.

"Dr Adams was an anaesthetist there, and I was often on duty in theatre when he gave anaesthetics. He even gave the anaesthetic for my appendicitis, with Mr Wilson Hall as surgeon. You couldn't say I didn't have prompt treatment, I reported my pain to Mr Hall at 9.30 and I was on the table at 11 o'clock.

"I found Dr Adams kind, helpful and courteous. He was an intelligent, competent anaesthetist. He had his own anaesthetic trolley, which I think he designed, I know the hospital didn't supply one. I can't say that Dr Adams went asleep when I was in the theatre, although he was always quiet. Unlike Mr Rainey, one of the surgeons, who had terrible tempers and would throw scalpels round the operating theatre and stand on any swab which fell to the floor to test if the nurses were counting the used swabs properly. He was a good surgeon though and I can see now that he must have been under stress."

3. A PROSPEROUS SENIOR PARTNER

In the mid 1930s, in his mid-thirties, Dr Adams had a flourishing practice of 2000 patients. Half were panel patients and their families, and the rest were private patients who paid half-a-guinea [52 1/2 p] for a visit. Panel patients were working men who contributed to a national fund at work, from which their general practitioner was paid. Introduced by Lloyd George in 1910, the scheme was a great boon for the 'breadwinner', but it did not cover hospital treatment, or the family.

A quarter of the town's population was over 65, rich, and beset by the ailments of old age. One GP said, "Far too many people in the Eastbourne of the day had too much wealth and not enough common sense."

Such patients needed reassurance about their general condition, and sought friendship. The typical couple had retired from the North Country, or the Home Counties, and as is the way the husband died after a year or two. The widow lived in an opulent home, a penthouse flat or luxury hotel, but was lonely. She wouldn't dream of picking up someone for company, and if a man was seen to go into her house, flat or room, a major scandal would erupt - unless the man was a doctor or a priest. Not only was a doctor's visit quite all right during daylight hours, it was more than acceptable at night too - just when a lonely soul most needed help. Not only would there be no gossip, but next day the neighbours would open a conversation to ask after the patient's health, and be most solicitous.

Thus their doctor's visit not only provided hope and company, it acted as an entrée to invitations to other flats or houses, or to the theatre, or other interests. A special relationship flourished between them and their understanding doctor. Understanding in that he would come at any time of the day or night, he would talk, and - even more - listen to them, and he was soothing, reassuring, and confidence-building, and for those who wished he would lay on hands.

Ann Whitehead says, "Some people said that he would lay his hand over yours, which I wouldn't like." Numerous patients thought it was marvellous. "And when you get older you are grateful for a reassuring hand".

Two members of the Eastbourne Ladies Coffee Corner said that their mothers told them he was a wonderful doctor, and the son of John Hector Roberts says his father was full of praise for Dr Adams, and wouldn't hear a word said against him.

On the other hand, another ELCC member said, "If he came into a house his eyes lit up if he saw anything valuable. Before he left I found myself offering him a silver cup which he was ogling".

Like most doctors, he tailored his charges to the patient's financial state, and there are many stories of him not charging the poorer families. A patient tells of the time, "He came to deliver our daughter. He charged £12, and when my wife told him she would have to pay by instalments, he immediately halved the amount."

Another patient: "Whatever he may have been guilty of he was a very good doctor at diagnosis. My parents knew both him and his mother through the Chapel. Some years before the war my mother was very ill with a high temperature, the attending doctor, Dr Pollard, told my father that he didn't know what else he could do for her. We called Dr Adams who came straight away, took one look, and went off to return with anaesthetic to do a lumbar puncture, and diagnosed meningitis. The sequel was that my mother was entranced with Bodkin. He called frequently, and she would impatiently await his visits. One day he made her get up, danced her around the bedroom, and notified her she was fit to resume her duties.

"It's hard to understand what attracted women to him, as he was a large red-faced chap, with ugly hands, although he had an attractive Irish brogue."

Nonetheless about 1933 Bodkin Adams fell in love with Miss Norah O'Hara. Her father was a family butcher: C O'Hara & Sons had six shops including 17 Meads Street and Carlisle Road, Eastbourne. Mrs Olive Pack, who worked as a bookkeeper at the Grand Hotel Buildings' shop in the 1940s says, "They had a thriving business".

Did it help that Margaret Gray, wife of Norman Gray, who aided Dr Adams with the Crusader courses, was Norah O'Hara's sister? By 1935 the romance had blossomed to the point where the girl's parents had announced the engagement and had even bought a house and tastefully furnished it as a wedding present. Margaret Kinman states, "Dr Adams insisted Miss O'Hara's father buy a house for them".

The next year Adams called it off. Whereupon, according to Jimmy Donne, the girl's father, Arthur O'Hara, said that his daughter had been disgraced and he threatened to horsewhip Adams in public, "Which he was quite capable of doing".

Why Adams ended the engagement will never be known, but the guess is that his mother put her foot down and said that she was not having her son marrying 'Trade'. To the middle class of the day to be a 'In Trade' was a social stigma. His mother had also entered her seventies and was concerned about where she would live if he married. As usual with Bodkin there were other views. Mrs Vivien Ackroyd says it was because old man O'Hara had said quite firmly that he would not change his will leaving all his money to his daughters.

Michael Clark confirms, "On their engagement Mr O'Hara bought a good house in Carew Road for the couple. The amazing thing is that they stayed on friendly terms and he remained Miss O'Hara's doctor to the end of his life."

Eileen Vine says the question of the professional classes not marrying 'Trade' was real in the Eastbourne of the 1930s. "The tradition was that the professional classes were relatively poor, because they did not soil their hands with trade."

Dr Adams' partner, Mr Edward Rainey, also had family worries and in 1935 moved himself to Norfolk. His place was taken by Mr Lawrence AH Snowball, who possessed not only an FRCS but an MRCP [the top physicians' qualification] and the only one in Eastbourne.

With Dr Gurney retiring the following year and Dr RV Harris joining the practice, with one bound Dr Adams became the senior partner. So, by the mid-1930s Dr Adams was fully established in practice, and involved in the Eastbourne social scene with invitations to the round of functions and gatherings.

Ron Parsons says, "Two ladies, patients of his, who lived at Church Street, Willingdon, would invite him to their cocktail parties where they asked him to mix up the cocktails. People used to complain afterwards of terrible hangovers, and it was found that he used cider (quite strong by itself) with vodka - a heady mixture". The typical action of the lifelong teetotal person with little idea of the effects of the various concoctions.

His contacts brought other potent benefits. John Wright Cheesborough, then a junior partner with solicitors Coles & James, says, "I thought Bodkin Adams made a practice of cultivating wealthy, elderly patients, ... of which there were many in pre-war Eastbourne, along Carlisle Road and into Meads".

He was certainly making a good living and his rich patients often remembered the Doctor in their wills - along with their chauffeur, cook, valet and gardener. This was quite usual. Before the 1939-45 war, a rich Meads family on £5 000 a year, would customarily leave their doctor £300 [some £10 000 in 1999], and while the bequests to Dr Adams were on the more modest side, £50 or £100, in keeping with his relatively junior state, they mounted up.

He was also picking up other sources of income. As the Eastbourne Water Company's doctor, they thought he was wonderful. "I never heard a bad word said of him, he looked after the men splendidly", said an ex-official of the company.

In 1935, however, came the first evidence that Dr Adams had a foolish side.

Since 1930 when she settled in Eastbourne, a wealthy widow, Mrs Matilda Whitton had been one of his patients. Over the years a friendly relationship grew up between doctor and patient, with her calling him "My John". The Doctor's mother and cousin would picnic with her on Beachy Head and when Mrs Whitton became incapable of driving herself the Doctor would loan her his car and chauffeur. There was nothing inherently reprehensible in their relations, although as with most of the Doctor's activities the motives could be read in differing ways. It could be that his kindly actions were in his patient's best interests, on the other hand voices were heard to say that it was done with the intention of being remembered in her will.

He did not even break any rules when he agreed to be her executor. Again it could be said that as all her family were away from Eastbourne he was merely taking a load off her mind, yet equally it could be argued that such a move served his purpose of touting for a bequest. Knowing Dr Adams, what probably happened was that she asked him to help because she didn't know who else to ask, and he didn't know how to refuse without upsetting her and thereby definitely losing out.

When she died, of high blood pressure, on 11 May 1935, aged 75, she left him £7000. Not only was it a substantial slice of her estate but she left £500 to his cousin and, in a codicil, £100 to his mother [altogether now over £200 000].

In spite of the will appearing to be valid the family contested it, but the High Court mainly upheld it, only the codicil was questioned and quashed.

Fighting the case was quite in keeping with his character. He would say it was his legally, it was what the deceased wished, and as it was a way of saying 'Thank you' for all he had done, it would be impolite to refuse the gift.

The publicity caused local gossip and some believe this episode was the first of the slurs on the Doctor's character. A few local doctors tended to distance themselves from him, feeling that it was not quite the decent thing to be the executor, and beneficiary, and to contest the will in open court.

Nurse Cruttenden: "I think he became a bit eccentric. While I was at PA his engagement was called off and I think he went within himself and perhaps his outlook seemed to change.

"Eastbourne in those days was just of sufficient size to get up a head of steam about rumours and yet not big enough to forget them and go onto something else."

Peggy Crowhurst confirms that as early as the late 1930s rumours were rife in the town about Dr Bodkin Adams, the bequests he received, and the manner in which his patients died.

Dr Adams (third from left) at the Langney Road YMCA centre for a Sale of Work in the 1930s {Associated Newspapers}

Could it be that he also upset the local doctors because he sent nearly all his surgical patients to London? He kept a list of the top London specialists for various conditions and it was his custom to accompany the patient to the consultation.

Before the NHS each main general practice in the town had one partner who considered himself a surgeon, one an anaesthetist, and another a physician, and they expected to cope with all the needs of their patients. They delivered them, treated them, and signed their cremation forms. It was frowned upon if a patient went from one doctor to another. A GP of the time said, "There was much jealousy and envy in Eastbourne medicine, and quite a spat in the *White House* practice when one partner 'pinched' a private patient from a colleague within the practice. Mark Lester [one of the partners] and later Duggie Ashforth were all right, but while Wilson Hall was a capable surgeon, he had a terrible temper".

There may be more to it, for Dr Adams was reputed to say to the, no doubt surprised, London specialist, "And how much will that be?" and paying him on the spot in notes. One interpretation could be that he was taking an extra worry from the patient at a difficult time, but others interpreted it as a means to add a few pounds onto the specialists' fee, when he finally sent in his account.

In most provincial towns before the NHS the quality of surgical practice was fragmented, the best surgeons were to be found in the big cities, and any difficult cases were sent there. Surely, therefore, we can say Dr Adams was definitely doing his best for his patients by sending them to London. Except that with local surgeons it would soon become common knowledge if he put a surcharge on the surgeon's bill, and he might lose the patient from his practice to boot – not applicable with a Bart's, Guy's, King's or St Thomas' surgeon.

Whether it was the result of these ways or other habits, Mr HG Estcourt, an Eastbourne surgeon and *White House* GP, commented, "Bodkin Adams was the most disliked doctor in Eastbourne".

Otherwise, life went well. The Crusaders' classes at *Kent Lodge* continued to be popular. Many young men say that they attended, among them the Revd David Stevens. Eileen Vine says, "I took one of the Crusaders classes and they were a valuable means of all social groups meeting up. Norman Gray worked hard to make them a success".

Close friends and colleagues continued to support Dr Adams. Ken Lawrence, cousin of Dorothy Lawrence, Dr Adams' receptionist, says, "She thought he was a lovely bloke". Numerous patients said how well he looked after them. A local GP confirms, "Bodkin Adams still worked till late at night, but he was foolish to himself because he kept few or no notes of his patient's details, or of the drugs he used, although I believe he was genuinely concerned with the patient's welfare. A family told me how when one of his patients, a Mr Hacker, died, Dr Adams had tears in his eyes as he came down the stairs from the deceased's bedroom."

In the spring of 1939 Bodkin Adams saw a different sight, a car he was never to forget. One of his patients had just taken delivery of a brand-new Rolls-Royce *Silver Wraith* limousine and had it registered at Eastbourne as JK 1600. The coachwork, to a high specification, was by the famous firm of Mulliner.

By now he knew a lot about cars, and JK 1600 was the ultimate in motoring comfort, but although he was comparatively wealthy he could not afford such a car. Did the thought cross his mind that perhaps one day he might own it?

For the moment he had his parquet-floored elegant house, set in a plot some 190feet by 60ft in choice, central Eastbourne. It boasted a large Surgery with chaise longue, a table, a roll-top desk, bookcase, some of his shooting trophies and two medicine cupboards on the wall to complete his domain.

Dr Adams was a substantial presence in more ways than one. Well covered, about five feet nine inches in height, he was some fifteen stone, had large almost swollen hands, wore round spectacles for his myopia, and baldness was just starting, displaying his pinkish skin. He kept putting on weight due to his excessive appetite for chocolate, which worried his mother, who consoled herself with the thought that he did not smoke or drink.

4. THE DOCTOR DURING THE 1939-45 WAR

As with so many folk, the outbreak of war in September 1939 brought change for the Doctor, and it was to have a profound influence on him later.

Junior partner, Vincent Harris, was called up straightaway being in the TA. His other partner, Laurie Snowball, became heavily involved in the surgical work at the hospital when surgeons, Geoffrey Estcourt, Desmond Cuffey and Henry Wilson, went into the armed forces. Over the autumn of 1939 Dr Adams coped with over half the work of the practice, and with the influx of evacuees into a 'Safe Area'.

The contrasting views about the Doctor persisted. Mrs Davies says that at the beginning of the war, "I was sent to *Kent Lodge* to arrange a medical prior to joining the WRNS. I found Dr Bodkin Adams such a forbidding person that when I went back for the examination I took a friend with me and wouldn't let her out of the consulting room".

On the other hand, a patient says that, "In September 1940 my wife was about to give birth and I was home on weekend leave. I called at his house about seven o'clock in the morning and he came to our home in my car - still in his pyjamas.

"Several members of our family were his patients. A niece about eight years old was very ill. When he visited he told her to wrap up in a woolly and there and then took her in his car to the hospital, for she had pneumonia. I do not believe he differentiated between his rich or his poor patients.

"Yes, several wealthy old ladies doted on him and wanted to give him gifts, as happened with other doctors and I'm sure still does."

During the 'phoney war' into the spring of 1940, Dr Adams prepared himself for the worst. "When I was in Bristol there was an outbreak of diphtheria and I was given an injection of antiserum and came up in a terrible rash, which laid me low for a week. So when the war came I had tetanus toxoid injections at a six weeks' interval, because otherwise they gave everyone a shot of antiserum to tetanus after any bomb incident".[1]

Inevitably, his world turned upside down again when the German Army reached the French coast in June 1940. Overnight Eastbourne moved from a 'Safe Area' into the Front Line. With the threat of invasion and air-raids [Eastbourne was the left flank of 'Sealion', the Germans' invasion plan] any evacuees were moved out, followed by most Eastbourne schoolchildren and many families. The population fell from about 60 000 to between 9000 and 15 000, and you can be sure that included in those who decamped were all Dr Adams' private patients. Among the exodus was the owner of that *Silver Wraith* who moved with it to Berkshire.

The Maternity Home closed and maternity cases near term were sent for delivery to Lewes or East Grinstead - another two guineas gone, although more than one baby decided to appear earlier than expected. Grass grew in the centre of the streets, and it was not exceptional to walk from the railway station along Terminus Road, the main shopping centre, without seeing a single passer-by.

Dr Adams found himself in the front line of the remains of his practice. Dr Harris was now in India, Mr Snowball became heavily involved with the air-raid rescue work, and Dr Williams had left. On 28 September 1940 Mr Snowball crawled under bomb wreckage in Cavendish Place to amputate the legs of a 17-year-old woman pinned by a steel girder. For this action, as it was in the presence of a burst water main, controlled only by constant pumping, and near an unexploded bomb, he received a commendation.

The 1940 Cavendish Place bombing, about 500m from Kent Lodge

Mr Snowball was also in charge of the Mobile Surgical Unit to cover Brighton, Eastbourne and Hastings, in practice it was hardly ever needed outside Eastbourne. Based on a converted bus, it was used for the resuscitation of bomb victims before moving them to hospital. Inevitably, it meant that Mr Snowball was busy and Dr Adams had to carry the practice by himself, although Gwen Snowball helped out.

Various arrangements were made under the EMS to ensure a smooth running wartime medical service. Based on national guidelines, they were agreed locally.

A local referee (Dr Philip Mathew for Eastbourne) decided, after consultation, which GPs should be allowed to volunteer for the armed forces, who was available for call up, and who should stay. It meant that practices lost partners and assistants equally, and the needs of the Services were met, yet a suitable mix of doctors remained to tend to those left in Eastbourne.

For those left in Eastbourne, including Dr Adams, the Acting Doctor Scheme for General Practice also meant extra work for less pay. Any patient, on the list of a doctor who had been called into the armed forces, was allowed to select a replacement from any of the remaining doctors who took the patient on his list 'for the duration', each doctor being credited with half the fee.

Dr Adams was particularly incensed that he was excluded from the pool payment system. He explained, "This was an arrangement to pay doctors a retainer to ensure sufficient doctors stayed in partly-evacuated towns subjected to bombing, such as Eastbourne. It was essential to provide standard medical care for civilians left in the bombed towns, and to have doctors on hand to treat casualties. In Eastbourne it was decided that twelve doctors would be recipients, I was the thirteenth, the only one not to receive any pay from the kitty". There seems little doubt that he thought the other Eastbourne doctors had ganged up against him.

This may have been a sore point which was allowed to fester after the war. In the meantime he decided to stay. He buckled down to the situation, by hunting out for patients, and by looking after his family.

First, he arranged for his mother to stay with friends near Hellingly, away from the coast, and then arranged for his own safety. At *Kent Lodge* he had an air-raid shelter built of reinforced concrete so big and strong that it would withstand anything but a direct hit from a big bomb and there he slept at night.

His air-raid precautions created quite a stir, John Cheesborough comments, "During the war Bodkin strengthened the basement of his house in Trinity Trees for use as an air-raid shelter". Laurie Snowball adds, "I sheltered from the air-raids on more than one occasion in Dr Adams' basement strengthened with concrete beams", and in Dr Adams' words, "Snowball and I slept there in safety through the worst of the raids".

He put his shelter time to good use by reinforcing and updating his anaesthetic knowledge. "I got my DA [Diploma in Anaesthetics] during the war. Had Magill[2] for the examination. I knew him at Queen's and had met him and Macintosh at Oxford." In 1941 he was the only Eastbourne doctor with the qualification.

Bodkin Adams continues, "Until Dr Linacre came, I was the only one who could intubate; needed for the facial injuries in the early part of the war. Pollard, Barron and West-Phillips were poor stuff and couldn't pass a tube into the lungs".

During the 'hit and run' air-raids of 1942-43 Dr Adams took a cottage in Lower Dicker, a few miles north of Eastbourne, where he installed his mother.

Other Eastbourne residents moved out of the town to the country villages around, which relieved some of the strain on the air-raid rescue services, but they were still within the catchment area for Eastbourne doctors. Patients were not allowed petrol for medical visits, and as doctors were given petrol coupons for that purpose, they were expected to visit. They had to plan their journeys with great care to avoid using up their ration of coupons. Night driving in the black-out had extra hazards, for there were no road lights, and headlights had to be hooded so that no light could be seen two feet above the ground.

So Dr Adams was kept busy, with a changed clientele and reduced circumstances. His housekeeper understood that, " During the war he went all over the place for his patients".

In the course of the war Dr Adams asked Ruth Saunders, a Princess Alice Hospital Sister whose family farmed near his Dicker cottage, to accompany him to a formal dinner. She says, "Forty years later and miles away from the South Coast, if I said I came from Eastbourne, colleagues would ask, 'Did you know Dr Bodkin

Adams?' and when I replied, 'Yes, and I even went out to a dinner with him once', they would reckon I was lucky to be alive".

Norah Relf was a maid in the Adams' household during the war. A relative says, "She wouldn't speak about the case, but she thought the world of the Doctor".

Mrs V Cooper says, "Dr Adams was our family doctor and he brought our son into the world in March 1942. There had been a lot of gunfire in the night, and although it was said this hurried babies along, mine wasn't affected. It seemed that Dr Adams would have to manage alone, but he gave me confidence and fortunately the nurse arrived in the nick of time.

"My husband was serving in the Army and, needless to say, not overpaid. Dr Adams did not send us the expected bill (this was before the NHS); he said that as my husband was doing his bit for the country, that was his way of helping. Whenever he did charge the bill was about half what we expected.

"On his fifth birthday our son wasn't well and we had to call for Dr Adams, who said it was measles, so we had to cancel the birthday party. Later that day there was a ring at the door and Dr Adams was there to hand in a model car, quite 18 inches long - a *Lagonda,* I think it was - he said perhaps that would assuage my son's disappointment. Dr Adams was a fanatic with cars and motor cycles."

As the world conflict wore on Dr Adams had his own sadness. "In December 1942 my mother started to fail and I knew she wanted to be buried in Coleraine. She died in March 1943 at Yew Tree Cottage and there was only one ferry operating, the Stranraer/Larne, and I took her body over – and there again was Providence – because afterwards they closed the ferry for D-Day. You know Southern Ireland, and Dublin in particular, had all the lights on, acting as beacons for the German bombers, so it was essential to stop communications at that time".

The landings in France meant that Mr Snowball's work for the air-raid services was drawing to a close. One of his last jobs included a night spent sewing up a plane load of paratroopers. A shell burst had peppered their aircraft on the way to Normandy, but it had been able to make an emergency landing at Friston airfield.

Nurse Pamela Fillery (Mrs Milne) calls to mind Dr Adams as, "a stout man with fair curly hair and a florid complexion". She can hear his soft lilting voice whispering to a patient he was anaesthetising during a flying bomb, V1, attack, "Just imagine you are in your little white cot by the sea and all will be well".

George Catt's mother was a patient of his practice, "He would often drop into the Old Town shop for a chat. He had an eye for the chocolate biscuits and mother would tick him off if he took one because they were rationed on points. He couldn't do enough for us".

By the autumn of 1944 Mr Snowball was able to play his part in the practice, and Dr Harris came back in 1945, holding the rank of Lt Col having been adviser in Dermatology to the 14th Army in the Far East.

Most of the evacuated residents, schools and businesses were returning to Eastbourne and the 6 College Road practice was getting back to some normality.

5. POST WAR RECOVERY

'Twill make Old Women Young and Fresh,
Create New Motions of the Flesh,
And cause them long for you know what,
If they but taste of chocolate.

James Wadsworth

Dr Adams explained, "After the war I was poor again and I needed to make some money. I would go round the hospital at eight in the morning to see the patients for anaesthetics that day, then do a surgery and visits, go to the hospital again some afternoons, then another surgery and then I would visit my practice nurses. I was so successful that I had six, and the only way I could keep in touch was to see them about nine at night. They were devoted to me.

"After I went to the Mayo Clinic in 1935, and with my reading, I had an understanding of people who had symptoms even though there was nothing to find.

"In my opinion they had over-reaction of the autonomic [a set of nerves controlling systems such as digestion]. I don't like the term 'psychosomatic' [the mind causing symptoms].

"Everybody's responses are different. I used to say that if you had a racehorse and a Clydesdale, and you slapped each on the back, one would disappear in the distance while the other would hardly stir, so people react differently to the same stresses. In some their autonomic systems over-react and bubble over so that one gets wheezing, or palpitations, and another stomach symptoms even though the X-ray and other investigations are normal."

He was also a great believer in auto-suggestion, this was novel, but basically not unsound.

A snapshot of those austerity days just after the war, when some rationing was worse than during the conflict, is described by Mr W Stapley, headwaiter at the *Grand Hotel* after its re-opening in 1946. "As those who experienced the rationing will know, cream served with sweet dishes had to be synthetic, not fresh. One evening Dr Adams was dining in the restaurant and he ordered a *Meringue Chantilly*, which consists of two halves of meringue filled with cream. He got up and left quite quickly. When I went over to clear the table, I found the *Meringue Chantilly* untouched, the Menu torn in half, and one half had been stuck in the middle of the cream. Written on the reverse side of the menu, in capital letters were the words, *THIS SHAVING CREAM IS UNFIT FOR HUMAN CONSUMPTION.*"

Dr Adams was the doctor at the *Grand Hotel* and he used the luggage lift near the Compton Street back entrance to avoid publicity for his patients.

Mrs Alice Ridings, housekeeper at the *Grand Hotel*, who retired in 1985, said, "Bodkin Adams had several friends among the residents. It was not unusual to see him making his way to their room for a sherry at lunchtime or in the evening".

Quite a few people recall seeing Dr Adams enjoying tea with one of his ladies at the *Grand Hotel*.

Dr Adams also had his hair cut by Mr Pickles, the gentlemen's hairdresser at the Grand. It was a popular choice because you could make an appointment for a convenient moment - and incredibly it was the cheapest place in town.

Mr Pickles gave as his opinion, "Dr Adams was good to people who could no more leave him anything in their will than Adam. He did a lot of good in the town. Unfortunately, he had a leering look, but of course a good bedside manner".

In 1946 Dr Adams drove Mr Henry Wilson, the surgeon, to London in his car. This was to meet Lady Michaelis who had donated £50 000 [over £1m in today's money] to fund a home for disabled ex-servicemen at her *Chaseley* home in Eastbourne. She was one of Dr Adams' patients who left Eastbourne during the war. Afterwards she lived in London and he would drive there to look after her, hence the lift for Mr Henry Wilson.

Solicitor, Richard James, was another who remarked, "He looked after my family." His wife Doreen added, "He was kindly, and looked after our two daughters well when they were young, but he was a silly man".

Mr James went on, "It was not exceptional when clients were making out their wills for them to say that they wanted to give Dr Adams a legacy, and I would say to them, 'Did he not give you a bill?' 'Oh yes' They would reply, 'But I want to give more.' And they did. Was it that he was single and had time to spare to chat up his old ladies?"

Mrs Eileen Goldsmith, a farmer's wife, whose family were at Black Robin Farm on the top of Beachy Head, says, "In February 1947 he was one of the doctors in our practice when my daughter fell ill. It was very bad weather and despite deep snow he was the one who came out to see her."

"Early in 1948", said Dr Ian Brown, later a Consultant Geriatrician at Eastbourne, "Bodkin drove me to Tunbridge Wells for a medical meeting, and talked about me joining the practice but, involved as I was at St Mary's Hospital, I declined. The next year Dr Adams' partner, Lawrence Snowball, invited me to assist at a major operation in the Esperance Nursing Home on a patient with bowel cancer. Dr Adams was the anaesthetist and I was mildly surprised when, half way through the operation, one of the nursing nuns wheeled a tea trolley into the operating theatre. Whilst Snowball and I sweated at the operating table, Adams lowered the cloth from his face and had tea from a large silver teapot, with a plentiful supply of meringues and cream cakes."

On 1 July 1948 Dr FBS Barkworth joined the 6 College Road partnership, and with the start of the NHS that month, Dr Adams was appointed a part-time Senior Hospital Medical Officer in anaesthetics to the Eastbourne hospitals. This was a career grade instituted for those whose qualifications and/or experience were considered insufficient for them to be graded a Consultant.

Bodkin Adams continued his shooting and maintained his prowess. He would say, "If 25 clays are put up I would expect to smoke[1] them all." He shot at Bisley year after year. Dave Keeley says that his boss often shot with Dr Adams at Hobden's Farm and he would accompany them. "Dr Adams was a good shot, mind you his guns included two cased Purdeys, synonymous with quality since 1814, and would have cost £18 000, apart from a Holland & Holland".

The Doctor continued to shoot all over Europe as well. On the boat to Norway the club would arrange to put up skeets from the deck so they could have practice on the way over. His favourite was duck shooting at Monaco, until Princess Grace put a stop to all live shooting there, when he confined himself to clay pigeons.

His gun cleaning oil consisted of:

Paraffin Oil 10oz,
Spirits of Turpentine $7^1/_2$ oz,
Rangoon Sperm Oil $2^1/_2$ oz,
Camphor $^1/_4$ oz.

His ritual was to clean his guns after each day's shooting, when he would first remove any fouling with tow and flannel on a cleaning rod. He then ran the barrel through with a bristle brush along with the special cleaning oil to remove any residual fouling. Finally he wiped out the barrel.

His housekeeper said, "He went to Scotland for the grouse shooting most years. He shot at Bisley, Wimbourne in Dorset, Beverley near Doncaster, and nearer home with the Sussex Police at Newhaven, at Battle, Westfield near Brede, and Catsfield Place. He went to club meetings at the Fountain pub by Bo Peep but I don't think he often shot there.

"He also had golf clubs, but his real love was chocolate. Kept a box on the seat of his car and another on his desk. If he opened a box they were soon all gone."

His practice flourished too - no doubt to the annoyance of other Eastbourne doctors who considered themselves a cut above him. By now it was bringing in about £7000 a year, and his wise investments and deposits another £2600.

Dr Adams' patients now included the Duke of Devonshire, Sir Oswald Birley, the painter, Admiral Sir Robert and Lady Prendergast, Sir Roland Victor Gwynne, Sheriff of the County, and Richard Walker, Chief Constable of Eastbourne.

Sir Robert lived at De Walden Lodge in Meads. As an example of his style, he had an extra horn installed in the back of his car so that he could honk at other drivers - to the embarrassment of his chauffeur.

As an example of Dr Adams' style he now wore Savile Row suits, and his private practice was going so well that he cut down on his NHS patients, although keeping about 800. "My family, living in Birling Street, were very sorry when Dr Adams wouldn't take us as NHS patients".

A local pharmacist says, "I had contact almost daily with Dr Bodkin Adams from 1948 to his death. Of my earliest recollections, I find this episode amusing.

"Bodkin Adams entered the pharmacy about mid-morning at a very busy time. 'Morning', He says, 'Colonel X is very ill, poor man. He is bedridden and, poor man, he is incontinent. I want to make him an appliance'. Mr Browne, the proprietor, said, 'Yes sir, how?' 'Well, I would like six feet of your red rubber tubing and I know you've got those washable condoms.' Mr B 'Yes sir, of course sir' and I am dispatched for the goods.

"He says, 'Give me some scissors Browne', and proceeds to cut half the teat off the condom and push the rubber tubing through the hole. Mr B, 'It will leak sir.'

'Not when we tie it with your red string Browne. Here I'll hold it, you tie it and we'll put some of your sealing wax, that you use on corks, on the string'. Mr B. 'Right sir'. Bodkin Adams held the appliance under the gas jet while Mr B did the waxing. Inadvertently, he dropped a large, fuming blob of wax on the Doctor's thumb. 'You bloody fool' yells Dr Adams, 'You've burnt my thumb'. He then hopped around our very small dispensary waving his arm about.

"This was too much for me and I shot off to the cellar to have hysterics."

Tom Searle, a pharmacist of Willingdon, also recalls Dr Adams. "I knew him quite well. His Irish, cherubic appearance and his reputation for a wonderful bedside manner were not always borne out. Bluntly, he could be a pig. He would throw the prescription across the counter with a 'Send it', no please or thank you."

Dr Adams continued to add strings to his bow, for example, he was the school doctor at Neville House in St Anne's Road (later the site of Eastbourne's telephone exchange), and doctor to the *Rustington Hotel.*

Occasionally his ventures did not come off. According to June Longley, he became the doctor at 'Rannies', the Eastbourne School of Domestic Economy in Silverdale Road. Unfortunately, the Principal, Miss E Randall, did not care for him and dismissed him quite soon after appointment. She said that his fingers were like 'sausages', and she did not wish him to be in contact with her students.

Even so, a local bank manager recalls going down to the bank vault with Dr Adams to examine a black box that he stored there, "And when it was opened it was absolutely stuffed with banknotes".

By now Trinity Trees had developed into an Eastbourne Harley Street. Dr Adams' residence, *Kent Lodge,* was 6 Trinity Trees; in the Doctor's time it always had a green front door. Number 12 was full of doctors' and dentists' surgeries - Mr HM Pimm dental surgeon, Mr B Beching (another dentist), Mrs MI Neal-Edwards (gynaecologist), Dr L Wilkinson (rheumatologist) - and at No. 16 was Thomas Turner, a retired surgeon. Across the road almost opposite *Kent Lodge* were Coles & James, Dr Adams' solicitors, at Claremont Chambers, 1 Trinity Trees.

Miss A Tucker, who trained at St Mary's Hospital, London, over 1920-23, and later nursed at the Hammersmith Hospital, describes the typical Dr Adams' patient. "I was at the *Olinda* Nursing Home, Grassington Road, when stroke victim, Mrs Edith Morrell was brought from Cheshire in July 1948. She was a wicked piece of work and most rude to the nurses. Dr Adams brought a bottle of whisky and sherry into the Home every Christmas, and he was much maligned." The *Olinda* didn't suit Mrs Morrell so Dr Adams moved her to the Esperance, which she also disliked, so she went to stay in her regular holiday suite at one of the hotels.

Her acerbity was probably related to her condition, worsened by arthritis, for in the 1930s she had played her part in the town, and was a house visitor at the Princess Alice Hospital, but her main interest was her garden. In James Carter she had a magnificent gardener who introduced the *Edith Morrell* and the *Marden Ash* dahlias. They were obtainable from specialist growers.

Dr Adams continued to care for Mrs Morrell after she returned to her home, *Marden Ash,* on 30 March 1949, attended by a bevy of nurses. In this ten-bedroom Meads mansion, he supervised her therapy, and her frequent will changing.

For an example of his relationship with patients: on 12 September 1950 Dr Adams went to Scotland on a shooting holiday, Mrs Morrell contrived a codicil on 15 September cutting the Doctor out of her will. He dashed back on 16 September, resuming his holiday two days' later, finally returning, 24 September. The codicil was torn up, 23 October. She died 13 November 1950 at the age of 81.

Mrs Edith Morrell in her garden {Popperfoto}

Douglas Wilson's wife, Gwenda Wilson (née Jones) who worked in a solicitor's office, witnessed the final will of Mrs Morrell. After his patient's death Dr Adams was given a case of silver and her ageing Rolls-Royce. Its registration number was JK 1600, and he transferred the number to subsequent cars, showing that it had a special significance for him. Some say the connection was with the telephone number of the *Grand Hotel* (Eastbourne 1600), but is it not more likely that he retained memories of the car from just before the war?

Mrs Ellen Chasey, of Lushington Road, was another elderly patient who had great faith in him. She suffered from asthma. His main treatment consisted of injections, an asthma spray, possibly *Rybarin*, and he prayed at her bedside.

Mrs Yvonne King says her parents ran the *Mansion Hotel* in the 1950s. "They thought Dr Adams was excellent, always very kind, caring and considerate. I was a little girl then and we had just come down from London where I had all the tests and they had prescribed diets because I was always sick before parties and other events. Dr Adams said, 'If you want her to be an invalid you're going the right way about it, she should try to live a normal life and before any occasion, such as exams, I will give her a little calming tablet.' And it worked. I thought he was a lovely gentleman. He had time for you. He came out any time of the night, often with his trousers over his pyjamas.

"At the *Mansion Hotel* it was noticeable that husbands would often bring their wives down for a week while they worked in London. Usually the woman was going through the change and was finding it difficult. Dr Adams would hold her hand and say, 'Now sit down and tell me how you feel'. Invariably, when the husband came back on the Friday he would comment that his wife was much happier and it must be the sea air, but it was a doctor giving a worried lady time to talk about her condition."

Mrs King adds, "He built up a rapport with many of his patients and they left him something in their wills, which was common then, now it all goes to Dogs' Homes. It was really bad luck that a number died about the same time giving rise to rumours partly fed by resentment that he should be benefiting.

"I recall his District Nurse was Nurse Turner, with whom he worked well."

Phyllis Turner was indeed his main District Nurse and she thought Dr Adams was, "... very good. Kind and gentle".

Mrs Grace Harriott, an Eastbourne district nurse in the 1950s, confirms that he was so busy it was often nine in the evening before he saw his nurses. "He was the only doctor who, after discussing a case, would shake hands with the nurse."

A senior ambulanceman, Mr AJ Burnage, reports that in the days when long-distance transfers of patients took place by train, Dr Adams was one of the few Eastbourne doctors who regularly came to the station to wish the patient 'Bon voyage' and to attend to any transit needs. It might be said that his actions were with an eye to the main chance, but he attended irrespective of the patient's status, and whether private or NHS.

Philip Cheal worked at C Brewer & Sons, decorators' merchants, in Station Parade. "Dr Adams was a frequent customer, but seldom spent much. 'Don't you have anything cheaper?' was a frequent question. He sometimes told us how he worked 18 hours a day for seven days a week for a stretch, and then took an expensive holiday, shooting, in Scotland. He was, of course, an expert shot."

A shooting companion of his at Fairfield (Westham) and Catfield was David Godden. About 1951 one of his daughters had a riding accident and developed septicaemia. Dr Adams looked after her and, it is said, saved her life when he had antibiotics flown over from the USA. Marlene Davey (née Godden) says that he looked after all her family wonderfully well.

Sarah Florence Henry, the cousin who had lived with him and his mother, died of ovarian cancer in June 1952, aged 52, at *Kent Lodge.* She was Mr Snowball's patient, but Dr Adams looked after her with great compassion. Her nurses describe him leaving half-a-dozen filled syringes when he went out, so that she would not suffer excessive pain. He described her as, "... a sweet Christian soul".

Joan Visick was a physiotherapist in Eastbourne in the 1950s who occasionally saw patients for Dr Adams. Her son recalls that in 1952, after the death of a patient with cancer whom she had been seeing with Dr Adams, her comment was that he had eased the patient's death. "This was said in the sense that he had helped the patient and was not in any way critical. She thought of him as a kindly doctor."

Local solicitor, John Porter, says that he first heard of Dr Adams from his brother who worked for a life insurance company in London and frequently used his services. "He had a high regard for his ability."

Mr Porter goes on, "A memory which will remain with me was of a telephone call from Dr Adams enquiring as to whether I had seen Mrs X that day and whether she had made provision for him under her will as promised. Obviously, I could not divulge such information and referred him back to the lady in question. Being relatively inexperienced I was horrified and astonished to receive such an approach from a doctor who at the time had an excellent reputation in the town. Subsequently I learned that what Dr Adams was doing was not uncommon among doctors in the town, namely to treat patients privately, but to render them merely nominal bills, on the understanding that the doctor in question would be looked after under the patient's will. As far as I am aware this is not contrary to medical ethics, but it was this sort of activity that gave rise to the suspicion that fell upon Dr Adams and led to his prosecution".

An Eastbourne GP of the time says, "Bodkin was a greedy man, a collector of trinkets, money and cars. I think he had the ability to be a good doctor, but his patients asked to be fussed, they wanted his time, and immediate availability. He had a remarkable ability to talk rubbish which reassured a frightened patient.

"He had a black notebook in which he kept a note of the consultants in every branch of medicine. He sent all his chest cases to Howard Nicholson of UCH, and Bodkin would have the great surgeons from London to operate in the Esperance Nursing Home. A standard remark among the other doctors was that they had to be good surgeons since he would be giving the anaesthetic, when he was awake, that is." And now he could take the patient for a consultant opinion in his Rolls.

Dr Adams was rapidly becoming the talk of Eastbourne. Another doctor confirms, "There was a considerable amount of jealousy in the town. Surgery was kept in the practice, so bringing consultants in from outside the area was disliked.

"His practice was more paternalistic than any of today. Dr Adams would do tests, for example ECGs [heart records], and if abnormal he would often not tell the patient. He would say that he glossed over the fact for the sake of his patient who would only worry. You have to admit that, unlike today, there were no significant drugs or operations to transform most heart diseases.

"A test on a young farmer from Hastings way showed he'd had a pulmonary embolus [a clot on the lung] and I told Bodkin, but he thought it could wait. When I told him he would be up before the coroner, he asked me to treat him."

Michael Clark says, "My wife Laura (née Bergman van Ling) was a nurse in the Princess Alice Hospital theatre, 1951-2, and she was always talking about the patients going blue when Bodkin Adams gave the anaesthetic."

Dr Colin Morley, Old Etonian and later an Eastbourne GP, told a story of Bodkin Adams and his anaesthetics from early 1953. "I was a houseman [junior doctor] at St Mary's Hospital when a little boy was brought into Casualty with a lacerated leg. After I discussed the case with the duty surgeon, Mr Peter Smith, he told me to get on with stitching it up, so I called in the duty anaesthetist who happened to be Dr Adams." Dr Morley recalled that Dr Adams spent most of the operation counting £5 notes and railing on about the iniquities of supertax [an additional 48% tax on incomes of over £20 000 in the 1940s and 50s] - not of riveting interest to Dr Morley who was on £350 a year. "After a while Dr Adams asked, 'Are you finished that end?' 'Nearly there.' I confirmed, 'Oh Good,' was Bodkin's reply, 'Because I've run out of anaesthetic'."

Although fairly fit, Dr Adams was having trouble finding a doctor for himself. A local GP explained, "I met Adams at a Medical Conference in London and was polite to him for a few minutes. He later wrote to ask if I would look after him. "Adams was an extremely lonely man. When he was ill he was embarrassed at being a nuisance, but only took what advice he wanted."

Dr Adams was, however, adding to his reputation in other ways.

Mr D Barden worked at the *Cavendish Hotel* during 1952-54, when he often saw Dr Adams. "He was a very smart and distinguished looking man, with his black hat, glasses, dark suit, black overcoat, gloves and, of course, his black bag and Rolls-Royce. He used to come to visit a Mr Reid, a permanent resident, who had a suite on the fourth floor, number 424, with a private nurse.

"Whenever Dr Adams came the nurse was told to leave, and I would take her down in the lift to sit in the lounge until the Doctor had left. This upset her greatly and she couldn't understand why. She told me that Dr Adams was a devious man with a charm and politeness which hid his inner self."

Other nurses agree that he tended to see his patients alone, although the interpretation was not always the same. "You had to stand to attention for Mr MacQueen", says nursery nurse Mrs D Dougall, "Whereas Dr Adams didn't stand on ceremony and would just want to be shown to the patient".

Norah and Nigel Skellett (he was Manager of the Eastbourne Birds Eye factory) said, "Bodkin Adams was the talk of the town in the 1950s, when Eastbourne was a select and fashionable place, very much what it had been before the war. Would you say that he was a proponent of euthanasia?"

For several years a joke went round the medical circles that Dr Adams' black bag contained just a blank will form and a hypodermic syringe of morphia. He certainly told the author, "You don't pay tax on bequests".

An Eastbourne doctor said, "I'm not suggesting that he deliberately set out on a program of getting a will in his favour and then killing the patient. He did, however, seem to cultivate a certain patient who 'needed' regular visits, and to have a manner that perhaps could be said not only to encourage a regular harvest of bequests, but that people would talk about it too."

An Eastbourne Consultant says, "A number of general practitioner patients in the 1950s and 60s were on monthly injections of *Cytamen,* Vitamin B_{12}, as a non-specific 'tonic' for 'anaemia' or 'tiredness'. Any incoming doctor at first thought it a most reprehensible practice. On closer acquaintance it became apparent that the patients welcomed the opportunity for a chat, and perhaps they liked the arrangement because they felt they were definitely being given something. It has to be said it didn't do them any harm, and to wean them off would not do them or their doctor, much good. So you could be hasty in your condemnations and there were worse practices, a few patients with no firm evidence of thyroid disease were on thyroid tablets for anything from obesity to fatigue." Another point is that tests to prove vitamin, or thyroid, deficiency were cumbersome in the mid-20th century.

So perhaps Dr Adams was not alone, but unlike the others he talked about his practices, and he was ostentatious about his wealth.

He supported local businesses. Morris Walker says, "During the years 1951-54 I was chief assistant at Douglas Catt's, the photographic and cine specialist of Terminus Road. Dr Adams was a regular customer and I got to know him well.

"He was an enthusiastic photographer and cinematographer and was always anxious to know about and, if possible possess, the latest equipment. We undertook a lot of his developing and printing and I was quite astonished to find that he did not produce good pictures.

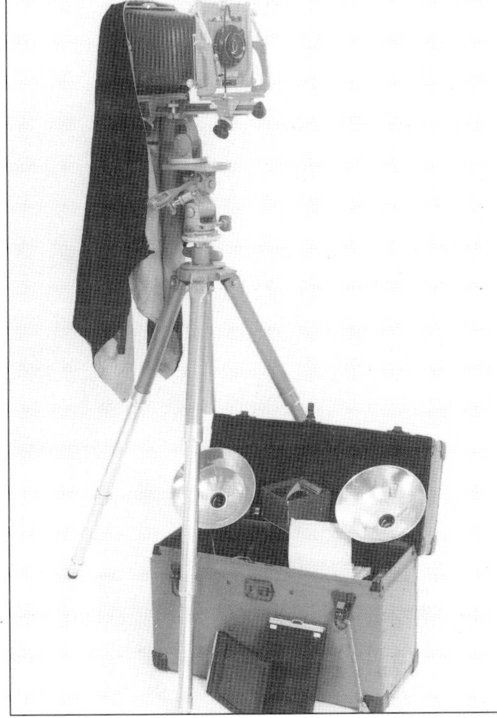

Large format monorail view camera owned by Dr Adams

"He loved to have the best of everything and I have a vivid memory of visiting his house, *Kent Lodge*, just round the corner, and demonstrating the very latest, Bell and Howell 16mm cine projector, fresh from the USA.

"His appearance in the shop was always an event. This fairly heavily-built, tubby, man with such quick light steps - almost dancing with enthusiasm - caused some amusement. He was always popular, full of stories and chuckled easily.

"I must reccunt one particular incident. After the war, well known German camera makers were beginning to produce new equipment and one day Dr Adams rushed into the shop flourishing a magazine advertisement and exclaiming, 'I must have it'. The camera was the Leitz Company's newly designed Leica. We had to explain that due to import restrictions it would not be available in Great Britain for some months. 'But I want it - I must have it'. He departed that Friday afternoon a disappointed man. Quite early on the following Monday he burst into the shop brandishing a spanking new camera, 'I got it'. He had made a weekend visit to Dublin and this was the result. Here was a man who simply loved to possess the latest and best whatever the cost. As with so many of his prized acquisitions, he had his name engraved on the metal case. He wasn't my doctor, but friends who had him thought he was good.

"He was, however, a truly attractive personality and in the shop we often smiled at his ways and always enjoyed his company.

"Bobbie Hullett, a patient of Dr Adams, was also a customer, although never in his company. I recollect her well as quite a striking woman. I also knew Mrs Morrell about 1937. Before I went into photography, I was an apprentice with John Pring & Co, the house furnishers. They helped to furnish Mrs Morrell's new home *Marden Ash* in Beachy Head Road, on the left side just past Darley Road."

Derek Keay, a radio engineer for Lindridges Ltd, radio and musical instruments, of Terminus Road, says, "Dr Adams was a keen radio listener, his favourite items were the news and information programs. He bought several radio sets, always Roberts' Portables. They were considered the 'Rolls-Royce' of radios and had a 'By Appointment' crest on the cover.

"I visited his house to keep these radios in first class condition as he was a most fastidious person and everything had to be right. We had little chats over a cup of tea and I found him a person who would talk to his staff and tradesmen and was most friendly to all. I have to say that regardless of all that has been said, I found Dr Adams pleasant to people who were doing work for him."

He did not sustain the wine trade. Dr Adams was said to be teetotal, and for all practical purposes he was, but after the war he would join in a social glass of sherry, which he looked upon as a medicinal appetiser. Mrs Pat Piper (née Tomlinson) agrees that he didn't entirely eschew alcohol.

Margaret and Nigel Lees say that their family firm, HT White's of Eastbourne, supplied Dr Adams with his wines and spirits, but these could have been for Christmas gifts. Richard Diplock was a manager of HT White's high-class wine shop in Compton Street. He remembers, "Dr Adams used to come in to collect a large box of liqueur chocolates which one patient gave him every Christmas, but as he was teetotal he never routinely bought wines or spirits."

The Doctor also played his part in supporting charitable causes.

Mr EG Turner, a chairman of the Eastbourne branch of the YMCA in the 1980s, said, "He was a life-long member and supporter of the YMCA movement. In Eastbourne he was joint-chairman for very many years and in the Hartington Hall days in Bolton Road it was his personal generosity which kept the branch going. As a specific example he paid all expenses for two young members, Ron Edwards and myself to go to a YMCA meeting in Paris".

George Turner goes on, "Mrs Prince was a great friend of the Doctor, as were the Chitty sisters, who owned the Sandhurst Hotel. Mrs Prince was a lonely, wealthy widow and every week Dr Adams went for a meal with her. She thought he was the King, but there was no question of any impropriety in any way. She was just one wealthy widow with a Rolls, who outlived him".

Other YMCA committee members Tom Alston (who was chairman after Dr Adams), John Dobell, and Frank Mepham agree he helped to keep the YMCA going. Mr Mepham, who organised the YMCA Sports, said Dr Adams would come for the Sports Supper, and generously gave lunch for the teams at Princes Park.

Mr Turner comments, "Dr Bodkin Adams didn't get on well with Lady Dodd and the Misses Campbell and Fovargue on the YM/YWCA joint committee, but he tolerated them to keep the YMCA going."

Philip Cheal added, "Dr Adams acted as chairman of many YMCA committee meetings which I attended. I recall that at one meeting the phrase 'controlling the Eastbourne YMCA' was used. At this he became very angry, banged on the table, and announced, 'No one controls this YMCA except ME'."

Mrs Barbara Selby mentions that in the 1940s and 50s she and her husband played in the Eastbourne Table Tennis Championships at the Town Hall. "Bodkin Adams used to sit on the stage and watch the matches. I believe he was a sponsor of the tournament". Philip Cheal confirms that the Doctor was Vice-President of the Eastbourne and District Table Tennis League.

Inevitably, among those who met the man some had reservations and were not too certain of him.

John Murray, of the *Kildare Hotel*, said Dr Adams was a regular visitor to the residents, in particular to a Mrs Robinson, of the building firm. "After he had been I would say to him, 'Does she need anything?' and he would reply, 'No, she's had her time'. It was said he would go round the hotels asking for any business."

Mrs Olive Pack worked at the butcher's shop in Little Common from 1950-97, and delivered the Doctor's Christmas turkey. "He was a strange gentleman, always dressed in black, and he used to pay me in cash from his black purse.

"I wouldn't say I was scared of him, but I was not keen to enter his house when invited in by his elderly housekeeper. At times he called at the shop, but no one was very sure of him; he was really weird. I could never understand how those ladies liked him as their doctor."

Mrs JF Allchorn (née Appleby) says, "In 1954 my mother took me to Dr Bodkin Adams' house in Trinity Trees to have my ears pierced for my eighteenth birthday. I remember the large house and being shown into a dark and sombre room. Dr Adams entered, he was a large man who seemed to have a beard and I must admit I felt a bit apprehensive - especially when he produced a large needle!

"However, the whole procedure was only a matter of minutes and I was very pleased with my gold earrings."

Supt Clive Evans recalled that when he was a bobby on the beat, patrolling Borough Lane, a nurse ran out of the Manor Hall Nursing Home to ask for help with a violent patient. They telephoned Bodkin Adams who came out with his coat over his pyjamas and he prescribed for the patient, although he didn't examine her.

Mrs Vivien Ackroyd knew Mrs Hunt, mother of Sir John Hunt of Everest fame, who lived in Selwyn Road. "She said Dr Adams begged her to allow him to advise on financial matters, whereupon she had told her maid never to let him in".

Usually, however, those who he looked after thought he was wonderful. Roy Bedford says, "My family thought that he was a very good doctor".

Mrs Adèle Snashall recounts her mother's experience. "My mother, Rita Gray, a very fashionable and go-ahead lady, arranged to have her ears pierced by Dr Adams. After work one summer day she pedalled to Trinity Trees for her appointment at the end of his surgery. On completing the procedure he gave her some tissues, '... to make sure blood doesn't drip onto your pretty dress'. After seeing her out the Doctor told her he was catching a train to Scotland for grouse shooting and waved her good-bye. Mum was smitten with his charm and wore earrings to her dying day. She thought him a true gentleman and never forgot his kindness and thoughtfulness, even though she only had a bicycle."

Sister Mavis Constable says, "He was popular with the nurses because when they went to him to have their ears pierced he didn't charge."

Scotland or anywhere, his shooting interest continued unabated. Colin Huggett says, "In almost every issue of *Shooting Times* of the early 1950s the Club Reports had 'First JB Adams' or 'Joint First JB Adams and DF Clay'. Doug Clay was a great shooting pal of his and they often went shooting together". Dr Adams also invited Richard James, to learn to shoot, at Berwick, along with Leonard Earp.

His cars were not forgotten. Mr Pickles said that when his previous chauffeur retired in 1952, Mr White came to Dr Adams from O'Hara's the butcher's.

Mrs Yvonne King added, "His chauffeur wore a cap and gaiters and was always washing his cars in the back of *Kent Lodge*. Living nearby we would say, 'Dr Adams must be going out, the car is being washed'."

Mary Alston says that her brother knew Dr Adams from the YMCA, and the Doctor often came into the family shop, which sold surgical supports. "He had the cleanest car in the town. Mr White was always washing it down." It was said that even if it had just rained he would still be able to go out in a pristine car.

Gordon Clark worked for Caffyn's in their Seaside garage as a panel beater in the bodyshop. 'We repaired Dr Adams' cars. I have never seen such a methodical, precise person. In a way he was comical.

"In the 1950s, he would send his chauffeur down with the car (he had a Morris Minor and a grey Rolls-Royce). After it was ready the chauffeur would come to look it over, and he would ask, 'Everything all right?' And off he would go.

"Within two hours Dr Adams would come in and, without a word to anyone (even if you said 'Good morning Dr Adams'. Not once did he say 'Hello'), he would go straight to his car, walk round it, look it over and walk out again. Shortly afterwards he would ring up the manager, usually Mr Frank Spooner, and complain about the slightest imperfection. One time he pointed out that the bumper of the Morris Minor was 3/8 inch [9mm] further away from the body on one side than the other and he wanted it put right. Only he would have noticed it.

"On one occasion he wanted a special boot lid fitted to the Morris Minor to carry his guns, but the old boot lid had to be specially delivered by Caffyns back to his home. Mr White, his chauffeur, told me that in a top room of *Kent Lodge* he stored every part that had ever been taken off a car of his and replaced. Numbered and labelled bits of cars, guns and cameras were spread all over the room.

"When he brought his car in for service we were told not to move anything inside the car or to touch the pockets. One day I looked in the glove pocket and found a booklet which noted everything about that car, every drop of petrol, oil change, battery charge, everything was recorded.

"He had a smash coming out of the back entrance of *Kent Lodge* into Lismore Road, when a car ran into the side of the Rolls, and I don't think it was his fault.

The Rolls was an old model and parts were not available so Caffyns made up a new door, new running board and a new wing, and he would come in at least once a week to see how it was doing. When complete the insurance company only wanted to have the new parts sprayed, but he insisted on a respray all over."

It was his chauffeur and Rolls-Royce JK 1600 that conveyed Princess Alice, Countess of Athlone, from the station to the Nurses' Prizegiving at the Princess Alice Hospital on 15 October 1953. Beforehand there was a luncheon at the home of Lt Col Roland Gwynne. The lunch was a success, but the matron, Miss Hilda de Pinto (later Wells), who was seated next to Dr Adams, complained that all he talked about was the huge amount he had recently spent on fishing rods. "However, his presence was necessary as a thank you for allowing the use of his Rolls".

A social event at Holywell Mount c.1950, host Jack Hullett is seated in the centre, Dr Adams is top left {Associated Newspapers}

Mrs Doris Sellens, later his housekeeper, says that he treasured a letter from Her Royal Highness, thanking him for use of his Rolls.

It is doubtful if Dr Adams ever fully integrated himself into the practice after the war. In most practices other partners would see patients when their doctor had a half day off, but Dr Adams kept his patients very much to himself. Patients of the College Road practice, Len and Agnes Starling, said that Vincent Harris was their doctor and Dr Adams seemed separate from the practice.

Dr Ian Brown, Hospital Superintendent at St Mary's Hospital from 1948, agrees that Bodkin Adams was a loner. "He used to telephone me at the hospital to ask if I would complete cremation certificates. He did not want to introduce other general practitioners to the family of a deceased patient in case the family might change their allegiance." Dr Adams knew Dr Brown was not in competition for private patients and Dr Brown was only too pleased to earn an extra guinea. Later he was to have some mild misgivings.

Dr Basil Barkworth says, "He was far from reticent about his material success. The other partners were critical of his very free use of dangerous drugs, and took him to task about sending bills to NHS patients. He couldn't see this was wrong if they were willing to pay him to visit them rather than wait in the surgery. We were wary of crossing him, he could be most wounding, and it was his own affair".

Dr Adams said, "I carried three sorts of tablets in my case: sodium phenobarbitone[2] [a sedative; does not relieve pain], a phenacetin type [mild pain reliever], and a placebo [tablet containing no active ingredient]. I would give the patient seven tablets of phenobarbitone and say, 'Take one at night', after a week I would give the pain relief tablet saying, 'You are sleeping well, continue' and after another week they could go on with the harmless tablet. Patients were pleased to find someone with an interest in them."

Hugh Weavers, who worked at the Princess Alice Hospital laboratory from 1949-59, says that he never understood why Dr Adams' style of practice was so unlike his partners. He remembers Dr Geoffrey Shera calling the staff together for a confidential meeting about Dr Adams in 1954. Dr Shera asked them to be vigilant because Dr Adams might be forging doctors' signatures to procure NHS services for his private patients. As Dr Charles Dunlop explains, in those days the EC10 prescription forms didn't have a doctors' name on them.

According to Dr Michael Emslie this request arose after his father, Dr John Emslie, was telephoned by Dr Shera asking why he had ordered such expensive vaccines for one of his NHS patients. Dr Emslie denied that he had ordered them, so they examined the prescription, but were unable to identify who had authorised it. Together they saw the patient, who stated that while he was an NHS patient of Dr Emslie, he was a private patient of Dr Adams, who had signed the prescription. The patient said he was not well off, that what Dr Adams did was for his benefit and he was grateful to him.

Drs Emslie and Shera hastened to Dr Adams to demand the meaning of the false signature. He apologised, saying that the patient was poor and he was trying to save him money. Dr Emslie told Dr Adams, "If there is any repetition this prescription will be produced to the police".

Such incidents could not help his reputation. Philip Cheal recalls, "For many months rumours had been sweeping the town suggesting that Adams had been helping old ladies into the hereafter by the administration of drugs and had benefited from their wills.

"I recall that several times money arrived at the YMCA which '... dear Mrs Blank so wanted the YMCA to have'. Gordon Downs, who was in charge at that time, was concerned at these episodes as no evidence was ever produced that a bequest had in fact been made."

Len Miller says that in the early 1950s he was engaged in legal transfers and, "... by 1953 everyone working in the office had noticed how many bequests Dr

Adams received. They were usually small sums such as £50-£100, but so many that we weren't surprised when the case surfaced later."

A secretary who worked at Coles & James, his solicitors, said the staff in their office also commented on the many legacies Dr Adams received.

Ernest George, a local solicitor, remarks that after putting in the usual newspaper piece about would any claimants to a will notify him, he was surprised to receive a letter from Bodkin Adams claiming that he had not charged this patient and was due a certain sum. "I had no proof either way, but decided to pay. An odd fellow I would say."

Michael Ockenden says that his father worked for Bruford's, the Jewellers, and not infrequently he would mention that a customer had come in to buy a piece of silver for Dr Adams.

Tom Searle, pharmacist, says "There were many rumours at the time, none as far as I know with any proof. One story went that he sat on the side of a patient's bed talking on the phone to the solicitor discussing the will".

On the other hand, as always with the Doctor, there is someone to say, "He was our family doctor and he lanced a boil behind my knee and here I am good as rain." Frank D Alford remembers having a bad dose of shingles "... for which he gave me some cream and the shingles vanished overnight".

Mrs Joan Hughes says that her father had Dr Adams as his doctor and thought him excellent. And Jack Putland says, "My aunt thought Dr Adams was wonderful."

Mrs Win Woodward, the Secretary at the Leaf Hospital, said that Dr Bodkin Adams punctiliously visited his patients in the Leaf at least once a week – "He would pop his head round the door and say who he was visiting."

Gabrielle Whyte says that her parents, both nurses, had Dr Adams as their GP, "... and he assisted at my father's varicose vein operation. He did on occasions make a visit to our house, and I remember his Rolls-Royce parked outside, which caused quite a stir".

John Tyhurst reports, "After being diagnosed by my NHS GP as having scarlet fever, I wasn't satisfied, so I contacted Dr Adams. He opted for German measles, which it turned out to be".

Dr Peter Cook, a casualty officer at the Princess Alice Hospital, says that Bodkin was oleaceous and ingratiating, but was undoubtedly prepared to give time and solicitude at any time of the day or night to his patients, many of whom were rich and grateful.

Dr Adams kept up his motoring interests. Mr Ron Spicer says that he was an expert engine tuner, and took part in hill climbs at Firle Beacon driving an MG in competition with, among others, Mr MA Knights, a local dental surgeon. Douglas Martin, another Eastbourne dentist, says he regularly met Dr Adams at meetings of the IAM at Withdean, "He would drive up in his blue Morris Minor with its distinctive squared-off boot-lid. From time to time Dr Adams administered a general anaesthetic at my surgery for his own patients. I remember the Doctor's 'whiff' technique with horror. He would induce deep sleep with nitrous oxide, whip off the facemask and expect the dentist to complete the operation before the patient came round. Though this was common practice in bygone years, it was not what a young dentist expected to cope with in 1956, when continuous anaesthetic methods were well established." This when Dr Adams claimed to have introduced nasal anaesthetics for dentistry to Eastbourne.

Other post-war changes were starting to affect Eastbourne. Life was easier, rationing had gone and the first signs of development were seen. The good Doctor remained unaffected, maintaining his mix of religion and medicine, whatever he thought would help his patients. Dr Michael Emslie says that Dr Adams would explain to patients, "If we pray to God together the medicine will work quicker". Yet again others said it was just a means of helping himself more than the patient.

He had not given up his obstetrics entirely. Sister Mary Bridger, who started at the Maternity Home in 1955, declared, "I have even seen Dr Bodkin Adams wielding a pair of forceps".

Mrs Jane Backhouse confirms that Dr Adams went asleep during operations at St Mary's Hospital in the 1950s, and a theatre nurse at Princess Alice Hospital says, "He was not a shining example of the profession, and he regularly fell asleep at operations. One day he dropped off his stool and this big hulk rolled on to the sterilising drums, scattering them with an almighty crash."

So Dr Adams continued along his way: beloved by his patients, especially his old ladies, somewhat isolated from his younger colleagues, tended by a housekeeper, receptionist, secretary and chauffeur, and followed by a cloud of suspicion and gossip. This was mainly about the number leaving him money, and while the gossips had to admit that Eastbourne, with its excess of elderly, would expect a high death rate, the rumours questioned the speed at which his patients died after willing money to him. Again it could be expected that some of the deaths would be sudden, but what if they were not occurring in their own good time?

Richard Gordon, [Dr Gordon Ostlere], "Smiling, soothing Dr Adams had an enviable private practice. In his charming Ulster brogue he would say to the widow across the couch, 'Do you know how much supertax I pay, m'dear? A thousand pounds! Now if I didn't charge any fees and you remembered me in your will, then it'll come to me tax free.' Quite a few obliged and the Eastbourne gossips, particularly the Meads bridge set, credited him with hundreds".

Richard Walker, the Chief Constable, mild and courteous, had like most of his force heard of the gossip, and being proud of the town's reputation had investigated discreetly without any real evidence emerging.

It was even said that Eastbourne police received three anonymous telephone calls in 1955 accusing the Doctor of murder. With no evidence being supplied to substantiate the accusations the calls were ignored. The Chief Constable was not about to launch a murder investigation without substantial evidence, and certainly not when the prime suspect was the doctor to some of the most influential people in the county.

Until, that is, the death of a middle-aged vivacious woman, with no history of serious illness, but many influential friends.

6. THE CORONER'S INQUEST

If they're lucky in addition
In their choice of a physician
And remember him when making out their wills,
And bequeath their Rolls-Royces
Then they'll soon hear angel voices
And are quickly freed from all their earthly ills.

On a Saturday morning in July 1956, the staff of St Mary's Hospital laboratory, Eastbourne, were working to get the results out before closing at one o'clock. A transfer box for late specimens arrived from the Princess Alice Hospital, with a urine sample from a Mrs Hullett, a patient of Dr Bodkin Adams, for barbiturate testing. The Koppani test, then used, took 45 minutes to complete and would not be finished in time. Robert Elliston, the senior technician, rang AG 'Jack' Newman, the chief technician at the PA, to ask if the test could be done as an 'Emergency On Call' - for which he would receive 12/6d [62$^1/_2$p]. Bob Elliston was informed that Dr Adams had said it could wait until after the weekend.

Mr Elliston said, "The specimen was refrigerated and tested on the Monday with a positive result for barbiturate. The incident was fixed in my memory because 62$^1/_2$p was a substantial amount when I was on a salary of £450 per annum. Another reason for not forgetting was that, in my experience of over 40 years in hospital labs, it was the only time that a doctor requested a barbiturate on a living patient and was willing to wait two days for the result."

Dr Adams was not up on tests and had asked for it only because Dr Shera said that if it was negative barbiturate overdose was unlikely, and in those days nobody could have done more for Mrs Hullett's presumed stroke. The test did not tell you how much barbiturate was present, hence a positive result could be detecting merely sedative therapy - and other drugs such as sulphonamides showed up.

Even so, it seems perverse to ask for the test, only to leave it until the Monday.

These events, an important part of the Bodkin Adams' story, had their beginnings in November 1955 when Alfred John Hullett, a wealthy Lloyds underwriter who would throw a party for 100 guests at the *Savoy Hotel,* consulted his doctor about a tummy complaint.

Jack Hullett had retired to *Holywell Mount* on the Eastbourne seafront at Upper Meads, as the estate agents would say, a good address. He spent lavishly rebuilding the house, and was a generous host. Dr Adams became his physician and a frequent social visitor to the house. Pearl Ayres, who worked there in the 1990s when St Bede's School took it over, says, "Hardly changed from Dr Adams' time, it still had an open veranda overlooking the sea with magnificent views".

After the death of his first wife Jack Hullett had talked with Dr Adams about his loneliness, and the Doctor suggested a cruise and as a companion a young widow, another patient of his and known slightly to Hullett.

Gertrude Joyce "Bobbie" Tomlinson, then 48, was the widow of Vaughan Tomlinson. He had been one of the four headmasters and co-owners of St Bede's School, Eastbourne. According to her daughter Patricia Piper (née Tomlinson), she had always been an anxious person; was shattered after Vaughan died of a heart attack in his forties in 1950, and at first did not want to go on living.

A cruise on the *Reina del Pacifico* to the Caribbean finished with an engaged Jack and Bobbie, who married shortly after their return in 1953. They settled into a happily married life at *Holywell Mount* where they welcomed many friends including actress Marie Lohr, actor Leslie Henson, singers Anne Ziegler and Webster Booth, Elsa Caffyn, the Bishop of Coventry, Richard Walker the Chief Constable of Eastbourne and his wife, and naturally, Dr Adams.

'Bobbie' Hullett walks in front of Jack's Silver Dawn Rolls-Royce at Eastbourne's 1954 concours d'élégance in the Winter Garden. Dr Adams is standing in front of the central pillar with a flash camera {Topham Picturepoint}

When in November 1955 Dr Adams came to examine 71-year-old Jack for his tummy symptoms, he speedily diagnosed a bowel cancer. He said to colleagues he knew it would be fatal so he didn't ask an Eastbourne surgeon, but called in top London surgeon, Sir Arthur (later Lord) Porritt, subsequently Governor-General of New Zealand, to operate at the Esperance Nursing Home. Jack Hullett told one of his nurses, Sister Mary Wagner, "Thank God I have a good doctor".

Mrs Piper, says "My mother thought Bodkin Adams was wonderful, as did Jack. Other patients thought well of him too, for example, Jack and Margaret Hawkins, who called him 'The Bod'."

Jack Hullett seemed to improve for a few months, but after a drive and a drink at his local, *The Pilot,* on 13 March 1956, he felt unwell and that evening called in Dr Adams. He diagnosed a stroke, or a heart attack, and gave him an injection of morphia to relieve his distress, but Jack Hullett died in his sleep early the next morning. The body was cremated.

He left £107 647; Dr Adams received £500, with the residue to his widow.

Mrs Hullett was devastated. Her daughter explains, "When Jack Hullett died it brought back all my mother's fears after my father's death." She became depressed and threatened to jump off Beachy Head. Dr Adams treated her with sedatives, primarily a favourite of his - sodium barbitone $7^{1}/_{2}$gr [450mg]. [1]He carefully doled out the daily doses so that she would not have enough for an overdose. Except, that is, for May 1956 when he went on a short holiday with her to Ireland, in a foursome with friends Mrs and Miss Hawkins, and because Mrs Hullett said she had forgotten her tablets he gave her enough to cover her stay.

Ronald Parsons says, "My wife, Do, and I knew Bobbie well at *Wishanger* in Willingdon, when she was the wife of Vaughan. Bobbie was neurotic, so there was an excuse for sedating her, but we always thought that he put her on drugs excessively. Having said that we never heard any complaints about his treatment of anyone and I know he was loved dearly by many patients."

Dr Barkworth recounts how he treated Mrs Hullett for the duration of one of Dr Adams' shooting holidays. "She was suffering from a neurodermatitis affecting her face, which was treated with sedatives without the slightest improvement; bear in mind, these were the days before steroid creams and tranquillisers." Dr Barkworth was thankful when Dr Adams returned and not at all surprised to be told a few days later, "I got rid of that rash of Mrs Hullett's". "What did you use?" asked Dr Barkworth, for Dr Adams to reply, "Petrolagar. I told her to rub it in every four hours and it was gone the next day".

Patricia Piper. "I found him a very kind doctor, everyone liked him, he had time to talk with patients and he was prepared to visit. On the other hand, it could be said that he was an ugly man with a leering look through his round glasses, and his appearance fitted a 'Wicked Uncle' tag."

Mrs Hullett's married sister lived in Dorset and so could not often visit, but she confirmed that her sister was thinking of suicide after the death of Jack Hullett. Typical of her letters was, 'I do not want to go on living without Jack'.

In the middle of July, 1956, four months after Jack Hullett's death, a series of dramatic events happened.

Mrs Hullett drew up her will on 12 July and signed it two days later. She had asked Dr Adams to be an executor, but this time he declined.

Dr Adams, who visited every day leaving religious tracts for her to read, received a cheque from her for £1000. Drawn on her account at the Westminster (Natwest) Bank, Meads, he presented it to his bank, the Midland (HSBC), on 18 July. He asked the cashier, Kenneth Pill, to expedite its clearance and explained, "This lady is not long for this world." Peter D Palmer, of the Midland Bank, says, "I was one of the people who handled this cheque and the writing was barely legible, I assumed that the drawer was a very old lady of advanced years".

The cheque was cleared the next day, Thursday, 19 July. That evening Mrs Hullett retired to bed early and was soon fast asleep.

On the Friday morning when the maid brought Dr Adams to see his patient he found her sleeping soundly and decided not to disturb her. It was when he was at a meeting in Lewes in the afternoon that he received a message saying Mrs Hullett was still asleep, so he asked a partner, Dr Vincent Harris, to visit her.

Dr Harris found her unconscious, looked in vain for an empty medicine bottle which might suggest suicide, and having obtained a history from the household that she had complained of a headache the previous evening, diagnosed a stroke [cerebral vascular accident]. He gave an injection of *Coramine* [a respiratory stimulant], and left a message for his partner. Dr Adams hurried back to *Holywell Mount* to find his patient comatose and, convinced in his own mind that she could not have saved up tablets for an overdose, agreed with Dr Harris' diagnosis. He arranged for a night nurse and stayed the night at the house.

Dr Harris thought that the patient should be moved to hospital, but Dr Adams said she had an intense dislike of hospitals and had made him promise that he would never send her to one. Her daughter confirms, "She definitely didn't want to go to hospital", and Bodkin Adams reiterated to the author that he had promised Mrs Hullett, "a dear friend", he would not to send her into hospital. He kept his bond and kept her at home. A brave, if not foolhardy, act in the circumstances.

Dr Harris also said that a second opinion should be obtained, but Dr Adams considered this unnecessary, again Mrs Hullett had said she did not wish to see another doctor. On the Saturday morning, however, he rang retired Dr Geoffrey Shera to discuss the case. Shera visited, performed a lumbar puncture which did not reveal a cause for the coma, and asked if she was on barbiturates, after which Adams agreed to send a sample of her urine for barbiturate testing. It was this which was sent to the laboratory in the late specimen transfer box, as described.

"Near midnight on the Saturday", says Dr Peter Cook, casualty officer at the Princess Alice Hospital, "I was told that Bodkin was looking for me. He asked to be reminded of the drug that we had discussed when chatting over tea on the Thursday, when I had mentioned an article in the *BMJ* about *Megimide* as an anti-barbiturate.[2] I told him that I had no experience of using it, but it might be in the dispensary. As we walked over I asked if he had a patient suffering from an overdose, suggesting to him that *Megimide* was more appropriately given in hospital when it could be titrated clinically against the level of unconsciousness.

"He confirmed that he had such a patient; we found the drug and he took it away. I expected to receive the overdose patient over the weekend, but never did."

Pharmacist at Browne's, Michael Clark, states, "*Megimide* was a short-acting respiratory stimulant, no longer in use. With his inexperience, and not wishing to give an overdose, Dr Adams gave a single 10ml dose. The drug was of little value in barbiturate overdose, but the dose he gave was sub-clinical and ineffective.

"Logically, this was not the action of a doctor with murder in mind, but that of a doctor out of his depth, clutching at straws, and using a drug he had not even heard of before. The sin was ignorance. As Dr Adams had taken the drug from the hospital, Browne's had to order *Megimide* for him to replace the hospital stock."

Mrs Piper says, "Kathleen Reade, my mother's best friend since schooldays, came over from Uckfield to look after her when she was ill." Dr Adams stayed at the house, attending to his patient throughout the day and night, administering *Crystomycin* [antibiotics] and oxygen, but there was no improvement.

Dr Harris had reminded him that if Mrs Hullett died the coroner would have to be informed, and a post-mortem would be ordered. Did he wonder whether he could certify the death as a stroke although he was uncertain of the diagnosis? He was in no doubt that if he did not give a certificate there would have to be a post-mortem, with all the attendant publicity. Perhaps the coroner would help?

"Holywell Mount", Eastbourne in 1994, where Mrs Hullett committed suicide

Early on the Sunday morning Dr Adams telephoned Dr AC Sommerville, HM Coroner, to ask whether he could arrange a private post-mortem. The coroner, still in bed, was more than surprised, and asked the time of the patient's death, to which Dr Adams replied, "Oh, she isn't dead yet". The coroner told him curtly that if death was to occur the routine system of notifying the coroner's officer should apply; so there was no sympathy for his predicament from that quarter.

It was an unusual enquiry. The timing alone shows that Dr Adams was a worried man, and that he wanted the details kept as quiet as possible. If, however, she had taken an overdose there would have to be an inquest.

By now Mrs Hullett was too poorly to move and deteriorating, whatever the cause, and she died early on the morning of the next day, Monday, 23 July.

This was the moment when if Dr Adams wanted to avoid referral to the coroner he had to provide a death certificate. This was clearly not feasible: he was not sure of the diagnosis, and as it might be suicide, there was only one course of action, to report the death to the coroner. Or was it only the accidental involvement of Dr Harris that stopped him writing out a routine natural causes certificate recording 'Cerebral Haemorrhage'?

Later that morning Dr Adams drafted a letter for Dr Harris and himself to sign. It was not a succinct medical report, but a long-winded, rambling account, typewritten in blue, which you could imagine Bodkin Adams composing.

After the superscription, the name, address and age, he continued,

> 'History: Married about five years to an adoring and rich husband who died suddenly four months ago after a major abdominal operation. Since then she has been ill generally and lost the will to live. I have attended her regularly, and strictly doled out to her sodium barbiturate so that she could get a good night's sleep. She could not possibly have secreted any of this. She repeatedly refused to consult a psychologist or other physician.'
>
> He went on to give details of 'nerve storms' which Mrs Hullett had suffered, that he found her in coma on the Friday, and examined the room for any empty bottles but could not find any. He mentioned the urine test for barbiturates, "which is not yet to hand", and the injection of *Megimide*.
>
> 'In spite of the above, after temporary improvement, her temperature rose steadily to 105.5°, her condition worsened and she died at 7.23 am on 23.7.56.
>
> 'In my opinion and Dr Harris's, death was due to a cerebral lesion probably involving her Pons[3] with secondary complications in the lungs.
>
> 'Because of the pathologist's findings being inconclusive, and cremation requested, we are reporting the facts fully to you as we do not feel in a position to issue a death certificate.' The last thirteen words were in Dr Harris' hand.

Dr Adams delivered it in person to Sgt John Bull, the coroner's officer at Eastbourne Police Station, who immediately telephoned the coroner.

Without delay Dr Sommerville ordered a post-mortem to be conducted by a Home Office pathologist, Professor Francis E Camps, and most unusually asked for a meeting with the Chief Constable, Mr Richard Walker.

Dr Camps' involvement in a death always had an ominous significance, synonymous with murder. Sgt Bull specially telephoned Dr Adams to keep him in the picture, explaining that Dr Camps was on his way down and did he wish to attend the post-mortem, but he declined the invitation.

Dr Camps started the examination of the body at midnight, assisted by Dr Richard Philps, the pathologist at St Mary's Hospital, Eastbourne. He removed parts of the body and returned to London with them.

Prof. C Keith Simpson, another forensic pathologist, who had been asked to keep a watching brief by Hempsons, Dr Adams' MDU solicitors, states in his book, 'Camps, normally a quick worker, spent a long time in the mortuary, but without finding any evidence helpful to the police'.

Percy Robert Handscombe, a buddy of Jack Hullett, had the task of identifying Mrs Hullett's body, and was the executor of her will.

The coroner, formally opened the inquest and immediately adjourned it to await the results of the tests. He later set the inquest for Tuesday, 21 August 1956.

The Chief Constable was well aware of the augmented rumours which swept Eastbourne while Mrs Hullett lay dying. Too many tongues were wagging to be ignored, but he also knew that Dr Adams had friends in prominent places, such as chairman of the magistrates, Lt Col Roland Gwynne, and his own deputy, Chief Inspector Alexander Seekings. He decided that for a transparently impartial investigation he would enlist assistance and he took train to London and taxi to Scotland Yard – for the first time in the history of the Eastbourne force. "A number of incidents, backed by very strong rumours, warranted my calling in the Yard". The investigations began, the gossip continued, and Eastbourne became news.

The Chief Constable held a press conference at which, under a grilling by the news hounds, he admitted that there was a possibility of foul play in Mrs Hullett's death and that investigations were in train into rumours about the deaths of other women in the town.

The next morning the national press headlines hit the country, ***WAS THE £1000 WIDOW MURDERED? DEATHS OF FOUR WOMEN ARE PROBED.***

Meanwhile Robert Handscombe had found a number of Mrs Hullett's letters in a deed box, but he kept them to himself because he thought that if she had died of a stroke he didn't wish to raise the whiff of suicide to upset her relatives.

One unposted letter addressed to him ran,

> *'Dear Bob,*
>
> *If I should die please be happy for me and know how grateful I am to you. Have anything you and May [his wife] want from here.*
>
> *Please do one more thing for me. Make sure Dr Adams' MG is paid for from Jack. I know it was his wish and I do so want it settled. Something of mine could be sold. It is all Jack's anyway.'*

The reason for not posting the letter was that the final paragraph was overwritten with 'I have done this 17.7.56'. From this letter it is clear that Mrs Hullett was contemplating suicide, and the £1000 gift to Dr Adams is explained.

It was only after some days, when the investigations suggested an overdose, that Mr Handscombe finally handed the letter to Inspector Brynley Pugh of the Eastbourne CID. The delay did not help Dr Adams' case, and it also produced confusion among the investigators.

At a second press conference the following day, the Chief Constable refuted the wilder reports of investigations into the deaths of umpteen widows, somewhat to the distress of the press and Police. "I have this morning seen a letter written by Mrs Hullett which, if we had seen it four days ago, might have altered the entire nature and extent of the police enquiries."

One shaft of humour lit Mr Walker's face when a reporter mentioned Beachy Head in the course of a question. His response was, "Keep Beachy Head out of this - it is the backbone of my business".

Peter Palmer describes an apt *Daily Express* pocket cartoon by Osbert Lancaster. "Two vultures are shown resting on the town nameplate and a placard reads: *Big Police Enquiry at Eastbourne.* A retired Colonel is saying to his wife: 'You mark my words, this is all Bournemouth's doing'."

It could be said, however, that the size of the enquiry was still in Eastbourne's hands and, if ever, now was the time to scale it down.

Dr Adams wrote a second letter to the coroner explaining that he had omitted to state that when Mrs Hullett went on holiday in May 1956 he had given her eight cachets of 7½ gr sodium barbitone '... the fact that she had these tablets did not occur to me until now'. What was the meaning of this letter? Was it the cracking of a guilty man who wants to protest his innocence? Did it just confirm what a careless, forgetful doctor he was? Or was he genuinely trying to throw some light on how Mrs Hullett could have committed suicide? If he was guilty wouldn't he have mentioned this possibility earlier, or was it part of a subtle game?

"Wealthy widow", Mrs Gertrude Joyce Hullett, aged 50 of *Holywell Mount* left £142 000. She bequeathed £100 and her 1954 Rolls-Royce, valued at £2900, to Dr Bodkin Adams. In the course of 1956 Dr Adams had five cars, two Rolls-Royce limousines, JK 1600 and AJH 532, plus two identical MG Magnette saloons and a Morris Minor. John Redfern said, "I believe the MGs were CJK 600 and DHC 200, or was it the other way round? He liked '00' at the end."

Matters were reaching the stage when almost any remark or action by Dr Adams was given a sinister connotation.

One day a local man noticed a vintage Rolls-Royce in Mansfield's Garage in Cavendish Place and asked the foreman, Percy Staplehurst, to whom it belonged. "He gave me the name, which I've forgotten, but mentioned that she was one of Bodkin Adams' patients and added that by chance the Doctor had also called that morning and having seen the car had asked why it was there. On being informed it was in for a minor service the Doctor asked Mr Staplehurst to make sure it was given a thorough overhaul, as the owner had informed him that it would shortly be passing into his ownership."

This was likely to be the Morrell Rolls-Royce, but others have recounted a similar chestnut about Dr Adams seeing Mrs Hullett's Rolls having a check up just before her death, and saying to the mechanic, "Give it a full service".

Gordon Clark says, "Mrs Hullett's Rolls was usually looked after at the Meads Caffyns". Mr AE Stevens was the works manager of Caffyns Meads Garage and, according to his widow Mrs K Stevens, "The only one there that Dr Adams would allow to touch his Rolls-Royce".

The Bodkin Adams' business was looking most suspicious to an outside eye as well. After discussions between the Chief Constable and the head of the CID, Commander George Hatherill, it was agreed that Detective Superintendent Herbert W Hannam should be assigned to the case.

Local businessman, Paul Harris, was telephoned by Richard Walker, the Chief Constable, and asked if he would meet him in the Police Station. "Walker said that he wanted me to be foreman of the Hullett inquest - no question of being elected. At least it meant that, at that stage, I had a great freedom to ask Dr Adams questions, and I was able to put to him directly, 'Did you kill Mrs Hullett?' "

In the course of a tedious five-hour hearing at the Town Hall on 21 August, the coroner took the opportunity to probe Dr Adams' actions, and he was critical of the way he handled the case. Dr Sommerville pointed out that less than four days supply of Mrs Hullett's barbiturate was a fatal dose, and knowing she was suicidal, what precautions did Dr Adams take? Dr Adams reiterated that he carefully measured out the dose to her on a daily basis. He accepted that after Mr Hullett's death no steps had been taken to retrieve any of his left over tablets, and that he gave Mrs Hullett extra supplies to cover her holiday in the May. "Even so when I got the call on the Friday, poisoning never entered my head."

The coroner asked why didn't he transfer Mrs Hullett to a hospital? Why did he fail to call in a Consultant Psychiatrist before the overdose? He repeated that he had given his word not to do so.

Dr Angus C Sommerville HM Coroner {Associated Newspapers}

He was also asked why he did not have a day nurse? He replied that there were enough staff about the house. Why did he consult Dr Shera, a pathologist, and not a physician? He did not think it necessary.

The Coroner read out to Dr Adams the manufacturing chemist's dosage for *Megimide*, which was 40ml. Why had he injected only 10ml, a quarter of the recommended dosage?

The coroner continued, "Doctor, in view of the fact that you have been practising for 34 years, do you usually take the advice of junior house surgeons when it comes to the administration of drugs?"

The Doctor's answers could be summed up as, "I honestly did what I thought was best for her".

Fourteen other witnesses were called including Robert Handscombe and Pat Piper. She gave evidence that she had received a letter threatening suicide from her mother. Mr John Oliver, manager at the Meads bank, told the court of the special arrangements for Mrs Hullett's £1000 cheque to Dr Adams, though it turned out that he had not seen the cheque himself.

Professor Camps informed the court that he had found a fatal amount of the sleeping drug, sodium barbitone, in Mrs Hullett's body and that, in all probability, no medical treatment would have saved her life.

The last witness was Superintendent Herbert Hannam, who was seated in the court. Rather surprisingly, the coroner called him to the witness box and asked amid silence, "The Chief Constable has invoked the help of Scotland Yard and I understand that you are in charge. Do you wish me to adjourn this inquest?" To which Supt Hannam replied, "I have no application to make".

Dr Sommerville told the jury in the summing up, "... the amount of *Megimide* administered was quite useless – a mere gesture." and added that they may come to the conclusion that there was an extraordinary element of careless treatment in the case. He offered them the choice of four verdicts: accidental overdose, suicide – with or without the qualification of a disturbed mind, or an open verdict. He pointed out that negligence had to be a reckless disregard for human life, a lack of medical skill did not fall into that category.

The jury had no difficulty in reaching a verdict of suicide, without a rider.

Mr Ronald B Price was on the jury: "The name of a drug mentioned - *Megimide* - sticks in my memory. It was suicide, but the jury thought adversely of him because he had to ask a junior doctor about the dose of *Megimide.* You thought he would know that. Out of his depth was the least way of describing his actions. The jury thought it a little dodgy; as the coroner said, carelessness."

Paul Harris confirms that the £1000 cheque and prescriptions for Mrs Hullett were offered in evidence and handed round at the inquest, but these documents were never seen again. The findings of a Scotland Yard inquiry by Commander Hatherill were not made public, and according to Peter Palmer an internal Midland Bank inquiry did not reveal what had happened.

Michael Clark, pharmacist, says, "At the coroner's court, the prescriptions and the £1000 cheque were lost, fortunately I had a signature for the prescriptions".

Mr Palmer points out, "... anyone who has attended a coroner's inquest will know that at the conclusion there are people milling around everywhere. The prescriptions and cheque had been left on one of the desks and the Eastbourne CID had not the slightest doubt that somebody, with Dr Adams' interest at heart, had pushed them into his briefcase and later destroyed them".

The author knew Angus Sommerville well and, although the Bodkin Adams case was not discussed directly, it was apparent by oblique references, at his irascible moments, that Angus thought Bodkin Adams was, if not a murderer, at least an abject creature who should be removed from practice. The coroner's actions at Mrs Hullett's inquest were designed to put people's minds at rest, and to let them know that something was being done, so they would go away reassured with all fears allayed. Human nature being what it is, they did no such thing.

The coroner's question to Supt Hannam had little to do with Mrs Hullett's suicide, but was germane to adjourning the inquest until after the investigations and any subsequent prosecution.

Conversely, the coroner's remarks about taking the advice of a younger doctor, and carelessness were hardly appropriate.

In times of medical advances it may be essential to take the advice of someone younger with more recent knowledge. The point could be made, why such a junior grade doctor? Even then Dr Adams could reply that juniors would be the ones giving the therapy in practice. The real reason, of course, was that Dr Adams wasn't on sufficiently close terms with the senior hospital doctors to be able to have an off-the-cuff chat about this new-fangled drug *Megimide.*

What happened was that he kept Mrs Hullett under observation to see if definite signs of a stroke appeared. When they didn't he was bound to ask himself, 'Had she, by hook or by crook, hoarded her tablets? Perhaps it might be worth treating for barbiturate overdose, but I've not dealt with a case for years – I know, one of the young sparks at the hospital who deal with these cases everyday was talking about an antidote, I'll find out the latest from him. On consideration, I'm not sure it is an overdose and I do not want any complications, so I'll not administer a full course. A good general rule is that one tablet or one ampoule won't kill, so 10ml shouldn't do any harm and might do some good. I must try to prevent an inquest to avoid the stigma to her and the publicity for myself.'

The carelessness tag, applied by the coroner to Dr Adams' failure to bring in a Consultant Physician or to send Mrs Hullett into hospital, also hardly fits. Her death was inevitable, with appearances worsened by a confused, but attentive, Dr Adams as he thrashed around carrying out her wishes while trying to reduce the impact on his reputation. Otherwise, her death represented either a well thought out suicide scheme (probably entirely Mrs Hullett's conception, or possibly collusion between her and Dr Adams) or a premeditated plan by Dr Adams to overdose her and let it look like a stroke. Not especially careless, unfortunate maybe, if the plan went wrong because of Dr Harris' involvement.

As Richard Gordon, the author, wrote, 'Dr Adams applied the tenderest of care for a stroke, the wrong diagnosis, when Bobbie Hullett had died from an overdose of hoarded barbiturate tablets'.

What the coroner failed to realise was that until the inquest the Bodkin Adams affair was all rumour and innuendo. It was all 'he said this or she said that', but once he had commented adversely on the Doctor's care, and had brought "Hannam of Scotland Yard" into the light of his court, he gave substance to the gossip.

Patients were stirred to ask whether there might be more to it than an odd prescription peccadillo? Relatives were moved to question whether the widows of Eastbourne were safe? Neither the coroner nor the Chief Constable seemed to be aware of the possible reaction, nor that it would spread outside Eastbourne and soon to be beyond their control. By the end of August, Michael Foot, editor of *Tribune* called the publicity, 'One of the most appalling examples of newspaper sensationalism and persecution in the history of British journalism'.

Struggling to his car through the crowds, Dr Adams was unperturbed, "The inquest has cleared up all the ugly rumours.... My conscience is clear, I have nothing to hide. I did all I could for Mrs Hullett. Yes, I have spoken to Mr Hannam because we were introduced".

The Doctor might have been more concerned if he had known how many more brushes he was to have with "Mister" Hannam in the months ahead.

7. SUPERINTENDENT HANNAM'S INQUISITION

As we witness the deceased borne
From the stately homes of Eastbourne,
We are calm, for it may safely be assumed
That each lady that we bury
In the local cemetery
Will resurface – when the body is exhumed.

The influx of the press into Eastbourne commenced shortly before the coroner's inquest, it was in full spate on the day, and overflowed in the days following.

Detective Superintendent Herbert Hannam didn't waste much time either. The *Eastbourne Herald/Chronicle* reported that, assisted by Detective Inspector Brynley Pugh and Detective Sergeant Charlie Hewitt, he was in Eastbourne on 23 August 1956, two days after the inquest, 'to investigate gossip over the deaths of rich women which has abounded in the town'.

John Cheesborough says, "While there was gossip about Bodkin's legacies, it was not until the Hullett case, when the press spread the stories of 400 deaths, that it developed into a *cause célèbre".* Paul Harris observes, "Rumours were rife, with the conjecture that in his own interests the Doctor might on occasions have helped matters along a bit". A nurse, who was working at the Middlesex Hospital in London says, "We knew all about the case in the autumn of 1956". People pointed out his house, and Eastbourne residents, who were children at the time, recall, "We thought it was wonderfully exciting to have a murderer just down the road".

The news was spreading too. A French magazine showed a seafront with rows of empty deckchairs, still imprinted by the shape of ample figures, and the caption, *'Où sont les femmes d'Eastbourne?'*

On 24 August 1956, Percy Hoskins, crime reporter of the *Daily Express*, met Dr Adams on the London train. He describes how he was mystified about the Doctor's unconcern. "At first I thought he was hiding his apprehension, but talking to him it became clear that his lack of concern was genuine." Hoskins warned Dr Adams that if the adverse publicity continued it could endanger his liberty.

On 29 August 1956 Pugh and Hewitt went to Pevensey to interview Mrs Mason-Ellis, a nurse to Mrs Edith Alice Morrell who, as we have heard, died on 13 November 1950, aged 81, and was a wealthy shareholder in the White Star line.

Supt Hannam assigned Inspector Marr and two CID Officers to Somerset House (the will repository) to probe every will made by an Eastbourne resident between 1926 and 1956. It became apparent that over the last 20 years Dr Adams had been named as the beneficiary in more than 130 wills, totalling some £45 000 plus gifts of two Rolls-Royce cars, furniture, jewellery, silver and other antiques.

It was also noticed that most of these deaths were certified as cerebral thrombosis or haemorrhage ['a stroke']; that most of the patients had been prescribed narcotic drugs, such as morphine or heroin; that most had been cremated, and any exceptions had been embalmed. For the police this was suspicious; the cremating or embalming could be to hamper any investigations.

In the course of the police enquiries many doctors, nurses and pharmacists were inadvertently caught up in the Bodkin Adams' net. Dr Ian Brown recollects how he had some misapprehension when Supt Hannam breezed into his office with a sheaf of cremation certificates, going back to 1948, relating to deceased patients of Dr Adams, which he had countersigned in good faith.

Tom Searle, a Willingdon pharmacist, said the police came to see him and made notes of the Doctor's prescriptions.

The Superintendent also encouraged local gossips to talk freely. He heard numerous stories about other 'suspicious deaths', but he was forced to ignore most of the chit-chat for there was no evidence, and the Yard's top detective had been brought to Eastbourne to find hard facts.

Typical of the Doctor's patients whose deaths were investigated by Supt Hannam were the Neil-Miller sisters, who lived at *Barton*, 30 St John's Road.

Hilda and Clara Neil-Miller, came from Scotland, and had no family except a widowed sister-in-law in Bournemouth. Hilda died on 15 January 1953 and Clara, on 22 February the next year. Clara left £5000 to Dr Adams, and had made out cheques for £500 and £300 in the months before her death.

According to journalist Rodney Hallworth, Supt Hannam and Sgt Hewitt interviewed Mrs Sharpe, the Millers' landlady, in consequence of a statement made by another Eastbourne doctor. Before they could complete their interrogations, however, Mrs Sharpe died in the autumn of 1956 and was cremated.

The origin of the 'other doctor's statement' was a tale he had heard from another paying guest in the house. She said that after Dr Adams had visited Clara, the night before she died, she had been left with her nightdress thrown up and the bedroom windows wide open on a cold night.

In another story it is an old lady at *de Walden Court*, who after a visit had been left more or less naked with bedclothes stripped off the bed and the windows left wide open during inclement weather. The veracity of this tale is muddied by it being said that money had been given to the Doctor instead of to the family. Could the open window method be a transparently distinct form of euthanasia?

Widow, Emily Louise Mortimer, was another of his patients to get a mention. In 1946, the year she died, she transferred shares worth £3000 to Dr Adams and made him a residual beneficiary of her will, bringing in a total of £5000.

Another 'typical' Dr Adams' patient was Julia Bradnum. Her niece told a *Daily Telegraph* reporter, "In May 1952 my aunt came to visit me. She was rosy cheeked and walked part of the way. Three days afterwards, 27 May, she was dead. I was astonished and upset. Three months before her death she told me had drawn up a new will. She left about £4000 to be divided up equally among six people, including myself, *and a new beneficiary*. When we heard of enquiries into deaths in the town we approached the police and made statements." By imputation the newspaper had Dr Adams on the rack, and after all the lady was 85-years-old.

Yet another was 88-year-old James Priestley Downs, a wealthy widower, and retired bank manager. He went into a nursing home in 1955 after falling downstairs and fracturing an ankle. Mr Downs died, on 30 May, a month after his accident, leaving £1000 to Dr Adams who certified the death as 'cerebral thrombosis'.

Many similar stories were retold around the town, but most were little more than the repetition of jealous remarks augmented by the number of ears and lips they had passed through. Some originated from family members who had lost out financially and had allowed their aggrieved feelings to ferment over the years.

The wagging tongues of 1956 recalled Dr Adams' earlier escapades going back to the 1930s, and the Whitton court case resurfaced. All the tales were repeated behind the chintz curtains of Meads and South Cliff, at coffee mornings, and as one lady put it, "even at charity bazaars".

The Fleet Street reporters, combing the town for any dirt about Adams, heard of Miss O'Hara in the gossip and called on her. The broken engagement had nothing to do with the inquiries into the alleged murders of widows, but it was meat to the sensationalism of the national newspapers. She was furious, so the story was published without her name, but everyone in Meads and South Cliff knew.

Dr Adams had never made any secret of the number of wealthy widows who remembered him in their wills. One of the possible reasons why the investigation came about was that he was quite prepared to declare his bonuses in public. He would also point out that other doctors had their care similarly recognised, and he resented the implication that he restricted his practice to wealthy families who were likely to leave him bequests. His NHS patients took up a lot of his time, and from them there was universal support and acclaim for his devoted care and attention.

It was inevitable that some patients and friends deserted him. Margaret Kinman says, "When the story broke about Bodkin Adams 'seeing off his old ladies' my mother said she knew all along he was up to no good, and during the trial my father denied that he had ever known Dr Adams".

Many, however, of all social strata, still believed in him. The manager of the Employment Exchange, in South Street, was one who swore by Dr Adams' care.

Miss M Fenwick-Owen says she was an Eastbourne councillor at the time. "When going round canvassing during election time, held in November then, people didn't want to talk about the staple politics of the day, such as dog mess or uneven pavements, for which I had all the answers, but about Bodkin Adams and how wonderful he was - a modern Robin Hood. They especially wanted to know when he was coming back, one question for which I did not have the answer."

There was a great deal of coverage in the Dutch press. Michael Clark's Dutch mother-in-law asked his mother, Irene Clark (née Browne), if it were true that Dr Adams had killed all these patients. She replied, "Absolute rubbish, he was far too nice a man to ever do that".

Supt Herbert Hannam, however, had convinced himself that he was dealing with a hypocrite, a mass murderer who, once he was sure he was a legatee, eased his patients into the next world. In the Superintendent's book there were too many cases of wills being made out to Dr Adams followed by the patient's demise.

Local solicitor, John Cheesborough explains, "Supt Hannam gave evening briefings to the press at the *New Inn* just by the Town Hall". Peter Palmer confirms that, when at the pub, he twice overheard the Superintendent use the expression, "I would certainly not like to be in a certain person's shoes, who lives at Eastbourne".

Most evenings the Superintendent, known as 'The Count' at Scotland Yard for his natty suits and cigars, would outline how his investigations were progressing, and the information he leaked to the press was the source of much of the speculation in the newspapers. 'Supt Hannam interviewed a relative of Mrs Matilda Whitton who had died in 1935.' 'Exhumations of the bodies of Julia Bradnum and Clara Miller were under consideration.'

Superintendent Herbert Hannam
The Count of Scotland Yard

Supt Hannam played a grim cat and mouse game with the Doctor, no doubt hoping the latter would crack under the pressure - and the focus of his attention became directed at Mrs Edith Alice Morrell.

Mr Walker, the Chief Constable, on the other hand, gave out that the enquiries were not murder investigations. "Because of the rumours ... in fairness to everyone I felt that an independent investigation should be made." The Eastbourne Police emphasised that to scotch the rumours would entail a long and searching probe.

Dr Adams commented, "I appreciate the Chief Constable's attitude. I am quite satisfied to await the outcome of those enquiries. My conscience is perfectly clear".

The Doctor's equanimity was in contrast to that of Mr Walker, who possibly regretted he had ever called in Scotland Yard, but realised it was too late to reverse the process. Richard Walker, Chief Constable of Eastbourne 1954-67, said in his old age, "Dr Adams didn't do me any good at all".

Dr Adams indubitably believed that Supt Hannam was in Eastbourne to exonerate him of the imputations stemming from the gossip. Whereas, to quote Lord Devlin, "Hannam was presented with a suspect and his search was for a crime. His job was not to question but to find the proof that would satisfy the law in as many cases as possible". It can be understood why Bodkin Adams was described as 'a trussed chicken waiting to be plucked'.

'Hannam of the Yard' had shot to fame in 1953 with the famous Teddington Towpath Murder case. At 48, he was at the peak of his career. Sartorially elegant, he enjoyed discussions with reporters and lawyers, and he was prepared to use publicity to assist his investigations; to pressurise the suspect, or to encourage witnesses to come forward. He was a skilled detective, who knew how to keep just on the right side of the law while applying every trick to break the nerve of his suspect or to assemble the evidence.

He was promoted to Superintendent during the Teddington Towpath case, in the course of which the defence barrister questioned the methods by which he extracted the signed confession. The counsel later explained that it was not that Hannam was lying, but it was the way that he secured the self-damning confession that was worrying.

He was a proficient note taker and by using a statement here, another piece there, and a juggling of the context, he was able to collect all he needed. Some of his colleagues referred to him as 'The Sorcerer' to explain the miraculous appearance of a confession in many of his cases when he saw the suspect alone.

John Cheesborough says, "You will gather from Hannam's cross examination in the trial transcripts, not only his arrogance, but his success in obtaining statements. It was his familiarity with the press, and his habit of making sure that other officers, such as Inspector Pugh, would be doing something else when he was interviewing suspects that caused anxiety at Scotland Yard".

Roy Bedford states that three Scotland Yard detectives stayed at his parents' hotel in Royal Parade, keeping an eye on Hannam and investigating the loss of the £1000 cheque. "The big joke was when they picked up a parking ticket".

Michael Clark, a local pharmacist also caught up in the investigations, remarks, "One of the troubles was Hannam's bombastic, overbearing manner. Pugh was frightened of him, and Hewitt just shrugged his shoulders. The Police, especially the cocksure Hannam, were convinced they could nail Bodkin Adams."

It is said that Sir Edward Pickering, editor of the *Daily Express,* decided to back the line of the paper's crime reporter, Percy Hoskins, in not condemning Dr Adams when he heard that Supt Hannam was in charge of the enquiries.

Detective Sergeant Charles Hewitt, the second string of the classic Scotland Yard team, was the fourth generation of his family in the Police. Industrious, painstaking and honest, he was tough when required, but had a friendly manner.

The third member of the team was the head of the Eastbourne CID, Detective Inspector Brynley Pugh. Even though the Doctor had delivered his children Pugh became antagonistic towards him, like others in the local force. John Cheesborough says, "Brynley Pugh had worked his way up by good conscientious police work over the years, but you could say he had an obsession with catching Dr Adams."

Another Eastbourne solicitor, Richard James, confirms, "Inspector Pugh was a good, honest, plodding, policeman. Unlike Supt Hannam, he was straightforward and trustworthy".

The Superintendent's probing into Dr Adams' affairs was greatly helped when he discovered that the majority of Dr Adams' private prescriptions had been dispensed by one shop, HR Browne, dispensing chemists, of Memorial Square, or more precisely, 44 Cornfield Road. In 1950 dispensing chemists (pharmacists) had to keep a Sales of Poisons Register as required under Acts of 1933 and 1935, and the Pharmacy & Poisons Act of 1933.

Michael Clark's great-great-grandfather established the firm in 1860. The fascia boards of the shop were inscribed in gold leaf, *H.R. BROWNE FROM THE APOTHECARIES HALL LONDON*; the old man had been the manager at the Worshipful Company of Apothecaries' shop in Blackfriars.

Mr Clark worked there from about 1950 to its closure in 1975. "Browne's dispensed for the Hulletts and Mrs Morrell. I made up Bodkin Adams' favourite sodium barbitone 7½gr in cachets for Mrs Hullett, archaic even then."

He goes on, "At the time all private prescriptions, and any repeats, had to be copied into a 'Prescription or Poisons' Book'. The details had to be kept for two years and be available for inspection by the RPS Inspectors, Coroners and the Police. The Poisons' Book was designated to record Controlled Drugs and Poisons ordered by doctors, dentists and veterinary surgeons for their practices. Members of the public could also obtain poisons, such as cyanide for the destruction of wasps' nests and strychnine to kill moles. In every case the person had to be known to the pharmacist as a *bone fide* purchaser."

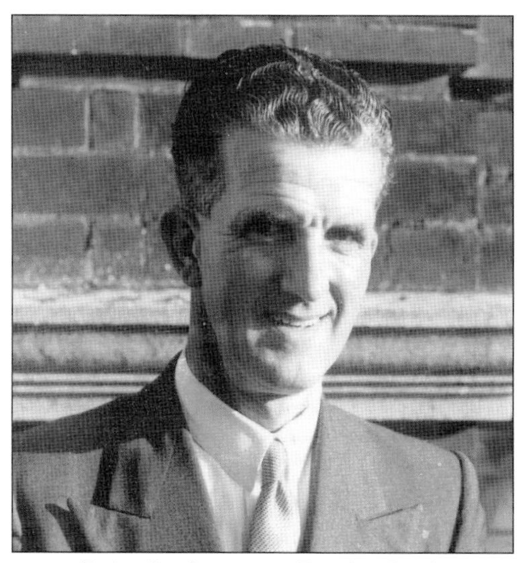

Detective Inspector Brynley Pugh {Topham Picturepoint}

It is not possible to examine every source of supply used by Dr Adams to order drugs, but as Supt Hannam found, most of the Doctor's drugs came from Browne's. Their Poisons' Registers reveal that in the late 1940s and early 1950s Dr Adams ordered fairly steady amounts of the opium-like drug, *Omnopon*, or papaveretum, (which contained morphia) and pethidine, another pain reliever, as well as barbiturates.

During the period, November 1950 to November 1951, he ordered 50 tablets of ⅙ gr of *Omnopon* on 9/11/50, 25/11/50, 31/1/51, 19/2/51, 4/3/51 (100 tablets), 22/3/51, 6/4/51, 19/4/51, 27/8/51, and 12/11/51. He also ordered 50 tablets of 25mg pethidine, and repeat orders of his favourite sedatives, Tab Barbitone et Amidopyrine, and Sodium Barbitone 7½ gr.

A point to interest Supt Hannam was that over the year there were only six *Omnopon* orders by other Eastbourne doctors in these Poison Registers. In other words, it might be interpreted that Dr Adams alone prescribed twice as much opiates as a group of similar doctors.

Michael Clark adds, "Brynley Pugh and Charlie Elliott took ages to obtain the details of the Drug Books for the prosecution, and got into a bit of a muddle. Every list they produced had to be altered, they had to correct their account three times.

"The defence also sent down a clerk to go over the Drug Books. I don't know his official position, although it was obvious he knew nothing about drugs when he started. However, after a day of work commencing at 11 o'clock, with a short break for a lunch at the *Sussex*, by 5 o'clock he had sorted it out. He had a complete record of all the prescription details he wanted and was word perfect".

There was a further slight set back for Supt Hannam. The Midland Bank cashier, Kenneth Pill, who had dealt with the £1000 cheque, now said that although he thought Dr Adams' words were, "This lady is not long for this world", he was not prepared to swear to that in court.

Dr Adams continued his work, halting only to take a short holiday in Scotland. He confessed to Percy Hoskins, "I was aware that news reporters were crowding into Eastbourne, they stopped me in the streets when I was on my rounds." Even more threatening to his freedom of movement were the four brushes he was to have with 'Mr' Hannam: on the 1 October, 24 and 26 November, and 19 December.

The Doctor was quite oblivious of any danger when on 1 October the Superintendent paused outside the garage of *Kent Lodge* as the Doctor was putting his car away. "Good evening, doctor, did you have a good holiday in Scotland?"

This led the Doctor off on a prolonged description of the sport, and progressed on to a general account of his life, in the course of which he referred to the rumours as 'God's plan to teach him a new lesson'. He finished with. "You are finding all these rumours untrue, aren't you?"

"I am sorry to say that is not my experience" was the Superintendent's answer.

"That is strange", replied the Doctor, "I live for my work, I gave a vow to God that I would look after my national poor patients, and day and night I will turn out for them, I never ask anyone else to do it for me. I think this is what makes people jealous of me. I start with the seven o'clock news of a morning ... and to-night I have been to a meeting of the YMCA in Brighton. If only others worked as hard as I do ... You haven't found anything else?"

Richard Gordon had Supt Hannam answering, "Nice Rolls doctor. Left to you by Mrs Morrell, with a chest of silver?" He probably said, "Doctor, I have been anxious about some of the gifts you received under wills from your patients."

"A lot were instead of fees, I don't want money, what use is it? I paid £1100 supertax last year ... Mrs Morrell was a very dear patient. A long time before she died she insisted that I should have the silver in her memory and I don't want it, I am a bachelor, I have never used it. I knew she was going to leave it to me and her Rolls-Royce car, she told me she put them in her will, oh yes, and another cabinet."

Supt Hannam. "Mr Hullett left you £500."

"Now, he was a life-long friend. He was a very ostentatious man about his wealth. There is no mystery about him; he told me long before his death that he had left me money in his will. I even thought it would be more than it was. ... Every one of these dear patients I have done my best for. God knows I have vowed to Him that I would relieve pain and let these dear people live as long as possible."

Supt Hannam. "Doctor, I examined the cremation forms you completed in your own handwriting for Mr Hullett and Mrs Morrell and you said that you were not aware that you were a beneficiary. This is quite a serious offence."

"Oh, that wasn't done wickedly. God knows it wasn't. We always want cremations to go off smoothly for the dear relatives. If I said I knew I was getting money under the will, they might get suspicious and I like cremations and burials to go smoothly. There was nothing suspicious really. It wasn't deceitful."

Supt Hannam. "I hope to finish all these enquiries soon ..."

Dr Adams ended their chat with, "Don't hurry. Please be thorough. It is in my interests. Good night and thank you for your kindness".

John Cheesborough's ironic comment was, "Of course, it was just by chance that Supt Hannam happened to bump into Bodkin Adams as he was putting his car away one evening. In fact the so-called chance meeting was perhaps a little too good to be true, it was carefully pre-arranged".

The next move in the softening up process was the search of the Doctor's house on 24 November for dangerous drugs. That Saturday Supt Hannam and Sgt Hewitt entrained to Lewes where they met Inspector Pugh and drove to Eastbourne. This roundabout way was probably to enable Supt Hannam to be brought up to date and for him to check that Pugh had a search warrant. It wasn't to avoid the press, for Hannam believed in keeping them in the hunt.

By the time the policemen went to *Kent Lodge* in the early evening, they were outnumbered by many reporters of all nationalities congregating outside the house.

The dinner-jacketed Dr Adams was preparing to go to out, but when Annie Room, his housekeeper, called him from his bedroom, Pugh produced a warrant empowering him to search under the Dangerous Drugs Acts.

The Doctor's first words to the Police team of, "There is no question of a statement for I have been told not to make one", did not put them off for they expected, with some confidence, a plethora of words.

John Cheesborough comments, "The evening he was arrested Bodkin Adams was due to present the prizes at a YMCA cricket dinner in 5 Bolton Road, just about where the Isobel Restaurant is today."

Philip Cheal adds, "I was a member of the YMCA cricket club. Our club captain arrived to announce that 'our President will be unable to attend as he has just been arrested for murder'." There are several surprising aspects of the Bodkin Adams case, but it is doubtful if many cricket club captains have been called upon to declare that the club's President was unavoidably detained because of a little matter of murder, even if the statement was premature at this stage.

Before making his search Inspector Pugh asked Dr Adams to produce either his Dangerous Drugs Register, or the journal in which he recorded the relevant details of drugs used, pursuant to the Regulations.

Dr Adams asked what was meant by dangerous drugs and on being told morphia, heroin and the like, he exclaimed, "Oh that group. You will find none here, I seldom use them".

He said that he kept no details of dangerous drugs, implying that Browne's kept any records, although since 1953 he was required to do so under the Regulations.

John Cheesborough comments, "When they went to *Kent Lodge* to look for drugs (which they knew would be in any doctor's house in the 1950s) Hannam sent Pugh 'to check that the blinds are drawn' so as to leave Bodkin Adams alone with him and Hewitt. This could be interpreted that Hannam was afraid of what Pugh might overhear". And who tipped off the reporters waiting outside?

Hannam brandished a list of drugs which Dr Adams had ordered for Mrs Morrell and, having referred to it, questioned him, "Doctor, did you prescribe for Mrs. Morrell 75 grains of heroin tablets before she died?"

Adams was alleged to have replied: "Poor soul, she was in terrible agony. It was all used. I used them myself. "

One of Dr Adams' tidy medicine cupboards {Topham Picturepoint}

With his reply Dr Adams little grasped that he had stepped on a slippery slope that could be disastrous, for the prescription list held by Hannam represented what would normally be considered a fatal dose of heroin. On the other hand if he hadn't used all the drugs for Mrs Morrell, what had he done with these drugs of addiction?

Dr Adams asked to look at the list and, presumably realising the amounts of morphine-like drugs mentioned, tried to retract his original statement and expressed the view that he thought some of the heroin might have been left over. "I am not dishonest with drugs. Mrs Morrell had all those because I gave the injections. Do you think it was too much?"

"That's not a matter for me, doctor. Did you take the drugs to the house?"

"No, the chauffeur picked them up from the chemists and I took them from the nurses".

Hannam asked him where he kept this type of drug and Dr Adams indicated two wall cabinets on either side of the fireplace.

Some Police accounts allege that the doctor was weeping at this stage of the search. One certainty was that the Police were not impressed by the chaotic state of his cupboards, with margarine and chocolate mixed amid the tablets.

A former patient says, "Dr Adams' housekeeper was a close friend of my mother, ... and we gathered that he was a little untidy in his ways, including his medicine cabinets, which was made so much of by the police".

According to Hannam, while the police officers examined one cupboard, Dr Adams went to the other, opened it and put two bottles in his pocket. This was just what Hannam had been expecting and the Scotland Yard man asked him sharply: "What did you take out of that cupboard Doctor?"

"I only opened for you".

"You put something in your pocket."
"No, nothing."
"What was it Doctor?"

To which Bodkin Adams was supposed to have replied, as he produced the two morphine bottles, "I know it was silly. I did not want you to find them". Asked where he got them, he allegedly replied: "One of those I got for Mr Soden. who died at the Grand Hotel. The other was for Mrs Sharpe, who died before I used it".

Dr Adams' solicitor, Mr James, now arrived and Pugh, having rejoined the group, requested the Doctor to accompany them to the police station.

Later that evening Pugh read to the Doctor thirteen charges. Nine were charges of forgery, mainly under the Forgery Act of 1913, and four were of false representations under the Cremation Act of 1902.

Examples of the forgery charges were:-

> On a day in January 1952 ... did obtain a quantity of prepared vaccine by virtue of a forged instrument, knowing the same to be forged contrary to Section 7a of the Forgery Act, 1913.
>
> On a day in May 1956 ... did cause to be delivered to one Beryl Galloway [a patient of Dr Lester] an elastic knee support by virtue of a forged instrument ... contrary to ... the Forgery Act, 1913.
>
> On a day in September 1956 ... caused to be delivered to Frances Abrams, a bottle of medicine and six seven and one half grain of sodium barbitone by falsely pretending the said Frances Abrams was authorised to receive the said articles as a NHS patient contrary to Section 32(1) of the Larceny Act, 1916.

The charges under the Cremation Act included:-

> On the 23rd February 1950, ... unlawfully and wilfully did make a false representation to wit: that so far as you were aware you had no pecuniary interest in the death of Amy Constance Clavering I'Anson Ware with a view to procuring the burning of the remains of the said Ware contrary to Section 8 (2) of the Cremation Act, 1902.

There were similar charges relating to Edith Alice Morrell, James Priestley Downs and Alfred John Hullett.

The drug charges were relatively minor. They consisted of Dr Adams signing NHS forms for private patients to obtain their prescriptions free on the NHS. Apart from one non-lethal dose of phenobarbital, they were for innocuous items such as aspirin tablets or elastic support stockings.

A pharmacist explains. "Forged prescriptions for surgical stockings went on elsewhere. You have to say it helped the patient, but when other doctors saw private patients and signed NHS prescription forms they confined these activities to their own patients and to exceptional circumstances. Dr Adams would put '*per pro* DAL Ashforth',or 'pp G Thrower', because the private patient he was seeing was an NHS patient of Drs Ashforth or Thrower, who were understandably furious with Dr Adams' action. Dr Adams could not believe that it was illegal because as he said, 'I didn't benefit and I'd pp'd it'. That you should only 'pp it' at the request of the person for whom you were signing appeared beyond him."

A retired GP confirms, "On rare occasions most doctors, having seen a patient at a private consultation, would prescribe NHS drugs for them if they couldn't afford the prescription. Just like breaking a speed limit for an emergency. Like Dr Adams, their belief was that the patient's well-being was supreme, the difference was that they did so only for their own patients and signed their own prescription forms, or they were on exceptionally good terms with the patient's NHS doctor".

The cremation form charges, potentially more serious, were that he had said he was not aware of any financial interest in the death when he knew there was something for him in the will.

By law, a doctor completing a cremation form has to state whether he would receive any pecuniary benefit from the death of the person. Bodkin Adams was alleged to have written 'no' or more likely a vague and wordy phrase such as *not to the best of my knowledge* when he must have known that he was a beneficiary.

Dr Barkworth says that for one of the Cremation Act charges there was no doubt that Dr Adams knew he was a beneficiary under the will. "He asked me to witness the will of a Mr Downs at Esperance. We were six in the room, Mr Downs, his solicitor, his housekeeper, the Sister and I, who were the witnesses, and Bodkin. All of us heard the will read out, including a bequest to Bodkin. It was duly signed and witnessed and a few weeks later the old man was dead." All described in the 19 September 1956 *Daily Sketch* as, 'Ten Attempts to Sign Will'.

Dr Adams would say that he could not be absolutely certain, the will might be altered, and if he had held up the funeral until probate he would not be popular with funeral directors or more importantly the relatives. Many doctors have a pretty good idea they will benefit, but until probate they cannot be sure.

Hannam had gone to the Doctor's house on a "fishing expedition", in the hope that Dr Adams would say something out of turn. Officially, Inspector Pugh held the warrant to search the house for illegal drugs.

The charges appear petty in a case where a man is suspected of multiple murder. Perhaps Hannam clung to the expectation that a weekend thinking it over would cause his suspect to crack.

The news of the Doctor's appearance before the magistrates spread over the town and the country. Dr Ian Brown says he was at an official function with the Chief Constable, when his deputy, Inspector Seekings, slipped in with the information that Dr Adams had been arrested.

After being given bail in the sum of £100, Dr Adams drove home with his solicitor. Even if the Doctor remained oblivious of his serious position, Mr James knew that these were holding charges, what you might call 'Your near back light isn't working' offences. Herbert James was concerned that the cremation charges pointed in the direction of further charges, this time of murder.

He questioned the Doctor who recalled that Mrs Morrell's name came up more than once. "Had he any records?" We know he hadn't, but he did think back to her son sending round a parcel of notes after her death. Dr Adams said he had meant to throw them away, but doubted if he had got round to it. Mr James searched the house and early in the morning found a torn, brown paper parcel, which had fallen at the back of a filing cabinet in the basement. It contained eight, ordinary, ruled exercise books. Mr James said he would take them home and read them. They would turn out to be more exciting than the Sunday newspapers.

Herbert Victor James did not act for Dr Adams on the criminal charges. His son, Richard, had been appointed a JP in 1948, and as they were partners in the firm Coles & James, all members of the firm were precluded from dealing with criminal matters. His actions were those of a close friend, and one who realised that if there was ever a time Dr Adams needed help this was it.

On the following Monday, 26 November, after a morning surgery, Dr Adams was driven by his chauffeur to the Eastbourne Magistrates' Court to face the original 13 charges, and further charges which were laid against him:-

> Failure to keep a Dangerous Drug Register, as required by Regulation 17 of the Dangerous Drugs Act of 1953.
>
> Obstructing a local police officer in the course of his duty, in that he endeavoured to conceal two bottles of morphine.

These were the result of the Doctor's antics on the Saturday night. It was unfortunate that he had not started to keep a Dangerous Drugs' Register, but the Regulations had come in since Mrs Morrell's death.

Supt Hannam explained that the matter was in the hands of the Director of Public Prosecutions and declared, "The Director has instructed me to ask the court to consider a remand without evidence".

Bail was set at a personal recognizance of £1000 and a surety of £1000, and on condition that the Doctor surrendered his passport. Two close friends, Norman Gray and Gilbert Foyle, stood surety.

After the remand, Dr Adams asked to see Superintendent Hannam, who was only too ready to oblige. Dr Adams said he understood that further charges were to be preferred against him and he wished to know what these were.

Supt Hannam, "I am still enquiring into the death of some of your patients, Doctor. I am not satisfied they died of natural causes".

Dr Adams, "Who do you have in mind?"

"Mrs Morrell is certainly one".

Dr Adams will be remembered for his reply which could be interpreted as a recommendation for euthanasia, "Easing the passing of a dying person is not all that wicked. She wanted to die – that cannot be murder".

Encouraged by the Doctor's phraseology, Hannam completed his enquiries on the cases to be submitted for a decision by the Attorney-General, the Crown Prosecutor. The only ones in which evidence had been taken on oath were Mrs Morrell, Mr and Mrs Hullett, and Mr Downs.

George Turner notes, "I was interviewed by the police at the time of his arrest and Inspector Pugh tried to pump me for information, so much so that I became annoyed. In my opinion they were out to get him".

According to journalist, Rodney Hallworth, the Attorney-General listened to the opinions of two doctors about the heroin dosage and what would happen to a patient if no subsequent action was taken with the doses described. Having heard that these were fatal doses, Sir Reginald Manningham-Buller turned to the police officers present at his office in the Houses of Parliament and said, "Go down to Eastbourne now and charge Adams with the murder of Mrs Morrell".

On 18 December, having obtained a warrant, Hannam, Hewitt and Pugh were again admitted to *Kent Lodge,* this time by appointment. When they entered the surgery they found two French newspaper reporters had got there before them, and it was only after they had been shooed out, that Dr Adams could be charged with the murder of Alice Edith Morrell.

The doctor was, to say the least, stunned. "Murder? Murder? Can you prove it was murder? I do not think you can prove murder. She was dying, in any event."

On his way out from *Kent Lodge* with the detectives, he touched his housekeeper's hands and pronounced, "I will see you in Heaven".

In Richard Gordon's words, "More damning phrases by Dr Adams which were unlikely to assist in his defence".

It has to be said that in everyday conversation his sentences were sprinkled with "It was Providence", and "I Swear to God" and "To the God in Heaven". Hence, to those who knew him the phrases meant very much business as usual, but such words could be contorted when worked on by a barrister in court.

After a night in the Police cells at Eastbourne, Dr Adams was formally charged with concealing drugs, failing to keep a Register, and obstructing the Police – plus the new charge that he "feloniously, wilfully and of malice aforethought did kill and murder Edith Alice Morrell". This created more than a stir amongst the hundred or so persons in the public gallery.

Most doctors subscribe to an organisation that will provide advice and organise a defence if they are charged with professional negligence. The Council of the Medical Defence Union was initially disinclined to take up the case of one so obviously guilty of murder, but justice prevailed. The MDU provided support for Dr Adams because it would be disagreeable to the profession to have a doctor erroneously convicted of murdering a patient. It was also alarmed in this instance because there was no suggestion of administering poisons to kill, the offence being a too lavish prescription of drugs used by most doctors in 1950.

The MDU arranged for Dr Adams to be defended by Mr Geoffrey Lawrence, QC who up till that time was not well known to the general public. He had acquired a high reputation within the profession, but had mainly embraced what was described as 'every sort of dreary dispute in which local authorities engage'.

Immediately following the arrest, Hannam applied for the exhumation of two former patients of Dr. Adams - Julia Bradnum, from Ocklynge cemetery and Clara Miller, from Langley cemetery. The procedures were accompanied by Supt Hannam's usual flair for publicity.

Jane Booth-Clibborn (née Nash) was at the Girls' High School in Eldon Road, Eastbourne. She recalls the head, Miss L Gunnery, standing on the platform at the start of a day in December 1956 and telling her pupils not to look over at Ocklynge cemetery that morning. "She didn't say what it was about, but it was a great temptation to look. We daren't go against Miss Gunnery, but hockey on the playing fields was more popular than on most days, and many girls gave a sidelong glance at the cemetery. We could see the canvas screens, but nothing else. I'd heard the rumours about Dr Adams, and my grandparents knew several of his patients in East Dean who told of his lovely bedside manner."

Some magazines declared: 'According to Dr Camps' findings, the women whose bodies had been exhumed had not died of the causes listed by Dr. Adams on the original death certificates.'

Conversely, Professor Keith Simpson, retained by the MDU to 'watch over' the exhumations, reported that, "Only one of the bodies was in good enough condition for Camps and me to agree on the cause of death, which was cerebral thrombosis – precisely what the doctor had certified".

Exhumation of Julia Bradnum, Ocklynge Cemetery. The Girls' High School is on the extreme right {Topham Pictureprint}

Camps' post-mortem examination of Clara Miller's body showed that she had probably died of bronchopneumonia and not coronary thrombosis [heart attack], which was on Dr Adams' death certificate. This was the only difference between Dr Adams' certificates and the pathologists' findings in the exhumed bodies and even that was not fully accepted by the defence. It was, however, still a natural cause of death, and pneumonia could follow a heart attack. Even so voices said she died of pneumonia because of the heavy sedation on a cold night.

The Dr John Bodkin Adams affair was building up to high drama, and living up to all that the national press expected of it. There was a fascinating interplay of 'there must be some simple explanation', coupled with the possibility that 'a cynical campaign directed against the vulnerable' had been uncovered. Here was this avuncular figure, a conspicuously reassuring family doctor, now apparently a horrific poisoner of helpless old ladies in a sedate resort. Yet by no means was everyone convinced, among them most of his friends and patients. "Eastbourne was divided between the Adams' supporters and his detractors", says Ken Harrison,

Borough Librarian 1950-58, "The latter were more numerous than the former, influenced by the media, which more or less condemned him from the start".

Betty Wenham remarks, "Considering that I had a broken ankle set by Mr AH Crook in 1943 when Dr Bodkin Adams gave the anaesthetic, and that he was our family doctor for some years before the trial, I think I may, perhaps, count myself a survivor. There were many scurrilous poems about him going round, including a parody of the Twelve Days of Christmas". It was said that John Wells, who was at Eastbourne College about that time, composed some of the verses.

George Turner, one of the founding members of the YMCA Hartington Hall centre, declared, "I never thought of anything other than the best as regards Dr Adams. I told the *Evening Standard* reporter that I'd known him all down the years and never once had to doubt his integrity".

Nurse Harriott explains, "I had been looking after an elderly patient of his in Greys Road who had died, so I was fearful of the police knocking on my door".

Dr Adams spent Christmas in a cell at Brixton Prison ready to be brought back to Eastbourne for the Magistrates' Court now fixed for 14 January 1957.

His views on Supt Hannam had shifted, "Mr Hannam was determined to get a conviction to become head of the CID. He had hung the Towpath Murderer on a fake confession which everyone knew from Wormwood Scrubs to Brixton.

"They took me away before Christmas and I spent 16 weeks in what was virtually solitary confinement. They hoped to break my spirit, but I knew it would all come out because it was a conflict between God and the Devil, and He wouldn't let me down. During the 16 weeks I received Christmas cards, and presents, and about 500 letters expressing sympathy and I replied to them all. Otherwise, I didn't do much reading or writing, I was on my own with few facilities."

Frank Alford recalls, "Dr Adams was my doctor in Eastbourne from 1945 until he was struck off. I wrote to him when he was in Brixton and received a reply which I still have".

Another transformation was seen when a patient left him £500 while he was in prison – now there was no gossip.

The Doctor later recalled his experience to Percy Hoskins. "When those gates clang … you lose your individuality and become just another number." Number 7889 was determined to be a model prisoner until his trial. Dr Adams concluded, "I had worked 16 hours a day – and the workings of God are strange – but it was too much and perhaps after eleven years it was time to take it easier".

Is there always someone who benefits from tragedy? The national press corps were keen to get their hands on copies of the death certificates for the 400 widows. Passing one copy round was not good enough, each newspaper had to have its own. The Registrar of Births, Marriages and Deaths at Eastbourne received a considerable sum in fees for the copies, and it is said that it was the only year the Eastbourne rates benefited from the Registrar's contributions.

8. THE MAGISTRATES' COURT

On Monday, 14 January, 1957, the committal proceedings began before the Eastbourne magistrates. Lt-Colonel Roland Gwynne was chairman of the magistrates, 1951-57, but on account of his friendship with Dr Adams he had to be eased out of the case, and Mr David Honeysett presided instead. Roland Gwynne had a reputation for being abrupt in court, but was a capable chairman. Peter Palmer says, "For many years 'Taffy' Honeysett had been a popular mine host at the *Lottbridge Arms*, in Mountfield Road, but the complex nuances of the Bodkin Adams' case were beyond him".

The full bench for this preliminary hearing was coal merchant's wife, Mary Bradford, hotelier's daughter, Eileen Comer, chairman of the local newspaper, Lionel Turner, preparatory school owner, Col Leonard Stevens, and Mr Honeysett. They had to decide whether the evidence warranted committal to a higher court.

The examining magistrates were laymen advised on legal points by their clerk, usually an experienced solicitor. It so happens that Harry Odell, the Eastbourne Clerk, was not qualified as a solicitor albeit very experienced. As a matter of course they would sit in public, although they could decide to sit in private.

They would hear all the witnesses for the prosecution, turning their statements into sworn depositions for use at any future trial. At this stage the prosecution only had to show that there was a case worthy of a trial; while the defence did not have to disclose their hand at all.

Before the Court House in Old Orchard Road was built, the courts were held in the Town Hall. As 70 seats were reserved for the press, queues for places started long before dawn. Brenda Sterry, a WPC at the time of the trial, reports that many, unable to obtain admission in the morning, immediately joined the queue for the afternoon session. The court was stiflingly full and on the first morning two women fainted and were carried out. John Markwick explains that it was only through his sister, Janet, assistant to Harry Odell, that he obtained a seat.

On the first day Dr Adams appeared dapper and cheerful, and waved to his friends who crowded the courtroom. He was to find, as JR Rappeport describes, 'Court work is another house. Not the house of medicine, it has different motives, goals, and rules'.

Ken Harrison has a few random recollections of the Bodkin Adams' days. "My office was in the temporary Central Library at Grand Parade, now Clive Court flats, and I often had to walk to the Town Hall for meetings. I shall always remember the crowds of journalists and photographers gathered outside the Police Station and Town Hall when the preliminary hearing was held."

Lord Devlin writes, "The parties at committal proceedings are not usually represented by counsel, but these proceedings were not usual". The Attorney-General was not there, of course, but the counsel who would take part in any higher court were there. Mr Melford Stevenson QC and Mr Malcolm Morris appeared for the Crown, and Mr Geoffrey Lawrence QC and Mr Edward Clarke for the defence.

The dilemma for the prosecution, the Crown, was that they had to show that Dr Adams was systematically killing off patients, but only one murder count could appear on the indictment.

One murder could not be proved by saying there were other murders; each case had to have proof beyond reasonable doubt, but if other murders were similar then doubt may be removed. So while the Crown only charged Dr Adams with murdering Mrs Morrell, it alleged that he killed Mr and Mrs Hullett in similar circumstances.

Dawn queues outside the court in Eastbourne, with PC Derek Wilkinson

After the Doctor's plea of "Not Guilty" to the charges, Mr Lawrence rose to ask that the court be cleared. He was already worried that the tremendous publicity would render a fair trial unlikely, and he was now disquieted in case the prosecution mentioned the Hullett deaths, which could prejudice the Doctor's chances if the case came to a jury trial. The chairman said that he would have to make any application in open court. This put Lawrence in a quandary for if he referred to the reason in public he would have disclosed what he was trying to stop the prosecution mentioning. After discussion the bench decided that Mr Stevenson should open the case with an account of the Morrell charge and the magistrates would reconsider the situation after that had been heard.

Opening for the prosecution Mr. Stevenson stated that he would produce evidence to prove that Dr Bodkin Adams had murdered Mrs Morrell for gain.

He explained that Dr Adams had attended Mrs Morrell for some two years before her death, which he certified as being due to a stroke. "She in fact died because she was poisoned by drugs, mainly heroin and morphine, which Dr Adams administered ... Dr Adams received under her will a valuable chest of Georgian silver ... and after her death a Rolls-Royce motor car. It is quite plain that before her death he believed he would be left these things".

Mr Stevenson continued, "Graphs have been prepared to show an abnormal level of morphine dosage administered to the dead woman - and, since Bodkin Adams held a Diploma in Anaesthetics, he must have known the effects of such drug dosage. Records showed that, on the day before her death, Dr. Adams had prescribed 18½ gr of morphia for the dead woman". Counsel also said that a solicitor would give evidence regarding Dr Adams' interest in pecuniary gain from the woman's estate; four nurses, who had tended the dying woman, would tell of drug abuse; a chemist would testify to prescriptions signed by Dr. Adams, and Supt Hannam would tell of conversations with the accused.

He went into details of her illness, declaring that it was rare for pain to accompany her illness. "We know from two sources of the treatment which Mrs Morrell received ... the nurses who nursed her ... and medical evidence of an authority that I venture to think cannot be seriously questioned".

As Peter Palmer writes, "In the case of Mrs Morrell, the Crown maintained that her illness and symptoms never required injections of morphine and heroin. Two eminent specialists produced graphs showing that whereas the normal dosage was ¼gr, the 18gr prescribed represented a fatal dose of that drug".

After describing the circumstances of Mrs Morrell's death, the will, and the Police investigations, Mr Stevenson gave way for Mr Lawrence to argue his point about the need for the magistrates to receive evidence of other deaths in private.

Mr Lawrence pointed out to the bench that as the case might go to a higher court where the evidence that the prosecution was intending to call might be ruled inadmissible, was it right that it should be heard in public now?

The magistrates turned to Mr Stevenson because if he had said he had no objection they would probably agree with Mr Lawrence.

Instead Mr Stevenson replied, "While I cannot consent to Mr Lawrence's request I do not intend to oppose it". This was the classic response of counsel who had nothing legally against a proposal, but whose client could be embarrassed by it. In this situation the magistrates should have been given a clear direction.

The magistrates did not know what to do. They decided to hear what Mr Stevenson had to say in private and having done so they declared it should be heard in court.

Alarmingly, the prosecution was allowed to introduce evidence unrelated to the charge at issue, but which tended to show a similar pattern - notably the deaths of Mr and Mrs Hullett. Alfred John Hullett had died in March 1956, leaving the Doctor £500, and Gertrude Joyce Hullett in July, 1956, leaving the Doctor £100 and a Rolls-Royce.

It was precisely this kind of evidence that Geoffrey Lawrence had asked to be held in camera - and had been denied.

As mentioned, this situation would not occur today. Magistrates had the power to hear cases in private, but since the Criminal Justice Act of 1967 any defendant at committal proceedings can opt for publicity or no publicity.

Mr Stevenson said that he would be introducing evidence relating to 'system murders'. This referred to a legal term, which, over-simplified, states that whereby one death could be natural causes, if there was another similar death the possibility of murder had to be considered, and if three or more similar incidents occurred it would be negligent not to investigate.

Any series of deaths would not suffice. To prove a systematic campaign of murder, they had to be strikingly similar so that any juryman would recognise the pattern.

Edward Clarke and Geoffrey Lawrence QC (right) at the Eastbourne Magistrates Court {Topham Picturepoint}

Mr Stevenson went on to say, "The first is Alfred John Hullett ... His death was caused by an injection of morphine some eight hours before he died. Nurses said that Dr Adams gave a large injection of a strong morphia solution." Mr Stevenson went on to describe the heavy breathing, the awakening at six o'clock in the morning, then saying something to the nurse, and Mr Hullett's death 30 minutes later.

The Crown stated it had evidence that Dr Adams had taken the morphia from his own stock, but when he replaced it he requested 5gr of morphia, which he charged to Mr Hullett. Essentially, the Crown was saying that he either injected 5gr, a large dose, or that he had not used that amount and was being dishonest about drugs.

The cremation form charges were also brought up. Mr Stevenson stated that Dr Adams had written 'No' on the form, in answer to the question as to whether he had any pecuniary interest, when really he received £500 in the will and had admitted to Supt Hannam that he expected more.

Mr Stevenson turned to the death of Mrs Hullett. "There is no doubt that she died of barbitone poisoning, but she died in circumstances which the Crown says amount to murder by Dr Adams, whether or not she herself administered the fatal dose." Counsel pointed out that she was only 50 years of age, and he mentioned the repeated prescriptions of barbiturate by Dr Adams. He added that a bank clerk would tell of being asked by the doctor to expedite the cashing of a cheque for £1000 signed by Mrs. Hullett, and that Dr Harris' would tell of his advice. He also reminded the magistrates of Dr Adams' call to the coroner to request a private post-mortem – "That was something far odder than the other things that had occurred".

The magistrates had previously granted Supt Hannam's application to examine the bank accounts of Dr. Adams , hence Mr Stevenson was able to quote from Dr Adams' bank statement. This showed that the £1000 cheque was paid into an account that contained £12 000, and he drew the conclusion that Dr Adams did not have to expedite clearance because he was short of money. The implication being that it was rushed through because he was afraid of losing the money if she died before it was paid into his account.

Mr Stevenson suggested, "The same pattern repeats itself". Rich patient, heavily drugged, under the influence of the Doctor, died following a final massive drug overdose, after Dr Adams knew he would benefit from the will. In two cases Dr Adams gave a false answer on the cremation certificate, and was only deprived of the opportunity in the case of Mrs Hullett because of the circumstances which led to an inquest. The same desire for money was demonstrated by his request for a rapid clearance of the £1000 cheque.

On reflection, these similarities were not exceptional. Rich patients were two a penny in Eastbourne, and the bequests to Dr Adams were small in relation to the estates. In Mrs Hullett's case the drugs used were not the same as in the other two, and the evidence for undue influence was weak. The proposition had to be that in two cases the final fatal dose was given from fear that they might linger, but in the case of Mrs Hullett the only worry the Doctor might have was that she might die before the cheque was cashed. Such a lack of similarity weakens the arguments for 'system' murders, and could demolish them.

A prominent Eastbournian points out, "There was extra public concern with Mrs Hullett because she wasn't one of Dr Adams' old ladies. What I can't understand is why he expedited the £1000 cheque, he wasn't in need of the money, so does it suggest he knew she was about to take an overdose?"

The prosecution called forty witnesses, but apart from a mild tangle with Supt Hannam, Mr Lawrence reserved his main cross-examination until any later trial. He was convinced that the magistrates would commit for trial whatever he did.

The witnesses included four nurses. Nurse Randall was Mrs Morrell's night nurse from the time she came home to *Marden Ash* in 1949 to her death in 1950, and she also gave the last injections. Nurse Stronach did a few weeks of night duty in June 1950 and day duty in October that year. Sister Mason-Ellis, who was the only married nurse at the time, was the relief nurse. Sister Bartlett, now Mrs Hughes having married since Mrs Morrell's death, came as the day nurse in August

1950. She worked 0900-2100h, relieved between 1430-1830h by Mason-Ellis, until the November. She slept at *Marden Ash.*

On 15 January the nurses gave evidence. One told of large drug doses. A second said she gave injections under Dr. Adams' instructions, but was not told what she was injecting. A third one said that Mrs. Morrell had been a 'difficult patient - and refused to allow nurses to be present in the room with the doctor. The nurses' evidence was interspersed with "I associated her symptoms with the heroin", "When the heroin stopped she had a quiet night", and "She became comatose days before her death". Mr Lawrence did have Sister Mason-Ellis agreeing that Dr Adams had suggested exercises and massage for Mrs Morrell.

A physician attested that Mrs Morrell had suffered a stroke, that she had some difficulty in walking, but suffered no serious or constant pain. Mr Stevenson immediately made the point that, under those circumstances, there was no need for Dr Adams to administer massive doses of narcotics to the unfortunate widow.

Dr Arthur Douthwaite, called as an expert witness by the Crown, said the spasms mentioned by the nurses would arise from the large doses of morphia or heroin. The $2\frac{1}{2}$ gr of heroin would have resulted in death, and the $18\frac{1}{2}$ gr of morphia, "was enormous". In respect of Mrs Hullett he said that a doctor should first think of barbiturate overdosage with coma in a suicidal patient on barbiturates, and he would disregard any request not to send her to hospital. For Mr Hullett he said some morphia would be the right treatment, but more than $\frac{1}{4}$gr would be risky, implying that if Dr Adams had given 5gr, as an initial dose, it would be fatal. Mr Lawrence soon demolished these allegations when Dr Douthwaite admitted that if Mr Hullett had been given 5gr he would not have woken up and had a conversation at 0600h. Later he admitted that it was most unlikely that a lethal dose had been given, and Dr Adams' diagnosis of a heart attack was probably correct.

The coroner, Dr Sommerville, gave evidence about Dr Adams' phone call requesting a private post-mortem on Mrs Hullett, and how amazed he was when he discovered that the patient was still alive.

A pharmacist, Michael Clark says, "I compiled all the facts from the Prescription Books for the trial, and I gave evidence at the Magistrates' Court. A point that struck me was that many lay people, such as juries, think that when doctors talk of a maximum dose it means 'anything over that dose and you are dead' which, of course, is not so".

Under cross-examination by the defence, Alfred Spenceley, former manager of a chemist's shop, and Arthur Butler an assistant, agreed that of the 17 prescriptions alleged by the Crown to be for Mrs Morrell, only 12 items were actually for her.

On 17 January Dr Peter Lionel Cook gave evidence that in July 1956 he had been a house surgeon at the Princess Alice Hospital and had became acquainted with Dr Adams, who was an anaesthetist there. On Saturday, 21 July, Dr Adams asked him about obtaining *Megimide* from the hospital dispensary, because he had a patient on his hands whom he thought was suffering from barbitone poisoning. *Megimide* was a new drug and when it had been obtained, he and Dr Adams read the manufacturer's pamphlet together, which gave both dosage and administration instructions, he never told Dr Adams that 10ml was the correct dosage. Dr Cook added that Dr Adams had discussed this drug with him two days previously.

Dr Cook comments, "All my evidence at the Magistrates' Court was incorrectly transcribed. It was laboriously taken down in longhand, with 'millimetres' (mm) written every time I used 'millilitres' (ml).

"This created confusion, which Geoffrey Lawrence exploited. I think he realised the significance of my evidence far more acutely than the prosecution.

"Geoffrey Lawrence, incidentally, was superb, he gave the impression that it was all routine, rather tedious, but unfortunately necessary, if irrelevant. When eventually he was asked if he had any questions he did not even look up but simply shook his head, conveying exactly the impression that he wished."

Dr Vincent Harris informed the court that he had seen Mrs Hullett in the first instance, when Dr Adams was unavailable, and on another six occasions when he had been present. He thought that although the symptoms were consistent with a diagnosis of cerebral haemorrhage, he had nevertheless advised that Mrs Hullett should be transferred to hospital. Dr Adams told him he had promised Mrs Hullett that he would never send her to either a nursing home, or hospital.

In answer to further questions, Dr Harris said that if Dr Adams had informed him that his patient had a suicidal tendency, or that she had been prescribed barbiturate medication, he would have insisted on a transfer to hospital. It was only on the Sunday that Dr Adams told him he thought that Mrs Hullett could be suffering from barbitone poisoning and that he had obtained and injected as an antidote, a new drug called *Megimide*. Dr Harris said he had not heard of this drug before and in consequence had no knowledge of the correct dosage.

Peter Palmer's conclusion was, "The evidence given by Dr Cook and Dr Harris indicated that there must have been collusion between Dr Adams and Mrs Hullett, and that her suicide was pre-arranged between them. As she seemed determined to take her life, perhaps Dr Adams thought it would be better if she died through an overdose of drugs rather than throw herself over Beachy Head. He would ensure that she would not recover consciousness or be transferred to hospital and he would issue a death certificate for, say, cerebral haemorrhage and this would avoid the unpleasantness of an inquest for her family. If, however, anything went wrong, as it did, he would cover himself by saying, that unknown to him, she had hoarded the barbiturates which he had given her while they were on holiday".

These conclusions seem based on Mr Palmer's interpretation of Dr Harris' statement that Dr Adams had not told him Mrs Hullett was on barbiturates, and on Dr Cook's statement that Dr Adams had discussed *Megimide* with him two days before. The implications being that Dr Adams hadn't mentioned barbiturates in case she could be treated, and that he knew all about barbiturate poisoning, including 'antidotes'. Dr Adams simply could not believe she had taken an overdose, although it had crossed his mind, and it would appear that Dr Cook was the one who brought up 'antidotes' in a chance remark over tea after reading an article in the BMJ. Dr Adams had not heard of *Megimide* before Thursday, 19 July. Even for him it would be strange to give, or allow Mrs Hullett to take, a barbiturate overdose the very night he had learnt of the existence of an 'antidote'.

On Monday, the sixth day of the Magistrates' Court, Supt Hannam told of Dr Adams' attempt to hide two bottles of morphia in his pocket when his house was searched. It was also the Doctor's 58th birthday and the local newspaper reported that 'he was handed a number of postal packets' in the court.

The next day, 22 January, Harley Street consultant, Dr Michael Ashby, who had prepared the graphs to show Mrs Morrell's heavy drug dosage, said, "I could not possibly conceive that Mrs Morrell could survive either the whole or the major portion of morphia or heroin, had it been given alone". He added, "I am not prepared to let myself be pushed beyond what I feel certain about. I am most reluctant to say that Dr Adams did kill his patient by giving those drugs".

When Dr Camps gave evidence he said his post-mortem on Mrs Hullett revealed that she died of bronchopneumonia, due to barbiturate poisoning. He also expressed grave doubts as to whether Mrs Morrell could have survived the prescriptions recorded as being given.

Michael Moss, a scientific officer at the Metropolitan Police Laboratory at New Scotland Yard, said that he had received some of Mrs Hullett's organs from Dr FE Camps and had found a concentration of barbiturates in excess of the fatal dose.

Much of this evidence was to prove irrelevant, although it all made sensational copy for the press, and could influence a future jury.

Mr. Lawrence was able to repair some of the damage done by the prosecution evidence in his cross-examinations. He showed, for example, that Mrs Morrell's chauffeur had himself been left £1000. He also verified that any cremation certificate had additionally to be signed by an independent doctor.

In his questioning of Mrs Morrell's solicitor Mr Hubert Sogno, Mr Lawrence established that Mrs Morrell had made many wills and codicils – some before Dr Adams was her doctor - and in all of them had expressed the desire to be cremated.

On 24 January Geoffrey Lawrence made a two-hour submission to the Magistrates, that in respect of Mrs Morrell "there were such flaws and defects in the Crown case it would be wrong to send it to trial".

Not unexpectedly his plea was unsuccessful. While some of the evidence was weak and the defence purposely did not test it, there was enough to justify reference to a higher court. With the pressure on the magistrates it was not realistic to expect them to do otherwise. To an outsider, entirely conditioned by the press, it would have appeared that the magistrates were failing to give vent to the undoubted head of steam building up over the rumours of a family doctor killing for money, and that they were involved in a cover up.

Local solicitor, John Porter, says, "Indeed, but for the surge of public opinion, I found it difficult to understand the basis in law which led the magistrates to commit him for trial at the Old Bailey".

Thus after nine days of hearings the magistrates took just five minutes to find that there was a case to answer, and they committed Dr Adams for trial at the Central Criminal Court – 'The Old Bailey'.

Mrs Eileen R Comer (née Hummerstone) was on the bench: "I was the youngest magistrate and probably put on the case to obtain greater experience. I had never heard of Dr Adams beforehand. We had to determine whether there was enough evidence for a higher court and we certainly thought there was, although whether it was murder, or mercy killings in that he helped them along influenced by the rewards, was for others to decide."

Jean Fuller, a niece of the chairman David Honeysett, says that while she didn't discuss the case with him she had the impression that he thought Bodkin Adams was guilty.

John Markwick comments, "I was amazed at the cut and thrust of the barristers' debate and how Stevenson and Lawrence could have such different views. Even the medical opinions seemed to be diametrically opposed at times".

Geoffrey Lawrence was keeping his powder dry for the Old Bailey. Even so, the outlook appeared bleak; four nurses said that the doctor injected morphine and heroin into a patient already in coma, and two eminent doctors were prepared to confirm that they were murderous doses.

Tom Jeffery was the police sergeant in charge of Dr Adams when he was held at Eastbourne during the court hearing. He felt sorry for him, having his shoelaces, braces and tie removed at night, and noticed that he was often on his knees praying. PC Ron Spicer, later an Inspector, says that at first Dr Adams was in the 'women's cell' which was easier to keep a watch on him. "What struck me was his calmness, considering the seriousness of the charges".

Another of the policemen guarding him who later became a senior officer, says his impression was that Dr Adams lived on *Bovril* and hot chocolate, and sang *Abide with Me* . "There was always an officer on guard, but his cell door was not locked and his meals were carried over from the restaurant by the *New Inn."*

The Doctor returned to his cell at Brixton Prison. Dr Ian Brown writes, 'He was a strong muscular type, but later put on weight. He wrote to his housekeeper Annie Room from Brixton while awaiting trial that, *We get plenty of food and alas without my usual active round I'm afraid I will put on weight'*.

Many friends wrote letters of encouragement, posted birthday cards, and sent him presents. Lady Prendergast, widow of Admiral Sir Robert Prendergast, had a basket of fruit delivered on his birthday. An Eastbourne businessman says, "While in prison Dr Adams exchanged correspondence with my parents who thought him a wonderful doctor". His replies were full of hope, confident that, with God's help, he would surmount his travail. *Do not worry. All will be well. British justice and the power of prayer will clear me in God's good time.*

A story is told which shows that Bodkin was convinced he would be found innocent. In December 1956 he had bought a new Morris Minor 1000 car, DJK 721, from Caffyns the car dealers. While in Brixton he contacted Reg Matthews (of Caffyns) through his chauffeur, James White, with instructions that his Morris Minor should be re-sprayed French Grey to match his Rolls-Royce.

Norman Gray was among those who stood by him. He visited Dr Adams in prison often enough to request a parking place at *Avenue House*, a health clinic conveniently near the station. Mr Ashworth, a patient, visited him in Brixton Jail, being chauffeured up to London in his Rolls, and his chauffeur, Mr White, was among others to show support. Dr Barkworth, one of his junior partners, went to see him three times in Brixton, "Each time he was completely confident of the outcome". The more senior partners didn't visit because they could be called as witnesses, and they were upset about the effects of the publicity on the practice.

Michael Clark, local pharmacist: "I knew Bodkin by sight from before the war and got to know him well in the 1940s. It was always rumoured that he was a trifle on the greedy side. Contact was very much JBA, it gave older people a sense of security and faith. Many patients believed in him and wouldn't accuse him of any wrongdoing and I only heard good from his patients.

"When he was committed to prison some Eastbourne acquaintances deserted him, but the majority didn't."

In replying to this letter, please write on the envelope:—
Number 4889 Name J.B. Adams
BRIXTON, S.W 2. Prison

Sunday

Dear Miss Langham.

Thank you very much for your letter, and message of comfort and encouragement. Certainly your quotation is a "Sheet anchor" and one which will hold and stabilise me right through to the end.
I have a clear conscience and faith in God's Power to answer Prayer, so all must be well. Certainly I have been

An example of a letter to a patient from Dr Adams in Brixton Prison. 'I have a clear conscience and faith in God's power to answer prayer so all must be well'

Thanks to the press campaign people who did not know him thought that he was guilty, but it is true that his patients would not believe anything to Dr Adams' discredit. "Unlike one mischievous woman. She had always extolled the Doctor's virtues, but she became vindictive towards him to an embarrassing and unbelievable extent before he was even charged".

Dr Chris Savile, who was appointed to the 6 College Road practice as a locum with a view to replacing Dr Adams, says, "I was perhaps the only GP ever to be appointed with the proviso, as one of my interviewers, Laurie Snowball, put it, 'Depending on the course of British Justice'."

9. THE OLD BAILEY TRIAL

"Usually as the facts fade from the memory curiosity dies. In this case it did not." Lord Devlin.

On the morning of 18 March 1957 Dr Bodkin Adams was taken from prison to the Old Bailey. Brought into the dock, he bowed to the Judge, Mr Justice Devlin.

The Clerk of the Court from 1955 to 1977, Leslie Balfour Boyd: "John Bodkin Adams, is that your name?"

Dr Adams, the prisoner, "Yes, sir".

Clerk of the Court: "You are charged that on the 13th day of November 1950 you murdered Edith Alice Morrell. Are you guilty or not guilty?"

Dr Adams: "I am not guilty, my Lord."

The Clerk of the Court turned to the jury to repeat the charge and the prisoner's not guilty plea and to state that it was now their duty, when they had heard the evidence, to decide whether he was guilty or not.

Court Number 1 was a large oak panelled room, with many pillars, holding about 250 persons. There were oak desks, tables and benches in profusion. The dock holding the prisoner was in the centre about the same level as the Judge, who looked down on the advocates. The witness box was to one side near the Judge. The jury to whom all the evidence was addressed and who would decide the verdict had a ringside seat the other side. The public gallery was high in the roof.

The leading counsel for the Crown stood up. The Attorney-General himself, as was the tradition for poisoning cases, set out the case for the prosecution.

Beforehand he warned the jury that it was also their duty to, "... listen to the evidence and give a true verdict according to the evidence. That means you must put out of your minds anything that you have heard or read about Dr Adams and about this case".

It was a decent middle-aged jury, ten men and two women. Juries should be prepared to hear all possible variations of what happened from both sides, but they should start from scratch. Not easy in this case when the newspapers had been full of 400 MURDERS headlines, and the jury had to devote their attention to just one.

Dr Adams faced two charges. The first that he murdered Mrs Morrell, and the second of murdering Mr and Mrs Hullett. The convention was that each charge was taken separately so he faced the charge of Mrs Morrell's murder first.

The Attorney-General went on "Murder is one of the most serious crimes known to the law. If you do an act, such as administering drugs, and you do it with the intention of killing, it is murder. This is a very unusual case. It is not often that a charge of murder is brought against a doctor. The submission of the Crown is that Dr Adams by the administration of drugs to Mrs Morrell killed her, and those drugs were given with the intention of killing her.

"A word about this doctor. You will hear that he was a Doctor of Medicine and a Bachelor of Surgery, that he has a Diploma in Anaesthetics, and holds an appointment as anaesthetist to a hospital. With his qualifications and experience, it is perhaps safe to assume the Doctor was not ignorant of the effects of drugs."

Perhaps this is a moment to have a word about the Attorney-General, Sir Reginald Manningham-Buller QC MP. Son of a baronet, educated at Eton and Magdalen College, Oxford, he had been an MP since 1943. It was said that he chose to become a barrister not out of any interest in justice but because it was a good ground for his political career. A large and imposing man, his nickname was Sir Bullying Manner, from the way that he handled witnesses. To be fair he was seldom abrasive, or even incisive, but he was persistent; he wore down his victims.

Sir Reginald Manningham-Buller QC MP the Attorney-General, known as "Sir Bullying Manner"

The Attorney-General was assisted by Melford Stevenson QC and Malcolm Morris, who had appeared in the Eastbourne court, but Sir Reginald led the case for the prosecution.

"Mrs Morrell was a wealthy widow, who left £157 000. She was 81 when she died in November 1950 in her house at Eastbourne. In 1948 she had a stroke and her left side was paralysed. The Doctor was in charge.

"She was attended by four nurses, and these nurses will give evidence. They will say they never saw Mrs Morrell in any serious pain. The Crown will also call a Harley Street authority who has formed the opinion that Mrs Morrell was suffering from hardening of the arteries, and who will say that pain is unusual in this condition. You will hear of large quantities of drugs prescribed for her by the Doctor. Why were they given? It is quite a different thing to try to help an old lady to sleep, than to prescribe for her large quantities of drugs including morphia and heroin."

The Attorney-General supplied the details: "Over ten months 1629 grains of barbiturates, 1928 grains of *Sedormid,* 164 grains [9840 mg] of morphia and 139 1/2 grains of heroin.[1]

"You will hear that these drugs if administered over a period result in a serious degree of addiction, a craving for them, a dependence on them. The Doctor was the source of supply. Did not Mrs Morrell become dependent upon him? Why were these drugs prescribed to an old lady who was suffering from the effects of a stroke but who was not suffering from pain? Perhaps the jury may think that the answer lies in the changes made in her will.

"Mrs Morrell's solicitor will tell the jury that she made three wills in 1947 and 1948, and in none of those wills was the Doctor mentioned. Then in April 1949 when she had been having morphine and heroin for some months, she made another will in which she bequeathed an oak chest containing silver to the Doctor.

"A year later the Doctor had a very curious conversation with her solicitor. The Doctor told Mr Sogno that Mrs Morrell had promised him her Rolls-Royce and she had forgotten to include it in her will. The Doctor went on to say that although Mrs Morrell was ill her mind was clear and she was fit to execute a codicil. Did it not show", suggested the Attorney-General, "a certain keenness?"

He continued, "You may think it significant and sinister that during the period he was prescribing substantial quantities of morphine and heroin the Doctor was concerning himself so much about her will".

Mrs Morrell was one of those who expressed her power as a compulsive and capricious will-maker. The complete story of her recent wills starts with a will of August 1946 which left £1000 to Dr Adams. He was not mentioned in the wills of February 1947, October 1947, or October 1948, but he did appear in those of 9 June 1949, 19 July 1950 and 24 August 1950, as well as the codicils.

She was comatose and still Dr Adams pumped in the morphia

The Attorney-General passed round copies of a graph, "You will see how the prescriptions increased. During the last 13 days of her life the amount of morphia was over three times higher than the preceding months, and the increase in the amount of heroin was even greater. If she had been in severe pain such doses might be justified, but she was not. The nurses will tell you she was comatose or semi-conscious. Why did the Doctor prescribe such quantities with no justification? The Crown submits that he did so because he had decided the time had come for her to die. She should have no further opportunity to alter her will".

The Crown now came to the night of Mrs Morrell's death. The Attorney-General set the scene. "Mrs Morrell was lying unconscious. At 10pm the Doctor filled a syringe with 5cc of a preparation."[2] At that moment the Attorney-General injected drama into the court by holding up a syringe for all to see. "He gave it to the night nurse and told her to inject it into the unconscious woman. She did so. The Doctor refilled the syringe – an unusually large quantity on each occasion – and told the nurse to give it if the patient did not become quieter. The nurse did not like giving another large injection, but it was her duty to obey the instructions. She gave the second injection, Mrs Morrell became quiet and died at 2 am.

"The prosecution cannot tell you what those injections were, but if she was dying from the morphine and heroin, it was murder. If these two injections accelerated her death, it was also murder. The only possible conclusion is that the Doctor killed her deliberately and intentionally".

The Attorney-General paused, for there was a weakness in his case. All he had to hand were the prescription lists kept by the dispensing chemists – all that was legally required in 1950. He was assuming that the Doctor would not re-prescribe until the stock was almost used up and that he gave all he prescribed to the patient. The Crown had constructed a list of drugs prescribed, and that was their case.

There was the chance that a prescription had not been administered and there was no information about the amounts in the body. He moved to close this loophole.

"The case for the prosecution does not rest here. When the Doctor filled in Mrs Morrell's cremation form, he wrote, *Not as far as I am aware* to the question asking whether he had any financial interest in the death of the deceased. Yet when a detective inquired about this the Doctor said, 'Oh that was not done wickedly. We want cremations to go off smoothly for the dear relatives. If I said I am getting money under the will they might get suspicious'.

"But for this false answer", boomed the Attorney-General, "There might not have been a cremation and we might know how much morphine and heroin there was in Mrs Morrell's body at the time of her death.

"The detective also asked the Doctor who administered the drugs to Mrs Morrell and his answer was that he did, with none left over.

"You will hear that the maximum amount of heroin which should be prescribed in 24 hours is $^{1}/_{4}$ gr, yet the Doctor prescribed no less than 8gr on a single day.

"The prosecution will call a medical authority, whose authority can hardly be doubted, who will tell you that Mrs Morrell could not have survived the administration of these drugs.

"I submit to you that the evidence I will call will prove conclusively that this old lady was murdered."

After two hours the Attorney-General sat down.

Most of the rest of the day was taken up by four witnesses giving formal evidence concerning the drugs prescribed by Dr Adams and dispensed by pharmaceutical chemists, such as Browne's of Eastbourne.

The fifth witness for the prosecution was less marginal. Nurse Helen Rose Stronach, the relief night nurse, was called at the fag end of the day, because she was the only one available at the time.

To Mr Stevenson Nurse Stronach confirmed that Dr Adams came every night and on his instructions Mrs Morrell was given a $^{1}/_{4}$ gr of morphine every evening.

Counsel, "Did you see him do anything with a syringe?"

Nurse Stronach, "He gave her injections".

"Did you see him?"

"We were not allowed into the room".

"Who forbade you?"

"I think it was Mrs Morrell's wish".

Counsel, "So you did not see the injection given, but you saw him prepare it?"

"Yes, but I have no idea what it was".

At this moment the judge suggested an adjournment to bring to an end the first day of the trial in Court Number 1.

Day Two Nurse Stronach meets Geoffrey Lawrence

Nurse Stronach continued her evidence from the witness box.

Mr Stevenson. "You told us that the Doctor visited Mrs Morrell at 11pm and gave her an injection after you had given her $^{1}/_{4}$gr of morphia at 9pm?"

"Yes."

"And at 11pm Mrs Morrell would be dopey because of your injection?"

"That is so."

"What was Mrs Morrell's general condition?"

"Very weak. She was getting duller in every way. On the last day I was on duty, 2 November, she was rambling and semi-conscious."

"Did you see signs that she was suffering pain?"

"She did tell me that she had pains, but I considered it neurotic."

Now came the first cross-examination by the defence. As in the Magistrates' Court Mr Geoffrey Lawrence QC was the defence counsel, assisted by Edward Clarke and John Heritage.

Mr Lawrence stood up. Of slight build, five feet five inches tall, he appeared youngish compared with the other counsel. He had been called to the Bar in the Middle Temple in 1930, was the Recorder at Tenterden 1948-52 and had been Chairman of West Sussex Quarter Sessions since 1953. Generally regarded as a formidable advocate and cross-examiner, he lived at Kents Farm, Hurstpierpoint. He had a good voice and would wait for a reply. If it was evaded he would put the question again, with minimal change and no hint of irritation, until satisfied.

Mr Lawrence opened with, "Nurse Stronach, how many patients have you attended since Mrs Morrell died seven years ago? A great many?"

"Yes. In private nursing we are in and out continually."

"For what you told the court this morning you were relying on your memory?"

"Yes."

"Mrs Morrell was an old lady, and at the end she was very weak?"

"Very weak."

"And she had attacks of irritability?"

"Due to her condition."

"Against the nurses?"

"Not only the nurses." Replied Nurse Stronach with some heat.

"It was due to the damage to the arteries of her brain?"

"Not only that." Was Nurse Stronach's response.

"To what else?"

"I should say a great deal to the amount of drugs she was having."

Mr Lawrence moved to another line of questioning. "You never gave anything other than morphia by way of injection. No heroin. No *Omnopon*?"

"No."

"And when the Doctor came of an evening and gave a further injection, you still say he did not tell you what it was?"

"I do say that."

"You have our word for it"

Mr Lawrence went on. "When one of the other nurses gave evidence at Eastbourne, she said that she knew what she was injecting, but could not remember; it was written in a book? You made a record of all that you did?"

Nurse Stronach confirmed the use of the records. "Yes, that is correct. We noted down every injection we gave. It is the usual and proper thing to do."

"And that is what you did?"

"Indeed we did. Every time we gave an injection we wrote it down – what it was, the time and signed our names."

Mr Lawrence spelt out the implication. "And whatever you wrote in that book would be accurate because it would have been done at the time?" And rephrasing it for emphasis, "Everything that happened of significance in the patient's illness would have been noted?"

"We reported everything, a proper report is written day and night."

Mr Lawrence. "And as distinct from your memory of six years later these reports would be absolutely accurate?"

"Oh yes, from each one of us."

"So." Suggested Mr Lawrence, "If only we had those reports now we could see the truth of exactly what happened night by night and day by day."

"Yes, but you have our word for it."

Almost before anyone realised what was happening Mr Lawrence has conjured up a thumb-marked, ruled exercise book, for the usher to hand it to Nurse Stronach.

"I want you to have a look at that book please. Is that the night report for June 1950? Is it in your handwriting? And is it signed by you?"

There was hardly any need for a reply, Nurse Stronach's eyes dilated and her mouth dropped, as she stared at her handwriting and signature. "It is."

Mr Lawrence. "There is no doubt about it? That is the very book of the records kept by the nurses who attended Mrs Morrell, and includes your own record?"

"It is." Was the faint reply.

Her replies became even fainter when Mr Lawrence replaced the first orange soft backed notebook with a red one, which Nurse Stronach admitted was a continuation, and further books of varying hues were similarly identified.

"At this stage my Lord." said Mr Lawrence, "I desire to say that we have the whole of the nurses' reports from June 1949 to 13 November 1950."

That startled everybody, for it meant the prescriptions became a minor issue and the nursing evidence now turned on the notebooks. Dr Adams looked smug.

Mr Lawrence continued his questioning of Nurse Stronach.

"Let us look at your first day. When did you come on duty?"

"I cannot remember the exact date."

"I'm not suggesting that you can, but we can look to see what you wrote in the report. Let us go through your entries: 'June 4th had milk and brandy. 11pm one *Sedormid* tablet, milk and brandy repeated; complains of pain and says she has not slept well. 3am patient awoke, refused to be turned over, said it hurt her to turn. 6.15am, patient awoke in a temper. Said she had rung the bell and I had not answered it. Said I left the bed all untidy and that I was a nasty common woman'."

Mr Lawrence put down the exercise book. "We have read your entire entry for that night and two things are clear – first, you did not give any injection, and secondly the Doctor did not visit."

Nurse Stronach, "Not according to this."

"It is what you wrote down. Look at your record for June 8th. Again there is no record of any injection and again no doctor's visit, is there?"

"It doesn't say he did not call. That's not proof."

"Before you saw this book, you told me everything of importance would have been put down, didn't you?"

"Yes."

"And that was the truth?"

"Yes."

"It is clear that in that spell of duty you never recorded any injection and never had a visit from the Doctor?"

"Not that I recorded."

"Are you saying that you, a trained nurse, who recorded every drop of brandy, would not have recorded an injection of morphia or a visit from the Doctor?"

"No."

Nurse Stronach, and the prosecution, did not have a leg to stand on, for the nurses' notebooks, found by Mr. James contained all the minutiae of life. The dry, but meticulous, details of the drugs administered were interspersed with mentions of mice in the bedroom, and complaints about the sugar rationing.

Mr Lawrence went on, "We will now look at your second period of duty in October. When you went back Mrs Morrell's condition had deteriorated. A month before she died your entry states, 'Patient restless' and, in your writing, '*Omnopon* given at 4.30pm.' You gave it?"

"Yes."

"Do not think I am blaming you, but earlier you told me that you had never given Mrs Morrell *Omnopon*."

"I believed that was true."

"This entry shows that your memory was playing you tricks?"

"Apparently so."

"Obviously so, is it not?"

"I cannot remember. It is a long time to remember these things."

"That is exactly what I suggest. It was a long time ago and mistakes of memory can occur and this is just one."

Mr Lawrence took Nurse Stronach over further entries in the book. "You wrote, 'Doctor visited, gave injection of morphia', so you did record the Doctor's visits and on this occasion you did know what his injection was. Another day, 'Patient had a good night.' No injection and no Doctor's visit. 'October 31st, doctor's instructions omit morphia and *Omnopon,* 1st November, much better day, awake and taking an interest in things'..."

Comatose patient orders partridge and brandy and soda

Mr Lawrence put the book down. "We have been right through the whole of your records and we have not found a single instance where you gave the injection of $^1/_4$ gr morphia you mentioned, you recorded only two visits by the Doctor, and you knew exactly what injection was given. Earlier this morning you told the prosecuting counsel that on your last day Mrs Morrell was rambling and semi-conscious. Do you remember saying that?

Nurse Stronach, not enjoying the occasion, "I do."

"We have your own record of that day. You wrote that this semi-conscious woman had boiled egg, bread and butter, bramble jelly, two cups of tea for breakfast, and for lunch she consumed partridge, celery, pudding and a small brandy and soda. Is that the picture of a semi-conscious woman?"

Nurse Stronach gamely replied, "Oh, they would only have been very small portions."

Mr Lawrence squashed that with, "I am not suggesting she had a banquet, but are they the actions of a comatose woman, or is it another trick of your memory?"

Nurse Stronach, in the witness box since the start of the day and her credibility in shreds, then said her most sensible words, "I have nothing to say."

Mr Lawrence finished with, "You also said that Mrs Morrell was always dopey because of the injections, and that turns out to be inaccurate too."

Nurse Stronach was briefly re-examined by the Attorney-General, after which the Judge asked about the procedures for ordering and storing the drugs. The Judge wanted to know whether the Doctor controlled the supply. Her answer led to more than the nurse, or the Judge, expected. Nurse Stronach said sometimes the Doctor took drugs from his bag, but usually he would write a prescription which Mrs Morrell's chauffeur would take to the pharmacist, and when he brought the drugs back the nurse stored them in a locked cupboard and she kept the key in her pocket.

Sister Annie Helen Mason-Ellis followed her into the witness box. Now that the nurses' notebooks were in the open she was inhibited. From the start of the Attorney-General's questioning, she was emphatic that she "could not honestly and truthfully answer about Mrs Morrell's condition." She was an ordinary nurse for whom this experience had turned into a terrifying ordeal.

Mr Lawrence did manage to get her to agree that from her entry in the books of August 1949 Mrs Morrell was on a standard dose of $^1/_4$ gr morphia, which continued unchanged for months. Just before the end of the day Sister Mason-Ellis also admitted that Mrs Morrell displayed an irritability from time to time and that it was essential she should have peace and quiet at night.

Day three "Don't say that or you'll get us all into trouble"

No matter how bright you are you need a bit of luck to succeed in this world and Geoffrey Lawrence had a slice the next day.

Three of the nurses travelled to and from Eastbourne and London by train, chatting to each other. This, when witnesses who have given evidence should not talk to witnesses who are about to give evidence.

On the train the next morning, the nurses were discussing the reports in the newspapers when one said to the others that if she was asked about storage of the drugs she would have to admit that they were not kept under lock and key. Whereupon another of the nurses burst out, "Don't say that or you'll get us all into trouble." A commuter on the train, disgusted at the nurses' discussion of the case, telephoned Mr Lawrence's office at the Old Bailey and told of the conversation.

When Mr Lawrence continued his cross-examination of Sister Mason-Ellis he began by asking, "Did one of the nurses on the train say to you, 'Don't say that or you'll get us all into trouble'?"

"I really cannot remember; I was not terribly interested if I may say so."

Which was met by another of Mr Lawrence's withering ripostes, "I am not asking you to remember something that happened six or seven years ago, I am asking you what you were talking about this morning."

It was becoming clear to the court that, while the nurses might be well intentioned, they could not truly remember exactly what happened seven years ago.

Arriving together at London Bridge Station, left to right, Sister Mason-Ellis, Nurses Randall and Stronach. They were in for a shock {Popperfoto}

Mr Lawrence continued to go over the nursing reports with Sister Mason-Ellis. The notebooks showed that Doctor Harris, Dr Adams' partner, had looked after Mrs Morrell at times, that the Sister knew the Doctor gave injections of a vitamin preparation (*Cytamen*), and that Mrs Morrell's "outbursts" [mainly railing against the nurses, calling them slum women and brutes, and saying she wished she was dead] occurred without any change in the amount of her drugs.

Mr Lawrence took her over Mrs Morrell's last few days. Sister Mason-Ellis agreed the patient wasn't in a coma, and that Mrs Morrell's son wrote to her after the death thanking her for what she had done and enclosing £50 that he said his mother wished her to have.

Sister Mason-Ellis' cross-examination by Mr Lawrence had lasted four hours, and on its completion the Attorney-General was on his feet to make three points.

"There is no entry by you recording that Mrs Morrell suffered severe pain?"

"She did not have any pain as far as I am concerned."

"And yet throughout the whole period you were attending her she was having pain killers – morphine, heroin and *Omnopon*?"

"She was."

"Have you ever administered them as routine injections for any other doctor?"
"No."

The next nurse to take the stand was Nurse Caroline Sylvia Randall, the regular nurse of Mrs Morrell and the "Don't get us into trouble" one on the train. Described by colleagues as 'a bit airy-fairy', she was the prosecution's star witness - the nurse referred to in the opening speech who would describe the last night in detail, including the sinister big injections. Unfortunately for the prosecution the notebooks disclosed they were nothing but good old safe paraldehyde.

The Attorney-General had her agreeing that she had never given all the drugs for other doctors, and Mrs Morrell received more injections, and had more twitchings, in the course of the last few nights of her life than any other time.

He persisted with questions about the injections of the last night. The Doctor gave one at 9.30pm, but the patient was restless by 11.30pm and not asleep by 12.30am. The Doctor had refilled the syringe and given it to Nurse Randall saying that if the patient was restless to give it. "You did give that other injection?"

"I did. At 1am."

"What was the effect?"

"She became quieter and passed out."

These were the final questions of the day, but the Judge issued a stern warning for the benefit of Nurse Randall, "You understand that you must not discuss with anybody the evidence you have given or are about to give. You would be wise to avoid the company of the other nurses and if I have grounds for complaint I shall take a very serious view of it".

The national newspapers carried pictures of four well-separated nurses sitting in different compartments of the train.

Day four Dr Harris started the *Omnopon*

This was Nurse Randall's day, or perhaps more precisely the day she spent being cross-examined in the witness box. By now the court was packed not only with reporters, correspondents, writers and public, but the well of the court was packed with barristers, all come to hear Geoffrey Lawrence's cross-examination.

At the start the Attorney-General continued the cross-examination about the paraldehyde, "How did you know it was paraldehyde?"

"I must have been told by the Doctor."

"Where did it come from?"

"I think the Doctor brought it in."

Having trailed the suspicion that the Doctor could have put anything into the syringe, inexplicably the Attorney-General moved to a new tack,

"What usually happens to the notebooks on the death of a patient?"

"I usually take them and destroy them after a while. We don't show them to the relatives. It's rather distressing."

"Quite. What happened to these books?"

"I don't know."

"Did the Doctor visit after Mrs Morrell's death?"

"He did not arrive before I left."

So the Attorney-General had hardly established that the Doctor secreted the books away, and it was time for the defence.

From his first question, Mr Lawrence established that Mrs Morrell was not a well woman and that she was on morphine in 1949, and that the object of the Doctor's treatment was to give her relief from her restlessness and to provide sleep at night. The treatment went on with little variation, except when Mrs Morrell was irritable when she would be given a little more.

"Dealing with the time Dr Adams was away in Scotland on holiday and his partner was in charge. The routine injections of morphine were increased and I quote, 'May have *Omnopon* $^{1}/_{3}$gr when necessary'. We have not seen *Omnopon* before, now it appears with Dr Harris. It is quite plain that on that night the medication was stepped up?"

"Yes."

"Later that night Dr Harris was telephoned because Mrs Morrell was wide awake and restless. He came and gave one tablet of *Omnopon*. 'To be repeated'. That was on Dr Harris' instructions?"

"Yes."

Mr Lawrence, "And *Omnopon* contains fifty per cent morphia?"

"Yes."

"And yet the effect is, 'Seems much brighter this am. Has taken breakfast well'. So Dr Harris has dealt with the restlessness by increasing the doses?"

"Yes."

"When later her condition got worse that was exactly the way the Doctor tried to deal with it?"

"Yes."

"So everybody's endeavours were directed to ensuring Mrs Morrell had some sleep, and Dr Harris used the same drugs as Dr Adams. It looks as though the doctors and the nurses were coping with the case very well?"

"Yes."

With Nurse Randall having to agree with all his points so far, Geoffrey Lawrence moved to dispose of the suspicious situation whereby the nurses were not allowed in the sickroom when Dr Adams was there.

"Mrs Morrell was not fond of the company of the nurses in her room?"

"No, the night nurses had to sit in the other room and creep along to observe her from time to time."

"It was Mrs Morrell's wish that you were not in the room with the Doctor?"

"Yes."

Mr Lawrence looked at a transcript of the previous day's hearing and asked,

"Yesterday in reply to the Attorney-General's question, 'Had you ever given routine injections of those drugs on the instructions of any other doctor?' you said, 'No' Now we have seen that you did that very thing on the instructions of Dr Harris, so that would not be quite right?"

Nurse Randall resignedly replied "No."

At the end of the day the Judge intervened to ask her one more question,

"What is the normal dose of paraldehyde?"

"It depends how you give it but I think 4cc or 5cc is a large dose."

The Judge, "One cc would be the normal dose?"

"It would."

"Is it a dangerous drug?"

"It makes you sleep."

At this point Mr Lawrence rose, "I must challenge what you said. The British Pharmacopoeia dose is 8cc. Do you know that?"

Nurse Randall, "No, I did not."

Mr Lawrence, "Of course, you cannot be expected to know all these things."[3]

Day five

This was the last working day of the first week. Nurse Randall continued her evidence through the morning and Nurse Bartlett was on in the afternoon.

Mr Lawrence completed this part of the cross-examination by asking Nurse Randall why the second injection, the final injection, was not recorded.

Reasonably, she answered, "I might have left it out because it was the last one and I had other things to do."

"You have no recollection seven years later why it was not in the book?"

"No, I haven't."

"Your memory isn't very trustworthy."

Nurse Randall, "It appears not to be."

All this questioning was carried out without any harassment of the witness, although for any witness who had made an unwary observation or was ever so slightly muddled in their thoughts it must have been a crushing experience.

Mr Lawrence went on to ask her about the remark, 'Don't say that or you will get us into trouble'.

"I do not remember saying it."

Mr Lawrence gripped the edge of the bench and asked gently, "Have you realised that Dr Adams is standing trial for murder. Are you being frank with me?"

"I don't remember."

"You don't remember something that happened on Wednesday, two days ago?"

"No, I don't."

"Is that the sort of memory you have?"

Nurse Randall, archly, "No, but if I didn't say it I wouldn't remember it."

Mr Lawrence, "Do you say that Sister Mason-Ellis was wrong?"

"I do."

Mr Lawrence tried another line of questioning. "When the Doctor went away on holiday in September 1950, Mrs Morrell was very upset?"

"Yes, very."

"Did she say she was going to alter her will and cut the Doctor out of it?"

"Yes she did, she was very angry at the time."

Mr Lawrence, "Among the others, how much did you get?"

Nurse Randall, "Three hundred pounds."

The Attorney-General took over questioning Nurse Randall about the nursing records, with mixed results. He managed to elicit an answer that Mrs Morrell had told her the Doctor had promised he would not let her suffer at the end, but when he asked, "Apart from the Doctor and Dr Harris, have you ever had instructions from another doctor to administer dangerous drugs when the patient was not suffering pain?" Nurse Randall replied lightly, "Yes, if they are very excitable."

The Judge turned to Nurse Randall. "Did you know the last injection was paraldehyde because the Doctor said so, or because of its distinctive smell?"

"I don't remember the smell of it."

"At any rate", continued the Judge, "there was nothing in your mind to suggest that it was not paraldehyde?"

"No."

"Had you ever got in your mind that it was morphia or heroin in the syringe?"

"No."

The Judge's apposite questioning concluded the morning session and Nurse Randall stepped down after a harrowing eight hours in the witness box.

Nurse Brenda Bartlett {Topham Picturepoint}

The afternoon started with Mr Melford Stevenson taking Nurse Brenda Bartlett (now Mrs Hughes) over the reports. We learn that she came as a day nurse to assist in Mrs Morrell's care three months before the death.

"In your first report there is reference to a special injection given by the Doctor, what was it?"

"He said it was a pick-me-up."

"Did you notice any signs of severe pain?"

"I did not."

"What was her condition like in the last few days?"

"She was semi-comatose."

Mr Stevenson, "And did you notice anything in regard to Mrs Morrell's movements?"

Nurse Bartlett, "She had twitching spasms."

She remembered the Doctor coming on the last night and giving the patient paraldehyde and the Doctor preparing another syringe which he gave to Nurse Randall.

When it came to Mr Lawrence's turn he again asked about the nursing reports, and read from one of the books.

"You have no record of twitchings or jerkings, 'Awake, restless, talkative', but no movements. Let us turn to the next report. 'Has been very alert and talkative this evening. Morphine and heroin given with no effect.' No effect?"

Sister Bartlett, "It had no effect at all."

"Did you know that paraldehyde is not an opium derivative, that it is a well established remedy for sleeplessness and is one of the safest drugs there is?"

She nodded, "Yes."

So the cross-examination continued: Mrs Morrell had bad tempers, and she would not allow the nurses in the room with the Doctor. Referring to all the other medications and measures ordered by the Doctor, Sister Bartlett followed the other nurses in agreeing that while the policy was to keep Mrs Morrell quiet, the Doctor's orders were that she was to be kept as mobile and active as possible.

The Friday afternoon soon drew to a close and, apart from the prisoner, everyone went home.

The case against Dr Adams as presented by the Attorney-General had sounded damning. The Crown prosecution intended the nurses to give the facts over the first couple of days, with the medical evidence following with an interpretation unfavourable to the prisoner. The Crown had expected the nurses' evidence to be short and not contested, whereas it had taken a week and been destroyed. The nurses' report books meant that the defence was able to dispute every fact and to demonstrate quite firmly that the nurses' memories for the happenings of seven years ago were vague, if not completely distorted.

To some observers the Crown's case had already collapsed. At the least it had been damaged and it was going to rely even more heavily on the medical evidence, due the following week.

OLD BAILEY THE SECOND WEEK

Day six Dr Adams had no motive

The day began with a succession of witnesses. Among those called in person was Mr Price, Mrs Morrell's chauffeur.

Crown counsel asked, "What kind of car had Mrs Morrell?"

"Rolls-Royce, sir."

"What happened after her death?"

"I took it round to the Doctor myself, sir."

Mr Lawrence's first question was, "A Rolls-Royce you say – what model?"

"1938, sir."

Letting it sink in that the car, if not quite vintage, was of ancient lineage, he went on, "Mrs Morrell was a generous woman?"

"Very generous to me, sir, and other people."

"How much did she leave you after three years' service?"

"A thousand pounds, sir."

After lunch the Attorney-General questioned Mr Hubert Sogno, solicitor, of Lawson Lewis & Co.

"Mrs Morrell became your client in 1948?"

"She did."

Attorney-General: "Did she make a number of wills?"

"She did."

"In April 1949, did you have a telephone conversation with the Doctor?"

Before answering Mr Sogno opened a brief case and took out a number of papers, which he perused. "I had. The Doctor said he was telephoning on behalf of Mrs Morrell who was anxious about her will and she desired to see me that day."

"Was a further will made?"

"It was."

The Attorney-General. "Did the Doctor call at your office subsequently?"

Hugh Sogno consulted his papers, "He called about a year later, March 1950, he said that Mrs Morrell had promised him her Rolls-Royce in her will and she had forgotten to do this. She now wanted to leave the car to him. I suggested that the matter should wait until Mrs Morrell's son visited, but the Doctor said she was uneasy and wished to get the matter off her mind. He told me I should prepare a codicil which could be destroyed later if it did not meet with the approval of her son. I told him that was quite impossible."

The Attorney-General ended, "And on 24th August there was another will?"

Mr Sogno confirmed that this was the last will. In it the Doctor was left an oak chest with silver and, if Claude Morrell, Mrs Morrell's son, predeceased her, an Elizabethan oak cupboard and the Rolls-Royce as well.

Mr Lawrence now took up his cross-examination.

"When the Doctor talked to you on Mrs Morrell's behalf did he make the point that you should go without delay and put her mind at rest?"

"He certainly asked me to go without delay. I am quite willing to assume that was his reason."

"Were you sent for again when the Doctor was away on holiday in Scotland?"

"I was. She instructed me to prepare a codicil the effect of which was to cut the Doctor wholly from any benefit."

Mr Lawrence, "And what happened to it?"

Mr Sogno produces an envelope, "It is in pieces. Torn up by Mrs Morrell."

Dr Adams wasn't in the will

"Did her tearing it up restore the Doctor back into the will?"

"Oh, no." said Mr Sogno, "It was not validly revoked before her death."

"Let us get this clear," said Mr Lawrence, "Mrs Morrell never executed a document which gave back the bequests to the Doctor?"

"She did not."

"So when she died the Doctor was not in any way a beneficiary?"

"That is correct."

"So anything the Doctor received was only by the favour of her son?"

"Yes. He said by all means the Doctor should have the chest and the Rolls-Royce because it was his mother's wish." And Mr Sogno again agreed that in all her wills it was Mrs Morrell's wish that she be cremated.

Mr Lawrence asked about the value of Mrs Morrell's estate and Mr Sogno confirmed that it was £157 000, of which Nurse Randall got £300, the gardener £500, and her chauffeur £1000.

"And what was the value of the chest of silver received by the Doctor?"

"Two hundred and seventy five pounds and five shillings."

John Porter, then a junior partner in Lawson Lewis & Co, had no direct connection with Mrs Morrell's affairs, but he believes, "Hubert Sogno's cross examination by Geoffrey Lawrence was a masterpiece on both sides. Hubert Sogno answered the questions put to him, without embroidery, and Geoffrey Lawrence eventually reached the question which provided the information that Dr Adams didn't benefit under Mrs Morrell's will." Mr Lawrence could sit down well pleased that he had removed the financial motive for murder by Dr Adams.

Inspector Pugh was called next by the Attorney-General, followed by Superintendent Hannam. The Superintendent's evidence, about the occasion on 1 October when he met Dr Adams outside his garage, was hardly underway when Mr Lawrence asked for the Judge's ruling on part of the evidence. The Judge ruled that much of the evidence allowed in the Magistrates' Court (about Dr Adams not wanting payment; that the gifts in wills were instead of fees; that the drug cupboard was untidy; and his attempt to conceal two bottles of morphia, with the words "I know it was silly") was inadmissible because it concerned cases other than that with which Dr Adams was charged.

Needless to say reports of the Magistrates' Court hearing had already appeared in the world's press and had almost certainly been read by members of the jury.

At the Old Bailey the Superintendent confined himself to mentioning only the discussion of Mrs Morrell's chest of silver, including, 'I knew she was going to leave it to me … '.

The Attorney-General asked about the cremation certificates. In reply Superintendent Hannam said that he told the Doctor about asserting he was not a beneficiary under the will when he was, and of the Doctor's 'Not done wickedly' comments, together with, 'Relatives like the cremation to go smoothly'.

The Attorney-General took Supt Hannam over the search for drugs at *Kent Lodge* on 24 November. This included the Doctor's statement, 'Dangerous drugs … I seldom use them', and showing Mrs Morrell's prescription list to the Doctor, when he had said he gave most of the drugs himself and they were nearly all used up. The day drew to a close with the Attorney-General asking whether any morphia was discovered on the premises, and the Superintendent admitted that there was only a small quantity in the Doctor's bag.

Day seven

In the morning the Attorney-General continued with Superintendent Hannam. He teased out more of the Doctor's incriminating statements, 'Easing the passing of a dying person isn't all that wicked', and when arrested his exclamation, 'Murder? Murder? Can you prove it was murder?' and there was his remark to his receptionist as he went out of the house, 'See you in heaven.'

In conclusion the Attorney-General asked the jury, "Was the Doctor's comment, 'I did not think you could prove murder. She was dying in any case.' what you would expect an innocent man to use, or was it what a murderer might say if he thought his crime could not be proved?"

Mr Lawrence took over and discussed the inflexion of the Doctor's voice in the phrase, 'Murder? Murder? Can you prove it was murder?' The Superintendent was quite open about this. He said that the Doctor was very shaken and distressed, and that he was not prepared to put an interpretation on any inflexion.

Supt Hannam behaved well. He was implying that the words were not in the sense of 'Can you prove *that*?', but were those of an astonished man. The risk of such a disclosure, from the Superintendent's point of view, was that the jury might not believe that a flabbergasted man could contrive a murderous scheme.

Detective-Sergeant Hewitt followed and stated exactly what the Superintendent had said. He admitted that they wrote up the notes together shortly afterwards, but the Judge accepted a composite record so long as both men had signed it.

The first witness after lunch was Thomas Reid, the Crown chemist, who told of an experiment with a paraldehyde-filled syringe which, left for a hour on a tray, filled a room with the smell. He went on to give his summaries of the prescriptions and injections, in essence, he showed a discrepancy of 30gr more morphine and 12gr more heroin prescribed than recorded in the nursing books.

At this stage most impartial observers were wondering whether it would be possible to determine what had precisely happened after such a span of time, with fallible memories, and now even records which didn't tally.

The next witness was Dr Harris, one of Dr Adams' partners. Ronald Vincent Harris, of Milnthorpe Road Eastbourne, had qualified at St Barts in 1933. He held a doctorate in Medicine. As well as a GP he was part-time Consultant Dermatologist at the Eastbourne & Hailsham Hospital Groups.

Mr Melford Stevenson questioned him about his visits to Mrs Morrell, "When the Doctor went away did he leave any instructions about treatment?"

"He usually told other doctors to carry on with whatever he had been giving."

"Why did you increase the morphia and heroin in September 1950?"

"She was extremely irritable because the Doctor had gone away and I increased the sedatives she was already having because of the cerebral irritation."

"Have you ever prescribed morphia and heroin together for a patient suffering from cerebral thrombosis?"

"Over short periods of time."

It was almost the end of a long day when Mr Lawrence gently began his cross-examination. Dr Harris agreed he saw Mrs Morrell on over 20 occasions, and that she was subject to attacks of restlessness and irritability that required sedation.

"Is it often that a woman of that age survives a stroke as long as she did?"

Dr Harris, "It is very rare."

Day eight Dr Douthwaite appears in style

Dr Harris finished his evidence the next morning. He confirmed for Mr Lawrence that rapid breathing was not associated with drugging, and that the twitching could be an indication of brain damage by the cerebral thrombosis.

The Judge followed by asking Dr Harris what drugs he would use.

He replied that in 1950 there were only phenobaritone, bromides and paraldehyde.

"In selecting your drugs would you have regard as to what the long-term effects might be?"

"One would, but it is not always easy to know how long that length of time is going to be."

The Judge asked whether morphia could be used for restlessness and was told one might use it. The Judge next tried to ascertain at what point a deputising doctor would change the treatment if he thought it was doing the patient harm. Dr Harris was equal to this and essentially replied that if one was seeing the patient over just a few days one would not change the treatment and in the case of Mrs Morrell to withdraw her morphia might make her extremely ill.

The Judge has one more point. "When you were talking about Mrs Morrell's deterioration in September, did you mean that you did not expect her to get better?" Dr Harris negotiated that question as well, "Well, in cases like hers there are phases which can be got over, or which might be the beginning of the end."

The next witness was the main medical witness for the prosecution, Dr Arthur Henry Douthwaite, a tall man, with a handsome profile.

Dr Douthwaite, of 49 Harley Street, London, qualified in 1921 from University College and Guy's Hospital. He held a doctorate in Medicine and was a Fellow of the Royal College of Physicians. He was a Consultant Physician at Guy's Hospital and Horsham Hospital, at some time a Senior Censor RCP, President of the British Society of Gastroenterology, and of the Medical Society of London. He edited textbooks, had written many articles, and his club was the Garrick.

The Attorney-General asked him how long life could last after a stroke.

"For many years."

"What is the proper treatment of a stroke?"

"As soon as one can one should mobilise the patient. Massage, exercises."

"And is there any justification for injecting morphia or heroin immediately after a stroke?"

"No justification whatsoever."

"Is it wrong to do so?"

"Wrong. In all circumstances wrong." You could imagine Dr Douthwaite's wattles wobbling as he shook his head. His pronouncements had such an absolute certainty and were in such contrast to the qualified comments heard so far that the Court was startled. Dr Adams alone was shaking his head sadly as though he had seen more strokes than Dr Douthwaite had eaten hot dinners.

The Attorney-General, "What about morphia alone?"

"Morphia should never be given to someone with a stroke, unless there is acute mania, and then only a single injection."

"What would be the effect of morphia on an old lady who had had a stroke?"

"It would greatly interfere with her rehabilitation."

"Is it necessary to immediately sedate someone who has suffered a stroke?"

"It is not necessary."

"Is it desirable?"

"Not in general, to ensure sleep then sedation is quite reasonable."

"Does that include morphia and heroin?"

"Completely exclude."

The Attorney-General, "Is it necessary to keep a patient with a stroke as quiet as possible?"

"Not in the day time."

"Is there a risk of another stroke if the patient is not kept quiet?"

Dr Douthwaite, "On the contrary, there is risk of another stroke from clotting."

"Would irritability be a justification for administering morphia and heroin?"

"Oh, no, completely contrary. It would give rise to addiction and they are not as effective as much safer drugs."

The Attorney-General, "Is morphia likely to produce addiction?"

"Very liable, certainly within three weeks."

"What would be the addicted person's attitude toward the supplying doctor?"

"Dependence on the doctor."

"Can you tell us the legitimate purpose of morphia, and the normal dosage?"

"For severe pain that cannot be quelled by other means, and one quarter of a grain. The British Pharmacopoeia gives the maximum dose as a third of a grain."

"At what intervals?"

"Perhaps every four hours, if really agonising pain it might be every hour."

Dr Douthwaite went on to say that the effect of a dose of heroin is a craving for more; and that it should never be given to old people unless they have an incurable disease. He explained that patients became tolerant so that the dose had less and less effect, so that larger doses have to be given to secure any effect at all. He confirmed that withdrawing the drug would make the patient ill.

The Attorney-General, "The only reason for the heroin was to 'keep her under'?"

Dr Douthwaite assented.

The Attorney-General, "Could the twitchings be produced by the heroin?"

Dr Douthwaite, as though he'd been waiting for this question, "Oh, yes they could."

The Attorney-General proceeded to ask about the injections of paraldehyde. "Could it be used to stop the twitchings?"

"Yes."

"What would be the effect if it were superimposed on morphia and heroin?"

"It would be likely to produce death."

"Dr Adams certified Mrs Morrell's death as cerebral thrombosis [stroke]. Are there any signs to justify that conclusion?"

"None." Spoken scornfully.

"What can be the object of giving routine morphia and heroin?"

"There isn't one."

The Attorney-General goes over the nursing books asking Dr Douthwaite how he would describe the dosage of heroin 1gr hourly.

"Very heavy, and an astonishing instruction."

"What would be the effect of the dosage administered in the last few days?"

"The only conclusion I can come to is that the intention on November 8th was to terminate her life."

Dr Adams closed his eyes and slowly opened them. It was Dr Douthwaite, however, who should have been thinking deeply. He had succumbed to the blandishments of the Crown team to provide the evidence they needed, for if he had not waded into Dr Adams, they might just as well have gone home.

Day Nine Dr Douthwaite calls all the other doctors murderers

The next morning Mr Lawrence took over the questioning. He did not attack Dr Douthwaite head on; he nibbled away at his stance. "I understand you are saying that the Doctor formed the intention to terminate life on November 8th and carried out that intention?"

Dr Douthwaite, "Yes."

"Have you ever expressed a more fateful opinion than that?"

"No."

"Before going into the witness box had you satisfied yourself that you had every piece of relevant information before you on which to base that conclusion?"

Dr Douthwaite nodded his assent.

Mr Lawrence, "You gave evidence in this case before the magistrates?"

"I did."

"When you were ignorant of her treatment before January 1950?"

"Yes."

"You gave your evidence on the basis that she had been in continuous coma?"

"Yes."

Mr Lawrence, quickly, "Which turned out on the facts to be quite wrong?"

"Yes, not in continuous coma."

"Had you made any inquiries before giving evidence against the Doctor yesterday about the circumstances of her stroke in Cheshire?"

"I knew she had her stroke when visiting her son in Cheshire, and I have said it would be interesting to know what treatment she had before she came under the care of the Doctor. I was told it wasn't available."

Mr Lawrence swung round to the Judge, "My Lord, I want the witness to look at a document". With his second conjuring trick Mr Lawrence produced the nursing records from the Neston Cottage Hospital.

He read out aloud " ... 'June 26th,' her first day there, 'Luminal two grains; slept very little'. A barbiturate", explained Mr Lawrence as he glanced round at the Judge and jury, "Mrs Morrell was under the care of two doctors, Dr Turner and a consultant Dr Hugh Spear Pemberton. 'June 27th, poor night. Patient very distressed and complaining of severe pain.'." Turning to Dr Douthwaite, "The very phrase you used yesterday as justifying the use of morphia. 'Two Vermon tablets given but patient unable to swallow them. Morphia 1/4 gr given. Patient slept.'."

Mr Lawrence reads on, briskly, and every night throughout Mrs Morrell's ten days in the Cheshire hospital there is a record of a morphia injection. He addresses Dr Douthwaite, "From these records it is clear she was an ill woman, she complained of pain, and after two nights of attempting sedation with barbiturates, the doctors resorted to morphia?"

"Yes."

"And every night she had morphia?"

"Yes."

"And after these injections, she slept?"

"Yes."

Mr Lawrence, "Yesterday, you were saying that no doctor should give morphia after a stroke except in acute mania and then only one injection. There is no suggestion of acute mania in the Cheshire hospital?"

Dr Douthwaite, "None whatsoever."

Dr MG Ashby (left) and Dr AH Douthwaite
The medical witnesses for the prosecution

"And does your condemnation which you declared from the witness box include the doctors in Cheshire?"

"If that was the treatment, yes."

Mr Lawrence, amazed at Dr Douthwaite's refusal to budge, throws up his hands with a, "Good gracious me", and there is laughter in the Court. The doctor's arrogance was not lost on the Judge or jury.

The defence counsel continues, "We are left with this, that two doctors who are not on a charge of murder, deliberately gave this patient injections of morphia, not a single injection, but night after night. Are you now condemning those doctors too?"

"If it was used to treat the stroke."

Mr Lawrence, "The pain was a consequence of the stroke?"

"Probably." Admits Dr Douthwaite.

"All these doctors, Dr Turner, Dr Pemberton, Dr Harris and the accused saw the patient. So far as you know you never saw Mrs Morrell?"

"I agree."

Mr Lawrence, "As a general rule it is true, is it not, that only the man on the spot knows the full picture? He has not got to be a perfect physician, that ideal which is stored in heaven or even in the mind of a Harley Street consultant?"

Dr Douthwaite failed to rise to the bait, but producing the Cheshire hospital notes was another telling blow just when the Crown was trying to get on its feet after being clobbered by the nurses' notebooks.

Mr Lawrence moved on. "Could six to twelve months be a reasonable outlook in terms of expectation of life after her stroke?"

"Yes, I think it would."

"Now the reasonable object of a GP's treatment would be to make her life as tolerable as it could be?"

"The first object would be to restore her health."

"That, of course, is the highest level. But no doctor in his senses would think that he could restore a woman of eighty to her pre-stroke health?"

"Oh, no, I agree with that."

"So the doctor has got to do his reasonable best?"

"Yes."

"And whatever you say about these drugs, the fact is recorded that until September 1950 she was being got up during the daytime?"

"Certainly."

Mr Lawrence asked, "Is it not necessary in relation to a charge of murder to see the whole case?"

"Quite."

"And by September she had exceeded the reasonable expectation of life?"

"I quite agree."

"Now if you are giving morphia to deal with pain, the time will come when you won't be able to deal with the symptoms on a level dosage?"

"I agree."

"And you are at the point where you can either stop the drug, which in an eighty-year-old might well have a risk of death?"

"I agree."

"Or give her more, which is exactly what Dr Harris did?"

"Yes."

"She was going downhill that September?"

"Yes."

"What to do in these circumstances is one of the most difficult problems that face a doctor?"

Dr Douthwaite, "Oh, yes."

"Your objection to morphia is because the patient may become addicted?"

"That is one of my objections."

"It is fairly obvious there is no perfect drug, and a short expectation of life mitigates the dangers of addiction?"

Dr Douthwaite, "Yes. May I say that my practice has always been that if a patient is obviously dying, it is ridiculous to worry about addiction."

Mr Lawrence moved to another line. "When the Doctor qualified, morphia and heroin were used as hypnotics [a drug that induces sleep]?"

Dr Douthwaite, "I accept that."

"They are not dangerous if properly used? When we say dangerous drugs, that is only one side of the picture, they are beneficial drugs are they not?"

"I agree."

"Indeed, they are one of greatest blessings conferred on the medical profession, and you led a deputation to the Home Office requesting that no ban be placed on the manufacture of heroin in this country?"

"I took a leading part."

"Have you tried to determine the character of the special injections?"

"I was interested in the drugs as set out in the summaries."

Mr Lawrence, "Can we disregard the special injections in your view?"

"As far as I am concerned, yes."

"Would you take it from me that the special injection in November was caffeine?"

"If you say so."

"Caffeine is a stimulant?"

"A feeble one."

"Wouldn't it have been odd for a doctor with murderous intent to have given an antidote – however feeble?"

"Agreed."

The day wore on and Mr Lawrence ground away at Dr Douthwaite's initial stance. Dr Douthwaite agreed there was no suggestion that the Cheshire doctors had any murderous intent; he accepted Mrs Morrell was alert; that her increased tolerance meant increased dosage; and that the symptoms were of senility.

"The Doctor stopped morphia at one time and gave heroin instead. Doesn't it look as though he was trying variation rather than increase of the dose?"

Dr Douthwaite. "I don't know what was in the Doctor's mind."

"Did you not before? When you saw murderous intent?"

Dr Douthwaite was silent. The examination continued.

Mr Lawrence pointed out that by his interpretation of Dr Douthwaite's evidence he was stating that on the 8 November the Doctor had decided to murder her. "Yet the only sleep she had on the 9th was 15 minutes in the morning and 20 minutes after lunch? If this sleeplessness went on she would have collapsed?"

Dr Douthwaite, "Heroin is useful."

"So it is sometimes prescribed?"

Dr Douthwaite again says nothing.

"The Doctor then give her hyperduric morphia. A slow acting type, is it not?"

"It is."

"On the eve of murder – a slow-acting drug? A strange choice for a murder?"

Dr Douthwaite shrugs his shoulder.

"And on the same day he gave her atropine." Mr Lawrence consulted a book. "'Atropine is classed as an antidote to morphine'. So on the second day you are saying the Doctor is carrying out his murderous intention he gave an antidote?"

You could almost sense Dr Douthwaite was about to say, 'all a part of the Doctor's fiendish plan', instead he answered, "Yes."

Mr Lawrence went on to the paraldehyde injections. "It was the Doctor's duty to produce sleep and he tried paraldehyde. One of the safest remedies there is?"

"Agreed."

"And 5cc is quite a common dose, even double would be permissible?"

"Quite."

Mr Lawrence, "Could anything else have been given at this stage?"

"There are several that could have been given with safety."

"Including paraldehyde?"

Dr Douthwaite drew the day's proceedings to a close by admitting, "Including paraldehyde."

Day Ten Dr Douthwaite has second thoughts

At the start of the next day Mr Lawrence concluded his cross-examination by asking, "I am not inviting a Harley Street opinion about the skill of a GP, but would you say on the history there is no need to postulate an intent to murder?"

Dr Douthwaite, "Where I live has nothing to do with my opinion or knowledge, but I am forced to postulate that, on the drugs given in November, there was murderous intent."

"You would not accept a possible alternative view?"

"Yes – we all have different opinions."

As the essential test of any evidence is to ask, 'Does the jury find it reasonable?' the Judge obviously felt that Dr Douthwaite had overstated his case. He intervened, "The jury must be satisfied that there is an act of murder. What is there in each act that forces you to assume murder was being attempted?"

Dr Douthwaite, "I have to postulate it in relation to the doses that were not given. She was given no morphia from 1st November to the 5th. By withdrawing the morphia he would reduce the acquired tolerance. I did not make up my mind on the desire to terminate life until I saw the return to morphia on November 6th was followed by a rapid increase."

The Judge, "Are you now saying the morphia was deliberately withheld in order that it might be reintroduced fatally?"

"That is what it appears to me."

There is a rustle in the court, this is a new line of thinking and the Judge wants to confirm it.

"When you consider a doctor's treatment, would the very last thing you think of be murder?"

"Quite true, my Lord."

"You criticise the Doctor's treatment? He embarked upon the wrong line from the beginning?"

"In my opinion, he had."

"But you are not suggesting murder as an explanation of that?"

"No."

"It could be that he didn't understand the right use of the drugs, or he had old-fashioned ideas?"

"Yes, it is possible. I cannot believe that a medical man of his experience and qualifications is not aware of the action of these drugs."

The Judge continued, "You start with a man who is taking the wrong line of treatment, not for sinister reasons, and you postulate that when he reintroduced the morphia on 6th November he must have intended to kill?"

"I am."

"And when she did not die the injections were increased and the dose increased until it did work?"

"Yes."

"And when she is still alive he gives more, so you draw the conclusion that he intended to kill? You regard the combination of morphine and heroin lethal?"

"Oh yes, the combination is more lethal."

"How soon would you have expected it to work?"

Dr Douthwaite, "One would expect death within one or two days."

The Judge, "Now we come to the paraldehyde. In your view death was certain so the Doctor gave the paraldehyde because he was tired of waiting?"

"Yes."

The Judge was concerned about this line of argument, which had not been mentioned before, and therefore Mr Lawrence should have the right to question the witness again. He turned to Mr Lawrence, "You heard me ask a number of questions and get certain answers. I was struck by divergences and if you were to make an application to cross-examine further, I would be inclined to grant it."

Mr Lawrence asked if might he consider the position over the weekend.

The second week had not gone much better for the Crown. They had lost the motive and had not even found the Cheshire hospital notebooks – another great production by Geoffrey Lawrence, and now their star medical witness was going the way of the nurses. At least the Attorney-General could look forward to rescuing his case himself by roasting Dr Adams when he had him in the witness box.

OLD BAILEY THE THIRD WEEK

Day eleven Dr Douthwaite had thought it all up on the spur of the moment

Mr Lawrence had clearly spent the weekend deciding on how he would tackle the Crown's main medical witness rather than watching the Boat Race, won by Cambridge. He decided to confront Dr Douthwaite again. "Am I right in thinking that your theory of murder is that the Doctor withdrew morphia to reduce tolerance and then gave increasing doses to bring about a fatal result?"

"Yes."

"If a GP had a case of spinal cancer the dosage would have been well within the experience of the profession?"

Dr Douthwaite, unbending, "It would suggest a desire to terminate life."

"Would you say that the general practitioner was a murderer?"

"No."

The Judge, interrupting, "You did say you would be forced to the conclusion that he intended to kill?"

"Yes, my Lord. I said the drugs were given to terminate life. I did not use the term murderer."

Mr Lawrence, explaining the term, "Murder, Dr Douthwaite, is killing with the intention of terminating life."

The Judge, "I am anxious that we should not introduce questions that may be partly matters of law. It may be that if a doctor gives drugs knowing that they will shorten life, but gives them because they were necessary to relieve symptoms, he is not committing murder."

Mr Lawrence, "Thank you my Lord". To Dr Douthwaite, "Would it be a summary of your view that every dose was an attempt to terminate life?"

"Every dose was given with intent, but every dose was not expected to kill."

The Judge, "You are inferring that the Doctor refrained from a higher dose in case it might arouse suspicion?"

Dr Douthwaite, "That's exactly what I meant."

Mr Lawrence, "Is this based on the theory of accumulation?"

"It is."

"Is it not well-known that morphia and heroin are non-accumulative drugs?"

"In the normal person, yes."

"There is no reason to postulate there was any accumulation."

Dr Douthwaite, "There is every reason."

Mr Lawrence, "Can you say what accumulation there was in the body?"

"No."

"It's all speculation?"

"The nearer to death, the more accumulation."

"This woman was in the terminal stages of life for a fortnight?"

Dr Douthwaite. "Yes."

The Judge interjected, "Do you mean she was dying before 1st November?"

Dr Douthwaite, "Yes, my Lord."

Mr Lawrence, "Let us come to your theory that the Doctor deliberately withheld morphia so that the patient was rendered more vulnerable. When did you first think of the theory?"

"When I studied the medical reports of the case."

Dr Douthwaite destroyed

"Before or after you came into the witness box?"

"Afterwards - I cannot remember."

"Up to day ten not a single hint of the theory has emerged from your lips? The truth is that this is all an afterthought?"

"No, as I said, I have been puzzled by the withdrawal."

"This part of your evidence never emerged until last Friday when my Lord asked you questions at the end of hours of evidence? In any case", thundered Mr Lawrence, "The medical theory upon which it is based is rubbish, isn't it?"

Dr Douthwaite doesn't answer.

"You know quite well that morphia and heroin are similar, both are opiates, and have cross-tolerance."

"To some degree, yes."

"To some considerable degree?"

"Yes."

"And vice-versa?"

"And vice versa, yes."

Mr Lawrence, "So this was not the case of a doctor withdrawing a drug to reduce tolerance and the patient not getting a similar drug?"

"No."

"We can see that over the days without morphia there are no withdrawal symptoms. Accepting that you would look for some innocent explanation, you cannot say you had to place a sinister interpretation on this alteration, can you?"

Dr Douthwaite, trying to keep his ship afloat, "I can only say I see no other explanation for it."

Mr Lawrence, "The truth is that you first gave evidence of one possibility and then thought of something else."

"I was turning it over in my mind and it crystallized."

"But that is your personal view, you can conceive that a reasonably minded physician of equal eminence might by no means find it necessary to postulate there was an intention to terminate life?"

Dr Douthwaite, "I have always accepted there may be contrary medical opinion." Adding with a grim smile, "I am expecting it."

"And would that medical opinion be entitled to as much weight as yours?"

"I do not question that."

Once again Mr Lawrence had skilfully questioned the witness in a logical fashion, which he had to follow, and which ended with the witness agreeing to more or less the opposite of what he said at the beginning. It was a good point that morphine and heroin were closely related and therefore the 'reducing tolerance theory' was, if not utter rubbish, not tenable.

Mr Lawrence pressed on to establish finally the possibility of other opinions, for conviction is unlikely if there is reasonable doubt, "You therefore admit to the possibility of a skilled genuine contrary view?"

Dr Douthwaite, "Yes."

The Judge followed with another intervention. "I do not understand your last answer to Mr Lawrence which was that you accepted the possibility of a contrary opinion?"

"I meant, my Lord, that doctors frequently disagree."

"If another doctor were to say he disagreed entirely with your views on accumulation would that be a genuine view?"

"I would be astonished if he does."

"You are saying that a single dose, not dangerous in itself, would be lethal because of the accumulation?"

"Yes."

The Judge, “Before you came to that conclusion, you excluded error, ignorance and incompetence?”

“Yes.”

“Could a view contrary to yours be due to error, ignorance and incompetence, but be honestly held?”

“Yes.”

“Then why do you say Dr Adams’ intent was to kill?”

Whatever Dr Douthwaite’s inner reasons for being so certain of Dr Adams’ murderous activities, his reply was, “Because of the Doctor’s qualifications.”

“You mean”, asked an increasing incredulous Judge, “That in the case of a GP it could be, but not Dr Adams, a GP with an anaesthetist’s qualifications.”

“That is my view.”

“So if the Doctor or any other doctor went into the witness box and said they disagree with this view, they could not honestly say that?”

Dr Douthwaite, firmly, “That would be my answer.”

The Judge, “You are going further than saying the treatment was wrong and dangerous, for that is not to say it was given with intent to kill. You say it could not have been due to error, ignorance or incompetence, it must have been to kill.”

“That is so.”

The Judge, “One more point. You have said the woman was dying on 1st November, the jury may have to consider what motive the Doctor had. They might say that if she lived too long she might alter her will depriving him of any benefits he thought he might get, by how much could he have shortened her life?”

“I would have expected her to live for a matter of weeks.”

The Judge, “If the Doctor is saying to himself, ‘She can only live for three weeks’, would he embark on a course which will take thirteen days to kill her?”

“He may well have.” Was the best response Dr Douthwaite could muster.

And so Dr Douthwaite’s evidence, which had started in such fine, ringing tones, petered out after almost ten hours in the witness box. He later described it as the most exhausting test of mind and body he had endured.

The next witness was Dr Michael George Corbett Ashby. Dr Ashby, of 148 Harley Street, was an FRCP. He qualified in 1941 from Oxford and the London Hospital. He was Consultant Physician at the Whittington Hospital, and Neurologist at New End Hospital, Hornsey Central Hospital, Colindale Hospital and Napsbury & Friern Barnet Hospitals. His clinical interests were the treatment of meningitis with cortisone; the perception of pain; and syphilitic meningitis.

The Attorney-General goes through the stock questions to the end of the day. Dr Ashby had not found morphine and heroin prescribed together without severe pain. He thought there was a danger of addiction in the Cheshire treatment. He would have tried to wean her off the drugs, and the doses were large. He did not think that the withdrawal of morphia from 1 November was anything sinister.

Day Twelve Dr Ashby says not possible to rule out natural causes

Dr Ashby is in the witness box all day, questioned by Mr Lawrence, Sir Reginald Manningham-Buller, and the Judge.

He said that he did not consider the patient could have survived the sedation recorded and she undoubtedly could not have survived the doses prescribed. The Judge added that he was not sure what value the prescriptions now had in this case.

Dr Ashby stated that his job was to guide the court as to what would be the result of certain actions and chemicals, he didn't feel in a position to say that on a certain day the Doctor decided to murder Mrs Morrell. He also accepted that the Doctor's instructions to keep her from getting restless, and the drugs given after 8 November could be interpreted as being for the patient's comfort, and that a patient who has had a stroke is likely to die of another.

He agreed that there was no maximum dose for opiates, and that Mrs Morrell never asked for an injection - suggesting that she wasn't addicted.

Mr Lawrence asked him could the death be due to natural causes, such as pneumonia or a stroke, and he agreed it could have been. When the Attorney-General questioned the possibility of natural causes, his reply was that while he did not think she could have survived the doses, the drugs might have killed her by a natural cause, such as terminal pneumonia. When the Judge pressed him to say that therefore the cause of death was the result of the drugs given, he replied, "With great respect, I can only say, it is not possible to rule out natural causes".

So, with the discrediting of the nurses' evidence and the exposure of grievous faults in the medical testimony, was the Attorney-General downhearted? Well no, for he remained confident that once he cross-examined Dr Adams the nursing records would 'boomerang' against the Doctor. Sir Reginald was said to have remarked, 'When I get Bodkin Adams in the witness box, he'll crack and run over like a lightly boiled egg'.

Day Thirteen Dr Adams not allowed to chat himself to the gallows

This was the day Mr Lawrence was expected to make his first speech to the jury. Instead he turned to the Judge and in the course of the morning, made a submission in law that the evidence produced by the Crown was not sufficient to support the indictment. He said that the Crown had to prove its case which was based on medical evidence. Two doctors had agreed that there was no intention to kill before November 1950, and as both said that there was a possibility that the death was not a result of the drugs, it was impossible for any reasonable jury to find that the prosecution had proved the case to their satisfaction.

If his plea had been successful the case would be thrown out, the jury would be discharged and Dr Adams would not have to give evidence. Legal colleagues believe that Geoffrey Lawrence also wanted to use the submission to air some points to the jury and test their responses to his arguments.

There was much discussion in the court as to whether this submission, in the presence of the jury, would go for or against the defence. It could be argued that even to consider there was no case must mean the prosecution case was flimsy, on the other hand if the Judge threw it out, did that mean there was more to the prosecution case than appeared?

The Judge decided that the case should continue because questions arising from the evidence of the two doctors could only be decided by the jury.

In the afternoon Mr Lawrence said that having talked much of the morning he would not open with a speech to the jury at this stage, but call his first witness, Dr Harman. He added, almost as an afterthought, that in the circumstances the defence had decided not to put Dr Adams in the witness box.

It should have been evident to the prosecution that in the light of Dr Adams' incriminating answers to the coroner, and the indiscreet verbosity he displayed to Supt Hannam, no adviser would allow him to give evidence and put a noose around his own neck. Before the trial Hannam had said, "If he ever stands in the witness box he will be easy meat for prosecuting counsel". You have some sympathy for Manningham-Buller; not only had his witnesses let him down, but the opportunity of retrieving the situation by his own efforts had disappeared.

John Bishop Harman of 108 Harley Street qualified in 1932 from Cambridge and St Thomas' Hospital. He held a doctorate in Medicine and his postgraduate diplomas included FRCP and FRCS. He was Consultant Physician at St Thomas', the Royal Marsden, and St Helier (Carshalton) hospitals. A member of the Editorial Committee of the National Formulary he was also on the Council of the MDU. His interests included the treatment of blood diseases and infections and the localisation of deep pain. One of his daughters, Harriet then aged six, became a lawyer and later an MP and Minister.

Dr Harman confirmed for Mr Lawrence that he had experience in the treatment of elderly people with strokes. In his opinion Mrs Morrell had a severe stroke and he was not prepared to condemn the use of morphia, and although the introduction of heroin was unusual he couldn't see anything sinister in it. He also thought that the drugs could be used to control irritability, and that at her age there was little point in trying to withdraw the drugs when the doctor's duty was to promote the comfort of such a patient.

He emphasised that paraldehyde was the safest of hypnotics, that the dosages used were within other practitioners' experience, that Mrs Morrell's final symptoms were not those of a morphia death, that he would have turned to paraldehyde, and that her death was quite likely to be due to her disease rather than the medication.

Day fourteen

As soon as Mr Lawrence finished the Attorney-General opened his day with an assault on Dr Harman. "Have you made a special study on morphia and heroin?"

"No special study."

"And is Dr Douthwaite a recognised authority on heroin and morphia?"

"He is."

"Have you ever prescribed such doses to a dying lady of eighty-one?"

"I have never prescribed them."

"And you would never?"

"I am not prepared to say."

"Did you hear Dr Douthwaite's opinion that each one of the later prescriptions was a lethal dose?"

"I don't agree with that. She certainly could have survived those doses."

The Attorney-General went on to unearth that Dr Harman had treated only a few addicts and had not seen a morphia convulsion, despite describing an attack to the court.

"Would the injections as described in the nurses notes be beneficial to health?"

"It depends on the circumstances."

Symptoms due to her condition not the medication says Dr Harman

After lunch the Attorney-General continued his onslaught on Dr Harman. "Do you say you never give less than 6ml of paraldehyde?"

"Yes."

"To a woman of eighty-one?"

"What I wanted to convey was that less than 6ml was unlikely to do any good."

"Are you saying that the administration of paraldehyde had nothing to do with her death?"

"I do."

"Are you saying that in your opinion the morphia and heroin neither caused or contributed to her death directly or indirectly?"

"Yes, that is what I am saying. Most of her symptoms were of her illness, not of the medication."

Dr JB Harman
Medical witness for the defence
{Associated Newspapers}

The Judge followed to ask a few questions of Dr Harman.

"Do you think that the instructions "to keep under" would accelerate death?"

Dr Harman replied, "No, it signified that the patient had reached the stage in which she would be distressed if she was not under some influence of drugs."

The Judge, "Therefore they were the right and proper instructions to give?"

"I would say it is quite common in such cases." Dr Harman went on to say that while it might have accelerated death, it was more likely not to have done so.

So the medical evidence failed to clear the uncertainties. Just as the Attorney-General's nurses had been discredited, so his leading medical witness, Dr Douthwaite, impaled on his pedantry, suffered the same fate, while Drs Ashby and Harman appeared to cancel each other out. Doubts had increased with one medical authority ready to place new interpretations on the Doctor's actions.

Day fifteen

Mr Lawrence rose to address the jury. "Let us remember that the Doctor is accused of deliberately murdering a patient, an old woman with possibly only a few days or weeks to live. Is it not extraordinary that a doctor should be accused of murdering a dying patient? The burden of proof lies on the prosecution, suspicion is not enough, likelihood is not enough, probability is not enough, certainty beyond reasonable doubt is required."

He reminded the jury that a wealthy, private patient would be far more remunerative to the Doctor alive, than the gifts given by her son after her death.

Mr Lawrence tackles the reason for Dr Adams not going into the witness box. "It is not the duty of the defence to put the Doctor in the box for the edification of the press, unless absolutely necessary. Can you understand the strain under which this professional man has been living for past months?

"These matters happened six years ago. Mr Sogno, the solicitor, remembered nothing about it except what he could recollect from his notes. The nurses had their notes put to them with results which showed how unwise it was to rely on your memory for events of seven years' previously. When the policemen went into the box, not one of them did not have notes in front of them.

"The Doctor has no notes. At the end of all that strain he would have had to cast back his memory over six years and at every stage there would have been the terrible realisation that one failure of recollection, one inaccuracy - however innocent - would have been seized upon and put before you as an indication of guilt. Surely the greatest justification is the witness in these note-books, made when the nurses' memory was as fresh as paint."

Mr Lawrence continued by stressing that the morphine was started in Cheshire, and that the patient had outlived the medical prediction for such a condition.

"The Doctor made life bearable. Even in the summer of 1950 she got about in her car, and sat out in the garden - with help because she could not walk without help. You may think the Doctor was doing his duty and not doing too badly.

Laughable to suggest that the Doctor would kill for £275.25

"It has been said it was wrong to use morphia because she became addicted, but a partly paralysed old lady, given to outbursts, had to have some sedation. In September Dr Harris found the situation was getting worse and increased the morphia. In the last few weeks is the Doctor to say, 'I am not going to help you'. What was in the Doctor's mind when he gave Mrs Morrell those drugs, was it to kill or was it to do the best he could to ease the misery of this dying woman?

"And the motive? It is ludicrous to say that the Doctor would kill for £276. And on the evening before her death, what does this diabolical murderer do? He turns to the safest drug on the market, paraldehyde.

"Members of the jury, what is left? Dr Douthwaite's theory. On any view it was a strange performance. Dr Douthwaite came here prepared to give evidence on the nurses' testimony and came to the conclusion that the Doctor had formed the intent to kill on 8th November. After two days in the witness box he told the Judge that he had a theory on the Doctor's withdrawal of morphine from 1st November. So strange was the situation that my Lord offered me the opportunity of further cross examination, and the theory of accumulation of morphia broke down because Drs Ashby and Harman dissent".

Mr Lawrence finished with, "Trying to ease the last hours of the dying is a doctor's duty and it has been twisted and inverted into an accusation of murder. Do not listen to what you have heard in the train, or read in the paper. For justice to be done make your decision on what you have heard in this court alone.

"The burden of proof lies on the prosecution. You have been called to sit on this jury in judgement, let it not be a memory that will haunt your conscience."

Day sixteen

The Attorney-General took over and essentially repeated his opening remarks. He stressed that while the effect of tearing up a codicil was nil, did the Doctor realise that would be the effect? He also suggested that no significance should be attached to Dr Harris continuing the morphia, "It was natural for Dr Harris to follow the Doctor's instructions. The Doctor comes flying back from Scotland not on account of her illness, but to look after his own interests."

He brought in Dr Douthwaite's theory about omitting the morphia after 1 November. "Why was that done? One would normally associate dose reduction with the patient getting better, not getting worse. This action puzzled Dr Douthwaite and led him to conclude that the intention was to terminate life." Dr Ashby said she could not have survived the sedation during the last few days and Dr Harman agreed that the policy was to give her an injection whenever she woke up. In the Crown's submission there is only one conclusion.

"Both Dr Douthwaite and Dr Ashby expressed the opinion that the jerky spasms were due to the large doses of heroin, yet the defence invites you to believe that she died of natural causes. I suppose you could say a man who is run down by a train might have had a heart attack as the train struck him, but in this case to ignore the evidence of the doses of heroin and morphia, the spasms, the injections of paraldehyde and say that death was due to natural causes would be to ignore the obvious. Members of the jury I submit that the proper verdict is one of murder."

The Judge, a doctor should relieve suffering even if it shortens life

The Judge is the final one to speak. Patrick Devlin, of Stonyhurst and Cambridge where he was President of the Union in 1926, took silk in 1945. In 1948 he became the youngest Judge of the Kings Bench Division.

Looking at the jury he said, "You are the sole judges of fact, but there are four matters of law about which I must tell you. The first is what is meant by murder. Murder is an act or series of acts which are intended to kill and do. It does not matter if death was inevitable, or if life was cut short by weeks it is just as much murder as if by years. No defence of this kind has been put forward in this case. What defence counsel was saying was that the Doctor's treatment was designed to promote comfort, and if it was the proper treatment the fact that it incidentally shortened life does not give any grounds for convicting him of murder."

The Judge continued, "The second point of law is for me to say whether some evidence is not worthwhile. I do direct you as a matter of law that there is no evidence that any drugs were administered except the injections recorded in the nurses' notebooks." In other words the prescription lists were not acceptable.

"The third matter of law concerns the fact that the jury must have heard a good deal about the Doctor. I should like to say this, and I say it with the approval of the Lord Goddard, the Lord Chief Justice, it would have been wiser if the preliminary proceedings before the magistrates had been held in private. Having said that, over the three weeks of sitting in this court you will have learned to distinguish between what is solid fact and what is gossip.

Mr Justice Devlin, a benign summing up {Daily Express}

"The fourth and final matter of law is that the burden of proof is on the prosecution. The accused is as innocent as anyone else in the court, he is entitled to the incredulity of any assertion that a doctor murdered his patient. You may feel that you should consider all the material that might seem relevant, but anything outside the evidence is outside your responsibility.

"An unusual feature is that the accused has not gone into the witness box. You heard Mr Lawrence tell the reasons why on his advice the Doctor did not go into the witness box, and you may have found those reasons convincing or not, but it does not matter. The Doctor has a right not to give evidence and it would be utterly wrong if you were to regard the Doctor's silence as contributing to his guilt."

It was in the midst of a short adjournment at this stage that Mr Herbert Victor James, Dr Adams' solicitor in Eastbourne, collapsed with a stroke in the solicitors' room at the Old Bailey.

The afternoon was spent by the Judge running over the salient dates. The hospital in Cheshire in June 1948, the prescription of morphia, the nurses, the conversations between the Doctor and Mrs Morrell's solicitor concerning the legacies, the Doctor's bequest compared with £300 for one of the nurses and £1000 to the chauffeur. The nursing records showing morphine and heroin given every day into September 1950 when there was a change of dosage coinciding with the doctors' opinion that she was going downhill. Later there were the injections of paraldehyde just before she died.

"You should be reminded that there was no suspicion at all at the time of Mrs Morrell's death. The nurses went on their ways, the Estate was cleared up, and it was not until the summer of 1956 that anything further is heard.

"There were the interviews with the police and the Doctor's comments when he was arrested, which quite rightly have disappeared from the case. You cannot attach importance to words said under great emotional strain."

The Judge went on, "Let me now help you to delete from consideration four matters which do not really help you to reach a decision.

"The first inessential you have heard was some criticism of the police action. Perhaps I may say that I have seen nothing at all in the conduct of the Scotland Yard officers that appears unfair or oppressive.

"Second, what help can you get from the long period of this illness before the 1st November, when it has been said the design for murder begins? You may think it is not a pretty story, a doctor angling for a legacy, but there is a very big difference between something of that sort and a charge of murder.

"You may come to the conclusion that the Doctor was a fraudulent rogue, but all fraudulent rogues are not murderers. If you think the truth is somewhere between the two, that the Doctor administered drugs not for any sinister motive but simply because he found it the easiest way to cope with a difficult patient, it doesn't justify the term murder.

"The third unhelpful matter is the doses of paraldehyde. If the Doctor had not been using morphia and heroin no one in their right senses can suggest that one or two injections of paraldehyde constitute murder.

"Now I come to the last of the inessentials, the discrepancy between the amounts of drugs prescribed and the amounts recorded in the note-books as administered. There is no direct evidence that the Doctor collected or received any of these drugs set down in the prescription books. As to the special injections, you may think some had been proved as vitamins, but whatever they cannot account for the difference between the amounts prescribed and administered.

"Supposing you were to think the Doctor dishonest about drugs, you may say he ought to have noticed when these prescriptions were made out that he was prescribing for quantities far larger than that which the nurses' note-books show had been given. You may think that someone was dealing dishonestly with them, and in fairness you have to bear in mind that two of the nurses told lies about this matter in the witness box. I am not making accusations against anybody, what I am inviting you to do is to disregard the whole matter as mere speculation."

It was late into the afternoon, when the Judge explained, "I now come to what are the essentials of the case. There are three points which have to be proved; that there was an act of murder, that the act caused the death of Mrs Morrell, and that when this act was committed the Doctor intended to kill.

"For the first point, we have a most curious situation in that the act of murder, normally so obvious, a knife or gunshot wound, in this case has to be proved by expert evidence. The prosecution identified acts about which you must be satisfied they amount to murder. The first is the reducing the morphia dose - Dr Douthwaite's theory. You heard Mr Lawrence asking whether you have sufficient confidence in a theory that the doctor did not think of until his examination was virtually completed. If the other doctor for the prosecution is not prepared to support it, and the doctor for the defence says is wholly wrong, you might think it would be dangerous to adopt the theory of Dr Douthwaite, whatever his qualifications and however he impressed you by the way he gave his evidence.

"The other act of murder according to the prosecution was the sudden change in the treatment on 8th November.

"Here again Dr Douthwaite was uncompromising. He was not willing to credit the Doctor with even ignorance or error. Dr Ashby's evidence on this point was borderline, and men of science cannot always give precise, clear, unqualified answers about an illness which occurred years ago and at which they were not present. Unless you go the whole way with Dr Douthwaite you must say that Dr Ashby's evidence was borderline, and in the matter of murder you cannot act upon borderline evidence and therefore you would not be safe in convicting.

"The second point is that the act of murder actually caused death. Mr Lawrence submitted that the act didn't cause death, she died of some intervening cause, whether it was another stroke or just old age. On this you again depend on the medical evidence. Dr Douthwaite was emphatic, he regarded the drugs as the cause of death. Dr Harman said that a lady of over eighty, suffering from a stroke, might die of anything at any time and no one could say without doubt of what she actually died. Dr Ashby came between these extremes in that he regarded the drugs as the most likely cause, but he couldn't rule out other possibilities.

"Members of the jury, it is for you to say whether you are satisfied that this lady did not die by natural causes, and if not the prosecution's case is finished."

Day seventeen

The next morning the Judge continued his address to the jury. "You will recall that we were trying to determine whether an act stood out, an act of murder. While Dr Ashby said that he could see no justification for the high doses given after 8th November, he admitted, in response to Mr Lawrence, that promoting the patient's comfort could be a possible interpretation, and he went on to accept that the Doctor may well have been forced to a point of no return. Dr Harman's view, members of the jury, is the other way round. He accepts Dr Ashby's view as a possibility, but he did not think that the doses would accelerate death.

"It was on this part of the evidence that Mr Lawrence made a submission to me, and the fact that I held it was a matter for you to decide does not mean that it was not a strong submission.

"If you decide in favour of the prosecution that there was a murderous act then you have to deal with the question of intent. First motive, and I take it that the motive was gain. Mr Lawrence suggested that the chest of silver was a paltry reward for murder, but you have to say the Doctor displayed a considerable interest in acquiring something under the will. Even so, here you have a woman who was dying, was he likely to adopt a plan which meant he would have his chest of silver seven days before he would otherwise have it? Mr Lawrence said that such a suggestion was ludicrous. Ludicrous is a strong word, but it is a strong point, and I did not hear the Attorney-General give an answer.

"The Attorney-General laid stress on the statements the Doctor gave to Superintendent Hannam, and you might have liked to hear the Doctor's explanation of phrases such as 'easing the passing of a dying woman', but you must not take isolated phrases into account, it is the trend of statements that is important. Take the chance interview in October, the Doctor answered, 'Don't hurry, please be thorough, it is in my own interest.' If he was a calculating murderer one might have expected him to be very wary in making statements, in fact he gave away a good deal at that interview when he said he knew about the Rolls-Royce and the silver. And when he was questioned at the time of the search for drugs there was that sentence, 'I am not dishonest about drugs'. It seems to show that it never crossed his mind that he might be charged with murder."

The Judge now concluded his summing up.

"Members of the jury, there are three points. The Crown must convince you that Mrs Morrell did not die from natural causes. If it fails, you acquit. The Crown must convince you that there was an act of killing. Again, if it fails to satisfy you of that, you acquit. Only if it succeeds do you go on to the third question, was the act done with the intent to murder? If it does not convince you of that, you acquit.

"Mr Lawrence has submitted that the whole case against the doctor is merely suspicion. No one can say the Crown were not justified in prosecuting on the material they had at the beginning of the trial, but it may well be that the Doctor is a man misjudged by those who suspected him. A man, who if all the facts were known, was guilty of folly, but who never in his mind came near to thoughts of murder. Who can say? Not you, members of the jury, it is not your task. You are not medical assessors charged with awarding points to the doctors, you sit to answer one question. Has the prosecution satisfied you beyond reasonable doubt that the Doctor murdered Mrs Morrell? On that question the Doctor has stood his rights and did not speak. I do not criticise it at all. I hope the day will never come when that right is denied to any Englishman. We afford to every accused, at every stage the right to say, 'Ask me no questions. Prove your case.'

"...the case for the defence seems a manifestly strong one..."

"I dare say this is the first time you have sat in a jury. This is not the first time I have sat in this chair. There have been times when the case for the prosecution was so strong that I have felt it my duty to tell the jury. On this occasion I have no hesitation in saying that here the case for the defence seems to me to be a manifestly strong one, but in the end the question is always the same. Is the case for the Crown strong enough to carry conviction and you have to answer it, and you will now consider what the answer shall be."

The jury was led off in the late morning, at 1116 hours precisely, to decide, 'Murder, can you prove it?'

In the corridors of the Law Courts lawyers and reporters led the discussions. 'The Judge was pretty definite.' 'Not much doubt in his mind.' 'You never can tell what a jury will do.' 'The Judge told the jury the defence had a strong case.'

The Doctor, in the custody of the warders, must have sensed the change. When the trial commenced the man in the street, influenced by the press, thought he'd done it, although the Doctor's numerous friends and patients were certain he was innocent. Many a doctor would say to himself, 'There but for the grace of God go I', and many observers in the court were asking, 'Who can tell?' 'Was it bad luck?' 'Was he so stupidly naïve to think people wouldn't resent his actions?' 'Whatever the truth, whether or not he had killed with intent was an imponderable.'

One person who had followed the trial intently was engaged in his own life and death struggle. Mr James, the solicitor, had been taken to St Thomas' Hospital, paralysed and unable to speak after his stroke at the Old Bailey.

Forty-four minutes later the jury came back. As one court official said, "Well before the time the usual jury take to settle their squabbles about where they are going to sit".

Each member of the jury answered to his or her name in reply to the Clerk.

The foreman was standing up, the Doctor was standing up, everyone else was on the edge of their seats.

Clerk of the Court, "Are you agreed upon your verdict?"

The foreman, "We are." A pause.

"Do you find the prisoner guilty or not guilty?"

Another slight pause.

"Not Guilty."

The Judge said, "Let the prisoner be seated."

There was one more moment of high drama. To the surprise of some present the Judge asked, "Mr Attorney, there is another indictment." This was the additional indictment charging the Doctor with the murder of Mr and Mrs Hullett.

The Attorney-General, "I have given most anxious consideration as to what course the Crown should pursue in relation to this further indictment charging Dr Adams with the murder of Mrs Hullett. The publicity which has attended this trial would make it even more difficult to obtain a fair trial. I have also taken into account the length of this trial, the ordeal which Dr Adams has undergone, and that the evidence is based on that given before the magistrates. The indictment also depends on similar unsupported evidence of the administration of drugs. Having given the matter the best consideration, I have reached the conclusion that the public interest does not require that Dr Adams should undergo the ordeal of a further trial on a charge of murder. Therefore I enter a *nolle prosequi* so that all further proceedings are stayed in this court."

All indictments are laid in the name of the Crown and *nolle prosequi* [do not prosecute] means that the Crown has decided it does not wish to prosecute. As Lord Devlin puts it, the Attorney-General's statement was specious, and if he meant that the Crown would not get a fair trial he had something. It was a method of getting the Attorney-General off the hook, although it did mean that Dr Adams was charged with but never tried for the Hulletts' murder.

One further technicality remained before Dr Adams could be released. The bail fixed by the Eastbourne Magistrates for the offences under the Cremation Act and the Dangerous Drugs Act had expired. Mr Lawrence rose to ask for an extension which Mr Justice Devlin immediately granted. The Judge raised his face and voice to declare, "John Bodkin Adams, you are now discharged."

The Doctor looked at the Judge, mouthed the words "Thank you my Lord", made his small bow and, half-guided by the warder, vanished from sight. Thus in the 17-day murder trial, he had spoken only eight words.

The Judge completed the proceedings by thanking the jury and discharging them from further jury service.

John Porter, Eastbourne solicitor, wrote, "I considered the not guilty verdict a fair and just decision".

Outside the streets were packed with people who waited for hours, but the Doctor had been secreted away. He had lunch, and at 1315h, wearing a dark blue overcoat and trilby hat, he got into a *Daily Express* car in the prison yard.

At an obvious side entrance another *Express* car was parked. A staff member of the paper, of the same build as the Doctor, with a coat over his head and accompanied by Percy Hoskins, the *Express* chief crime reporter, rushed into this car which drove off at high speed, chased by a posse of news sleuths and photographers. Meanwhile the Doctor's car drove to the offices of the *Daily Express* in Fleet Street.

Crowds outside the Old Bailey waiting to catch a glimpse of Dr Bodkin Adams after the trial {Topham Picturepoint}

There he was interviewed by *Express* reporters to ghost his story for the next day's issue. Offers of champagne were greeted with, "My son, I do not drink". A similar negative response greeted offers of another lunch and a tip for the races.

About midnight, Percy Hoskins took him to a secret hideaway at Westgate-on-Sea in Kent. Dr Adams spent some weeks there while the *Express* squeezed every drop out of him. They printed a signed statement from him the next day thanking those who had helped him; 'to Percy Hoskins, for his courageous stand against what must be the biggest witch-hunt in history, to Mr Geoffrey Lawrence, for his devastating cross-examination and masterly speech to the jury, to Mr Edward Clarke (for preparing the defence), and for the backing of the Medical Defence Union'. Over the next week the paper serialised an account of the Doctor's life.

The *Daily Express* paid Dr Adams £10 000. Twenty-six years later, after his death, the money was found in a bank vault, untouched in the original envelope.

So the Crown's case that strongly addictive drugs were used in massive quantities to kill, confirmed by incriminating statements, with gain the motive, was lost.

In the past several judges have expressed the opinion that old evidence is poor evidence and never was this shown to be truer than with the nurses' testimonies.

Mr Lawrence's conjuring trick with the nursing report books was one of the most dramatic moments of any trial at the Old Bailey and rocked the prosecution on its heels. His cross-examination, which gave the impression that handing out morphine and heroin was all in a day's (or night's) work, and that no one had any right to expect the nurses to recall anything worthwhile from seven years ago, was a bravura performance, displaying his agile mind and a mastery of his brief.

The surfacing of the nurses' notebooks was especially unfortunate for Nurse Stronach, who just happened to be in the box as the first nurse witness. For the day on which she had said that Mrs Morrell was semi-comatose and the Doctor had given a big injection, the notebooks showed the patient sat up in bed and partook of partridge for lunch, and there was no visit from the Doctor.

It was reported that the single word 'partridge' had more effect on the jury than all the expert witnesses.

Ten vital moments, including six incredible twists and turns, saved the Doctor.

1. The prescriptions on which the Crown relied were shown to be worthless by the nurses' notebooks. The very reports that Dr. Adams had left littering his basement.

2. The shame of the nurses who lied in the witness box. In the end the nurses' evidence aided the defence.

3. The unlikelihood of any sane doctor murdering a patient who had only a few weeks to live for silver worth £275.

4. The motive went when it was revealed that Dr Adams did not benefit from the will.

5. The discovery that the last 'big injections' were probably paraldehyde, the safest of all sedatives.

6. The production by the defence of the Cheshire hospital nursing notes showed that other doctors started Mrs Morrell on morphine and that she had pain.[4]

7. The destruction of the main prosecution medical witness after he denounced as murderers all doctors who prescribed morphine for a stroke patient.

8. Mr Lawrence's decision to keep Dr Adams out of the witness box, which stopped him chatting himself to the gallows. At this point in the trial even his earlier incriminating statements were taken with a pinch of salt.

9. Dr Harman stating that the patient probably died of her illness rather than the medication, which suggested that alternative professional opinions were valid.

10. The Judge, in an exceedingly benign summing up, agreeing that a doctor should relieve suffering even if the measures taken incidentally shorten life.

10. THE AFTERMATH

On his first day back at Eastbourne Dr Bodkin Adams went into Browne's shop, and declared, "I'm free. It's thanks to God and British justice".

He had spent nearly three weeks in the hideaway flat in Westgate-on-Sea, returning to Eastbourne on 28 April, exactly 130 days after his arrest for murder.

"As a friend and neighbour," declared Mrs IA Snell welcoming him back, "I cannot speak too highly of him."

Mrs Joyce Bobby, of Meads, had lunch with Dr Adams shortly after he was set free. "He scribbled me a note which read, 'May the skin of a gooseberry make an umbrella big enough to cover all your enemies'. He was a charming man."

He was still front page news. Philip Cheal says, "I recall attending a show at the Devonshire Park Theatre, and when Adams appeared in the stalls most of the audience turned to watch him take his seat." Mr Cheal added that the Doctor speedily resumed his interests, supporting a junior international table tennis match at the Pier Pavilion quite soon after the trial.

Peter Palmer writes, "On 2 May, shortly after his return home, I saw Dr Adams at *Kent Lodge.* Sitting among the substantial furniture, it was hard to believe that this was where the drama between him and Hannam had taken place.

"It was interesting to hear his version of events. He told me that he had always been convinced he would be acquitted. He hoped that the period in custody would be taken into consideration and that the charges against him would be dropped." [On 21 May 1957 he was committed to the Assizes and ordered to pay costs.]

"He intimated that these offences were trivial. In respect of the forgery charges, Hannam was scraping the barrel. If he had been able to contact the doctors beforehand, they would have agreed the prescriptions, which were all for amounts of under a pound. As to the cremation certificates, patients had often mentioned that they intended to leave him something, but when their wills were read, his name wasn't included. He said he answered question 4 of cremation form B with the words: *Of this I cannot say.* This sounded to me", declared Mr Palmer, "More like the girl in the music hall who sang:- 'I didn't say yes and I didn't say no'.

"He went on to say many other doctors in Eastbourne received bequests in wills, but these often went unrecorded in the local press." Dr Adams would allege that Mr MacQueen had twice the amount he had received from bequests, and that Dr Kent received more money in one will than he had been left in all the time that he had been in practice at Eastbourne - yet there was no gossip. Needless to say, Ronnie MacQueen and Basil Kent were much smoother personalities than Adams and were thought of kindly by both colleagues and patients.

Mr Palmer goes on, "I said to him that he was fortunate the records of Mrs Morrell's illness had survived. Dr Adams said he had always been an inveterate hoarder and in *Kent Lodge*, there was a lot of similar material, which went right back to when he had started as a doctor at Eastbourne.

"Dr Adams' comment on the drug charges was that there had been recent changes in the law and before the trial few general practitioners kept a record. He believed it was only the publicity about him that gave colleagues time to produce a register or book as required under the Dangerous Drugs Regulations."

The nurses were bitter about the notebooks. While Sister Mason-Ellis said, "The routine was for the nurse to hand them over to the doctor if he wanted them, but he usually didn't", Nurse Randall considered that nurses' reports belonged to the nurses and should have been torn up after they had no use for them.

The Eastbourne Medical Society wanted rid of him as soon as possible. A letter dated 30 April 1957 on headed paper of *The White House,* 97 South Street, to the Secretary of the Society, and calling upon Dr Adams to resign, was signed by EW Hall, RC MacQueen, L Muir-Smith, PW Mathew, and BS Kent.

On 21 May at a meeting in the Princess Alice Hospital Board Room the essentials of the letter were put before the Society as a resolution,

> *In consequence of the unnecessary extra publicity which Dr Adams himself and his housekeeper have given to the recent case before the Courts, by their newspaper articles, the Eastbourne Medical Society do not consider this to be in the best interests of the Profession, and to have been a very un-ethical procedure. We therefore call upon Dr Adams to resign from the Society.*

This was carried by 34 votes to 2. In reply Dr Adams wrote,

> *I should like to clear up what is evidently a misunderstanding. May I assure you I did my utmost to avoid publicity of any kind, and all that occurred was completely beyond my control, nor have I personally benefited from it .*

Nevertheless, he tendered his resignation, the only doctor to be drummed out of the Society. Perhaps this was why he pursued such articles in the courts.

In 1956 Dr Adams had sued Associated Newspapers for libel because of the juxtaposition of two articles in the *Daily Mail.* One referred to the investigation into the rumours of mass murder of wealthy women in Eastbourne, and the other to a report of an inquest verdict that one of Dr Adams' patients had committed suicide. Dr Adams' counsel claimed that the association created the impression that he was involved with both and had been identified as the poisoner. The case was settled by the newspaper tendering apologies and a sum for damages and costs.

He wasn't able to stifle all the undercurrents. Dr Ian Brown recounts that when a medical colleague was fishing for salmon in a Scottish loch, he sought the advice of his ghillie. "I've been trying for hours without success, and I've used all my best flies - any suggestions?" "Try this one, sir. It's a Bodkin Adams - a sure killer".

On 30 June Dr Adams resigned from the NHS. Dr Barkworth was one of the partners who had to ask Dr Adams to leave the practice. A practice nurse notes, "I never heard a bad word about him from the patients in the surgery waiting room".

He also behaved with dignity when asked to resign from the YMCA committee.

Peter Palmer adds, "I saw Dr Adams again on the 23rd July. By then he had heard that the other charges against him were to be pressed and he said that Hannam was determined to have his pound of flesh. He seemed to derive considerable satisfaction on hearing that Hannam had failed to make an arrest when enlisted by the Halifax force for a murder enquiry. Dr Adams got up, unlocked the wall cabinet, and showed me a bottle of drugs, which had been contained inside. He explained that this was what he had done on that fateful night in November. He said to me, 'Every move I made was being watched by three CID officers, would I or anyone else have been so foolish as to try and hide bottles of drugs?' He said he wanted to fight the charges, however, he had been advised that no jury would accept his word against those of three police officers, so he would have to plead guilty. He said he would always be indebted to The Medical Defence Union, as without them, he did not know what might have happened to him."

Mr Palmer concludes, "At both interviews with Dr Adams, I noticed that all the time he looked at you directly in the eye, which some people consider, is the action of an innocent man".

On Friday 26 July, Dr Adams appeared before Mr Justice Pilcher at the Sussex Assizes in Lewes. The Crown had dropped the forgery charges and Dr Adams pleaded guilty to all thirteen remaining charges about drugs and cremation forms. Mr Justice Pilcher said that he took a very serious view of these offences, and he would have imposed a prison sentence, but he would take into account the ordeal and imprisonment he had undergone. He would impose fines which totalled £2 400 in respect of these offences. In conclusion, Mr Justice Pilcher said to Dr Adams :- "You clearly have had a very worrying time". Thus ended the Crown case.

Michael Clark says, "The 1957 proceedings at Lewes, where I gave evidence, had an air of, 'We didn't get him before, but we'll get him on these counts'."

Dr Adams was of the same opinion, "Afterwards they were determined to get me and put up that I did not keep records of drugs. I got all my drugs from Browne's, the Chemists, and they had all the records. They also said that I had signed a cremation certificate – an important document – that I would not have any financial advantage but I wrote *not to my knowledge* . How could I know so soon after the death? They said I had a good idea. My counsel advised that I should plead guilty, and for that reason, although I wanted to fight it, they were able to say that I had committed these offences and I was fined 2 000 guineas".

Dr HJ Walker, of Brighton, who had given evidence in court about refereeing cremation forms, said that no doctor had ever admitted he might receive money on all the forms he had examined. A Medical Officer of Health, who refereed cremation forms for almost 50 years, also said he had never seen a form that stated the doctor would benefit. "In a way it is an improper question. You shouldn't be asking patients if they have left you money, so you shouldn't know."

Following Dr Adams' conviction, the Home Secretary, Mr RA Butler, made an Order on 10 September under Section 29 of the Dangerous Drugs Regulations 1951, preventing Dr Adams either holding or prescribing dangerous drugs.

On 27 November after appearing before the General Medical Council he was struck off the Medical Register.

The 1957-58 Annual Report of the Eastbourne Hospitals Management Committee did not even mention Dr Adams. The previous year, a report of Dr Pollard's death, another part-time anaesthetist, ran to eight lines. Dr Adams' name was removed from the list of medical staff and under *Medical Staff* it was reported,

'During the year there was only one change in the personnel of the hospital. Dr PH Venn was appointed Consultant Anaesthetist and is welcomed to the staff.'

Some say, wasn't he brave to return to Eastbourne? Others that he was just thick-skinned. As far as he was concerned he was innocent (the guilty plea at Lewes was a technicality at the behest of his solicitor), and everything would come all right. "Why, even Lord Devlin said I had almost a clean bill of health."

Always a loner, Dr Adams was a lonely man after the trial. An Eastbourne businessman says, "After his release he called on my parents, who had been patients, every week. Quite non-professionally, I think he needed friends."

Dr Adams did miss his practice and he filled the void by cruises and holidays, including some exotic spots for the 1950s, such as *Reid's Hotel* in Madeira.

In 1957 there were restrictions on the amount of travel money that could be taken out of the country, so his GP gave him certificates for foreign travel on account of his chest, but mainly because his doctors felt the more he was out of the country the better.

Richard Gordon writes, "I went to Torremolinos and the hotel barman said, 'There is another English doctor here, Dr John Bodkin Adams, so you'll have someone to talk to'. Though officially as innocent of killing patients as any other doctor, he was a broken man. This did not seem to worry him. Fat, chatty, jolly, beef-faced, moon spectacled, in a trilby hat, brim turned up all the way round, he busily organised bridge for the over-wintering widows who adored him. 'Nothing like a round of bridge with friends'.

"He had just been struck off, but he was having a wonderful time with the old ladies. He called them all 'my dear', and they thought the world of him."

Dr Barkworth says that while Dr Adams was known to play bridge, he was never a regular devotee and merely used it to provide useful introductions.

When he was struck off his patients were divided up among the other doctors. John Underhill, 92 in 1998, says "Dr Adams was my doctor until he was struck off when Tony Churcher took over". George Catt's mother went to Dr Harris.

Mrs Alice Ridings said, "After the trial Dr Anthony Churcher became the doctor for the *Grand Hotel* guests, while the staff were the responsibility of the *White House* practice". Dr Churcher was also the hotel doctor at the *Queen's Hotel.* The intention had been to have a number of GPs working in rotation, but it was found that the guests liked to see the same doctor the next day after they had been ill in the night.

An Eastbourne GP who helped to look after Dr Adams' patients comments, "Adams' patients did not like investigations, but were a pleasant lot, although they would continue to see him. An awkward predicament did not arise for I did not object to them seeing him. They knew he could not prescribe and I had no power to stop them seeing him since they regarded Dr John as a friend. On reflection, it sounds naïve but he would go to tea with them and stuff himself with cream buns. His chauffeur, Mr White, would go round and wash the patient's Rolls."

John Seath, a local pharmacist who had a subpoena to give evidence to a GMC hearing, adds, "When he was struck off he continued to see patients, but only provided 'over the counter medicines' for them".

Early in 1959 Dr John Linley Adams applied for a post as Consultant Physician at Eastbourne. He wondered aloud to a London colleague as to whether he would be considered in view of his name. The response was, "Of one thing you may be quite certain, you will be short-listed. They will be so curious to see Dr Adams II". He got the job and hyphenated his family name to Linley-Adams.

That year saw our Dr Adams' affection for warmth continue with another trip to Madeira, and in the sunny autumn of 1959 he took a holiday in Dorset.

Dr Bodkin Adams in November 1960 {Topham Picturepoint}

Mr D Deamer writes, "It would be after the trial that I went shooting with Dr Bodkin Adams at Catsfield and got to know him well. On two occasions I went to Northolt with him for the British Clay Pigeon Shooting Championships. He would send Mr White, his chauffeur, round for me in the Rolls-Royce. We stayed the weekend at the *Bull Inn* at Gerrards Cross. One weekend we were sitting over dinner talking and he said to me, 'You do know about my little problem?' I said I had read about it. He went on, 'My counsel, Geoffrey Lawrence, thought I wouldn't make a good witness with my looks.' As at times he did have a brusque manner, I asked, 'Didn't things look bad for you at one time', to which he replied, 'When I was in the cell, I knew the Good Lord would look after me'.

"He had a pair of Purdeys and a Holland & Holland. He sold me an Aya, a Spanish gun, which was quite good. His basement was like an armoury, he had boxes and boxes of cartridges. He would often fire off over 150 at a shoot.

"At one time he was the Treasurer of the shooting club, but he wasn't very good with figures, so as I was at the Midland Bank I helped him to balance the books. In return, he took my wife and me out to dinner.

"There was a BBC TV program about an American doctor and the commentator said something like, 'So he'd done a Bodkin Adams'. Dr Adams sued, and came into the bank with a £2000 cheque, with the words, 'Look what I got out of the BBC'. The Doctor was collecting the odd £500 into 1969."

On one occasion he donated £500 to buy medical equipment. Perhaps it was from the same source, but he said it came as a result of a good share deal. He was only able to sue for defamation occurring after his acquittal.

Mr Deamer concludes, "He loved his shooting and even did well at Olympic skeet shoots where the clays come at all angles".

Conversely, his love affair with the MDU went cold, "It was only when I gave up the MDU, who just had a lawyer asking each year whether I could be reinstated, and hired myself a better barrister that I was finally re-registered in 1961".

Dr Adams added, "I believe that the wife of one of the local doctors was heard to say at a bridge party that they never thought I would be reinstated, and if they'd known it was likely something would have been done."

Three years was a long time for such offences. He was restored as soon as the GMC realised that most of the condemnation stemmed from the press campaign.

John Porter says, "I, for one, felt justice had been done when Dr Adams was restored to the Medical Register. It seemed to me that his striking off, considering the nature of his breach of regulations, was an over reaction".

District Nurse, Mrs Grace Harriott, says, "He was always kindly to the patients, many of whom came back to him after he was restored to the Register."

Mr D Deamer confirms, "The old ladies idolised him and they flocked back after he was restored to the Medical Register. What people liked about him was that he would go out at the drop of a hat at two o'clock in the morning." The Doctor also inspired loyalty, Mr Deamer adds, "I recall his housekeeper was a faithful retainer."

He was not restored as a partner, and his practice was not the measure of his pre-trial one, and the numbers fell, but patients continued to leave him money, without any strings. On occasions he even did a holiday locum.

The local doctors were unsure just how many patients Dr Adams had after reinstatement, but he told one GP he couldn't claim expenses against tax, implying that the fees paid were insufficient for him to pay tax on his private earnings.

However, despite representations made to successive Home Secretaries, the ban that had been made under the Dangerous Drug Regulations was never rescinded, so Dr Adams was not allowed to prescribe or dispense morphine or heroin again.

No one seems to know what he did for patients needing morphia, it is possible that he had an arrangement with a GP to refer such patients. He could prescribe phenobarbitones which had been the basis of many of his treatments.

Another of his problems was that the notice on the gate post at *Kent Lodge,*

Dr JB Adams

At Home 12-12.30

was always being pinched until he gave up putting it back.

Although he resumed his practice, more than one of his friends observed, "I don't think he ever fully recovered from the court case".

In the early 1960s Michael Harding became a neighbour of Dr Adams when he ran a hotel at 22 Trinity Trees, since converted into flats, Windermere Court. "It was near to *Kent Lodge* and guests would often ask in an awed whisper, 'Where does Dr Adams live?' About 1962-3 whenever there was a medical emergency with an elderly guest Dr Adams would always come to see them if asked and was absolutely charming. The guests were invariably happy with him and when, the next day, I explained that they had been seen by *the* Dr Bodkin Adams you can imagine what a buzz of conversation went round the dining tables that night. He never charged, but would say jokingly, 'It's a bottle of Scotch you'll be owing me', not that we ever gave him one."

Mrs Mary Seiffert says, "I met Dr John Bodkin Adams about 1970 when I was asked to give private physiotherapy to the Ashworths, two wealthy elderly patients of his, who lived in a flat at Park Gates in Chiswick Place.

"They were a charming Old World couple and were devoted to 'Dr John' speaking of him with great reverence. He was always offered sherry if he visited while I was there. As I remember he spoke quite softly with an Irish accent. Both my patients were totally convinced of Dr John's innocence."

Another example of his practice were the Whinnetts. He had been an architect. Other GPs saw him when he had pneumonia while Dr Adams was struck off, but none ever saw his wife, Rose. She would go to *Kent Lodge* to see Dr Adams every weekday at 1145h just before his surgery started at noon. Obviously she had become dependent on him, but the couple had no money and some doubt if he was ever paid. They died about 1990 and left their attending doctor £1000, which had probably been intended for Dr Adams.

He continued with his religious observances. He could be seen most days of the week kneeling deep in prayer at St Saviour's & St Peter's Church, or Holy Trinity, or a United Reformed church, or St John's Polegate. It is said he and Miss O'Hara attended St John's because the Revd Peter Johnson was also a doctor.

Mr Anthony Stevens says, "Working as a junior draughtsman in my late teens, I was given a surveying job at St Saviour's Church, South Street, around 1970.

"I was about a week at the church and most days a gentleman spent several hours sitting alone in the front pews of the main chapel. I remember him as a sombre figure, dressed in dark clothing carrying a Homberg style hat. We were mainly alone in the building for lengthy periods, but we never spoke; I was busy with my work and he, whether in deep contemplation or prayer, seemed unapproachable. In fairness we would probably not have had much to talk about as I had the fashionable shoulder-length hair, purple flares and a Che Guevara T-shirt.

"At the end of the week the partner in the architectural practice told me that it was Dr John Bodkin Adams. He also had to tell me of his infamous court case, for I was unaware of the Doctor's history, because of my age and I had been brought up outside Eastbourne."

Michael Clark says, "In his light he was a good Christian. Religion played a big part in his life. He prayed at the bedsides of sick patients, and it was not unknown for them to maintain that the faith he instilled was of great comfort to them. As a

Humanist I can understand how the sick with faith can face up to pain, suffering and mental anguish".

A local doctor: "He still had faith during his custody. 'Cast down but not abandoned' as he would say, and the nurses' notebooks and the nurses' chatterings on the train were given as examples of not being forgotten by God."

After the trial he immersed himself in the sport of shooting. Always important, it became his main interest and he took up administrative posts in various shooting clubs. He was still a good shot, but got very annoyed if he had a poor day.

Mrs Joan Read, Secretary of the Bisley Gun Club, writes that members often spoke of the day when this irascible Irishman had shot badly and threw his gun in a ditch in a fit of temper, only to send his chauffeur back to retrieve it. "I believe he was quite a good shot when younger, and he was President of the Club from 1975 to 1983."

Dr Adams said, "I was one of the Founder members, number 32, of the British Clay Pigeon Shooting Society, on the Council, and only the second Honorary Vice-President. In the 1970s I still shot every week at Westham and three other places in Sussex. Once or twice a year I helped to organise a Bisley Shoot. It was the only really good shoot in the South East. About 65 entered, at £10 a head, the prizes took about £225 and expenses £200, so it meant a profit of £225.

"I gave a cup for a Badminton type of Z shoot (five shot off irregularly, standing about 30 metres behind), but it wasn't in the same class as some of the Continental Z shoots and could be easily won."

Dr Adams continued to travel for his sport. In 1960 he was in Belgium with the English team, but did not distinguish himself. Scandinavia was a favourite spot, and Dr Ian Brown writes, "In 1966 I was on a study tour in Finland which included a visit to the hospital at Jyvåskylä. I found that Bodkin Adams was a fellow guest in the hotel; he was participating at a clay pigeon shooting competition".

John Junor, the newspaper columnist, claimed that on one occasion he sat next to Dr Adams on a plane coming from Ireland.

An Eastbourne GP recalls, "He took me out shooting once and since I couldn't hit anything we went to Holland & Holland where an expert worked out that I needed a cross over stock. Adams found a gun locally and gave it to me."

Michael Harding says, "For me what was incredible about Dr Adams was that this myopic, tubby middle-aged doctor should be such a good shot. One day he invited me to the clay pigeon pits at Bo Peep. When we got there, he suggested a small wager, 'We'll have a few clays and have a little money on it'. 'How much?' I queried, 'Five pounds?' 'Oh no', he replied in his Irish brogue, 'I was thinking of something more like five shillin's'. Even in the 1960s five shillings [25p] wasn't very much, but was I glad. As an ex-Army officer I thought I was fairly adept with a shotgun, but I didn't stand a chance with this rotund Pickwickian character. He smoked me. When I was having a bad run, comparatively, he would exclaim, 'I wouldn't mind having you as an enemy', and sometimes he would look along my line of fire and say, 'You're shooting it up the arse'. Mind you, I was shooting with a Spanish gun and he had a Holland & Holland, a lovely balanced gun, worth thousands of pounds even then.

"Tom Turner, a retired surgeon, lived in 16 Trinity Trees and he would summon us to collect cling peaches (an exotic fruit, with white flesh) from his conservatory. I don't think Bodkin had the slightest interest in hothouse plants but he had been invited so he went and enjoyed the luscious fruit."

Mrs Doris Bertha Sellens saw an advert in a local paper and started as housekeeper to Dr Adams in 1967. "I was able to put my furniture in my room at *Kent Lodge*. He was quiet and never interfered, which was what I wanted, and he knew that nothing would be repeated." Dr Adams was at pains to point out that she lived in a separate part of the house, but he invited her to his Christmas lunch.

Mrs Sellens said she did everything. "I did all the shopping, washing, cleaning and answered the telephone. I had the back lounge, waiting room, consulting room (surgery), dining room and hall to be kept nice, in fact all apart from the bedrooms. At one point he nearly took on extra morning help, but he didn't do anything. He was too afraid of someone coming who would talk."

Dr Adams skeet shooting at Westham {D Deamer}

Dr Adams did not entirely forsake his other habits, obviously well ingrained. About 1977 he wrote by recorded delivery to a solicitor asking whether bills could be settled for the late Miss Langham, as he had not submitted an account since 1926. Miss C Hardwick says that Clare Langham, who had been a teacher at St Paul's School, had terrific faith in Dr Adams and had left him a bequest. Dr Adams missed out on this occasion for the solicitor involved said there was no proof.

He did not miss out on many financial opportunities. It was with a smile on his face that he sought counsel's opinion about whether he could claim his costs of the murder case against income tax, since he had been charged in his professional capacity. The legal advice was that the action was unlikely to succeed, so he lost out on that one too.

No one in the shooting fraternity had a bad word for The Doc. Mrs Barbara Hutchison, whose husband, Don, shot regularly with him says, "He was very kind and generous. A youngster in the club wanted a shooting jacket and told The Doc he was saving for it. 'How much more do you need?' he was asked, and the next week The Doc said, 'No more saving, I've bought the jacket for you'."

Even the members of a shooting syndicate in Scotland, of which Dr Adams was a member, just had a chuckle at him. All agreed he was a good shot, but while they would pool in cases of whisky for refreshment Adams always chipped in just a bottle of sherry. Yet people were sure that he financially supported local Clubs.

Sometimes the Doctor was able to combine his skills. At a shoot at Berwick, when Edward Cottington was firing the clays, the guns were waiting but nothing happened. Bodkin went to investigate and found that Edward had knocked himself out when hit by one of the clays so the Doctor was able to render assistance.

He hadn't changed in other ways. Dr Brown mentions that when he passed the examination for the IAM Dr Adams phoned to congratulate him. "He was a member of the Institute, and once drove me to a road safety discussion at Battle. During the journey he talked incessantly about how 'the authorities' had got it in for him. He genuinely believed he had been victimised."

Mrs Peggy Lawrence says that her parents were his patients and when he heard that relatives had been doctors at Leicester Royal Infirmary, he said he wouldn't charge them, "In any case", he added jokingly, "I prefer cars to cash."

"He was a nice old boy, I got on well with him", comments Henry Kirkland. "He was a staunch supporter of the Eastbourne Ulster Society and generously donated a President's medallion when we held a conference in Eastbourne."

One lasting result of the Bodkin Adams' case was the 1967 Criminal Justice Act, sections of which took into account many of the lessons learnt. Mr Justice Devlin had said, "As regards to the committal proceedings at Eastbourne, and I am not criticising the Eastbourne magistrates, it would have been better if they had used their powers to hold the proceedings in private".

The legislation radically changed English Law so that committal proceedings are no longer reported in the press, unless the accused agrees.

Had the Act been in force ten years earlier there would have been less adverse publicity, although the local magistrates would still have been under great pressure to send him up. It might have induced the defence to produce the nurses' notebooks at an earlier stage when he might not have stood trial at the Old Bailey.

As mentioned, the case also resulted in changes in the Dangerous Drugs Regulations. Before 1953 only recording the purchase of such drugs by the dispensing chemist was required. From 1953 it was necessary for doctors to keep a drug register, and later the so-called Schedule IV poisons required a signed and dated record of patient details, the preparation, and the total dose used.

11. "THEY'LL BE ROUND IN SWARMS"

Dr Adams kept up with his old friends, such as Norah O'Hara, and he was there to meet her when she landed from cruises in the 1960s. It is said that an Admiral's widow was so upset when she learnt that he had been on a sunshine cruise with another lady friend, that she "shut her door in his face for ever".

Mrs Sellens said, "Norah O'Hara lived in the penthouse at Linkswood latterly, but had property in Seaside Road. They could never have lived together, but as old friends they were fond of each other in their way. She was a misery, always telling him that he was dropping peas on the floor".

Dr Adams could not entertain at home so he regularly dined out. Each lady friend was taken to a different restaurant. He would go to *Le Chantecler, Le Roi Neptune,* the *Grand,* the *Beachy Head* and the *Sussex* hotels as well as places outside Eastbourne. Mrs Valerie Wilson recalls seeing him at *Grimaldi's*, a restaurant in East Dean where, as Mrs Grace Taylor puts it, Miss Betty Craddock of *Little Hill* trifled with him. A GP says that he was at the *Sundial,* Herstmonceux.

Ms M Plant writes, "I was a waitress at the *Boship Farm Hotel* from 1973 and on three occasions Dr Adams dined there. He was always accompanied by an elderly woman, and was quite obnoxious in his attitude to the waitresses who served him. It was of interest to me to see him and witness his attitude".

"Among his other friends", says Mrs Sellens, "Was Mr Leeson, a local butcher. He was also a patient and one of his young staff developed red spots. Dr Adams sent him straight away to a Harley Street specialist who got rid of the rash and the lad kept his job. They thought he was a very good doctor.

"Don Hutchison, a farmer at The Dicker, was a shooting pal at Battle and he would send him lovely sausages.

"Mr White was a real marvel. He washed his cars, Miss O'Hara's car, Mrs Stevenson's car, and the Ashworth's Rolls."

On 4 December 1963 Dr Adams had been fined £10 with £20 costs for careless driving in North Westmorland. It was said he 'had a clean licence'.

He wasn't prepared to risk another constabulary confrontation when he was involved in an accident about 1971. A lady says, "In Cornfield Road, when you could turn left or right at the bottom, he was in front and suddenly turned to go left so I touched the rear bumper of his A40. What I really remember, as he jumped out of the car, was a really big, menacing figure saying, 'We will settle this without the police'. I was more worried about my little boy in the back, and agreed, but he took us for everything. I learnt later that he was always getting into car scrapes."

He continued to enjoy driving. In June 1973 he went to Bisley and back twice over a weekend. Was he considering a more permanent move, for in 1974 he was granted planning permission for a six-storey block of flats in place of *Kent Lodge*?

Mr E Lopez says that Mr Chris, restaurateur and doyen of the Greek community in Eastbourne, who ran *Le Chantecler,* a leading Greek restaurant in the town, was a friend and patient of the Doctor, and consequently most of Eastbourne's Greek community had him as their doctor. A local pharmacist adds, "Mr C opened a new restaurant, *Le Roi Neptune* in South Street, and as I was friendly with him he invited my wife and I to a free meal on the opening evening. We arrived there met by Mr C. 'Ah, Harry I've got a nice table for you with friends'. I could not imagine whom, but soon found out - JBA and Miss O'Hara. The Doctor, as charming as ever, rose, bowed to Laurie and shook my hand for the first and last time. The meal was delightful, but the conversation was all Miss O'Hara saying, 'John you're dribbling on your tie', 'John close your mouth when you chew' and so on. Laurie remarked, 'I don't wonder he didn't marry her'.

"One day a chum of mine, a Medical Representative, was bemoaning that having visited all his usual surgeries, his call sheet was blank. I thought of JBA and said, 'Give him a try'. He went and came back delighted. JBA had asked him in, listened, accepted various inhalers, and told him, 'Young man, I have written papers on asthma.' After that virtually all the Reps visited JBA and got shown his guns and cups. They all seemed to enjoy their visits."

Many GPs say they would meet him at lunches hosted by pharmaceutical firms in hotels.

Colin Huggett (who wrote as "Marshman" in *Country Weekly*) knew the Doctor well from clay pigeon shooting. "About the mid 1950s Ray Tolhurst, Peter Field and I started the Fairfield Club at Westham. He turned up every week. We all called him 'The Doc' and he shot at many places locally – Berwick, New Barn with Doug Clay (who owned it), and Catsfield, with Mike Collins. Another club was Diamond Guns at Heathfield." He also went clay pigeon shooting at Willingdon a few times, but found it a bit hilly.

"Don Hutchison was a good pal of The Doc's, and although he never took his shooting too seriously, he was very popular." Another name was Peter Miller from Eastbourne, he went shooting and was friendly with Dr Adams. "The Doc helped many a newcomer." says Colin Huggett, "He would say, 'I'll lend him a gun and stand the cartridges, if you'll stand the clays'.

"The story in one of the books about The Doc which has him pointing a gun at a reporter is a load of rubbish. I never saw him come near to pointing a gun at anyone. He was meticulous in maintaining the regulations and safety requirements of the sport, as is anyone who is accepted by a club.

"He had many good guns, I remember him lending a 20 bore to a young member, who shot 23 out of 25, and The Doc saying he was selling it to someone in Holland with 100 cartridges and he would mention the score. No one had a bad word to say about him in the shooting fraternity. He would give anyone, anything. At a function in the *Red Lion,* at Stone Cross, when the club presented him with a lovely mug in appreciation of his work, there were tears in the old boy's eyes. He couldn't be all that bad.

"We didn't talk about the trial, people thought it was not worth bothering about. He came over as showing kindness, we gave him respect, but he was one of us.

"I'll never forget", recalls Colin Huggett, "The Doc saying 'Always practise your swing. You're shooting well, but you must practise more often. What you should do is take your gun to bed and practise aiming it at the picture rail'. When I mentioned this to my wife she said, 'It's bad enough you going off shooting, which I don't mind, but I'm not having the club and your guns in the bedroom'.

"To sum him up I would say he was a sportsman."

In 1964 the Doctor went with the British Clay Pigeon Shooting team to the Tokyo Olympics. Mr Ray Ward comments, "He was a very good shot, but not quite Olympic material".

Barry St-John Nevill, Doctor of Music, says, "I first saw him in Trinity Trees at the end of 1964 stepping into a chauffeur-driven Rolls.

"In the summer of 1965 I was at a reception at the Congress Theatre with that great star of yesteryear, Clarkson Rose, and his wife Olive Fox. Present was the then star of 'Sunday Night at the London Palladium', Don Arrol, and Bodkin Adams' name came up. Bodkin was highly praised by 'Clarkie' who said, 'He is the best doctor in Eastbourne and he's Olive's doctor'. In a *sotto voce* comment heard by everyone but the couple, Don Arrol commented, 'Poor f------ Olive!'

"From what everyone who knew him, or was a patient, has told me, he was greatly liked and respected as a more than competent doctor. Bodkin was, I understand, a companionable man, who enjoyed playing cards at the *Grand Hotel* and having a chat over a drink."

Being back on the Medical Register the Doctor could call Consultants to advise on his cases, just like other GPs, and following the court case he was more likely to seek the help of other doctors about drugs and where to refer his patients. Dr Keith Liddell, Consultant Dermatologist, said "JBA used to bring his patients in his car to a private consultation, and he always accompanied the Consultant to a Domiciliary Visit".

A Consultant was asked to see a patient for Dr Adams and when he finished the examination the attending nurse asked, "And when will you be coming again, doctor?" The Consultant, who did not think there was much wrong with the patient, replied, "I'll have a talk with the Doctor, but not this week." "Oh, I see", huffed the nurse, "Doctor Adams attends every day."

A retired Consultant ENT Surgeon says, "I recall seeing one of his patients in a flat along the seafront whom Bodkin thought had suffered a nose bleed, hence an ENT surgeon. When I examined the patient I found he was coughing up the blood from his lungs, a serious diagnosis in an elderly smoker. The interesting feature was Dr Adams' approach. He met me at the flat, said I must not tell the patient the diagnosis, and with great charm introduced me to the patient and then withdrew. Afterwards, I told him it was very difficult to see a patient without explaining the diagnosis. As we finished talking, he put his hand in his pocket and when I said, 'My secretary will send a bill', he insisted, 'I prefer to settle now'."

Another retired Consultant remarks that no matter how many letters you sent about any of Bodkin's patients, he would always send a thank you letter back.

He often requested consultant advice for his own illnesses and fears, mainly because his GP would not pander to Dr Adams' multiple requests. "After a consultation he would ask, 'And how much is that I'd be owing you?' and when you said, 'Oh that's all right', he would produce a bottle of wine from somewhere out of the depths of his coat or trousers and hand it over." He saw DM Wallace for blood in his urine and told everyone he was cross that his staghorn calculus [kidney stone] could not be removed leaving the kidney intact.

"I have always been keen on clay pigeon shooting", says Nat Barnardiston, "So when I moved to Eastbourne in 1976 I contacted my friend, Hedley Visick, who I knew had a similar interest. A few days later I received a phone call from a man who, in a Northern Irish accent, introduced himself as 'Dr Adams'. He was most friendly and invited me to join the Club; at the time the name meant nothing to me.

"The following Sunday morning I joined Hedley at Westham where we waited our turn while the first squad set off for the skeet field. Amongst them was the stocky, almost ogive, figure of the Doctor who, with the minimum of movement, succeeded in scoring a 'possible' - 25 out of 25. When he returned to the clubhouse his friends greeted him with, "Well done Bodkin", a form of greeting which might be regarded as an affectionate needle by those who were clearly outclassed by his shooting expertise. The mention of this unusual name began to trigger distant memories. Hedley was quite dismissive when I enquired about the Doctor's past, saying, 'it was all a terrible misunderstanding'. Other members of the Club were equally unwilling to discuss the topic, so I decided not to pursue it.

"Incidentally, I have noticed that a high proportion of successful shots and dart players have the same physique. He often used a 20 bore, which is considerably more difficult than a 12 bore to shoot well in skeet and down-the-line disciplines.

"I haven't forgotten his generosity both in encouraging the less gifted shots, and at the Christmas parties, latterly held at the *Bourne Inn*, where he invariably bought most of the rounds and showered wives and girl friends with gifts, particularly crystallized fruits and large boxes of *Black Magic* chocolates. My wife always seemed to win the raffle, but perhaps being Irish had something to do with that".

Sometime after the trial Dr Adams rejoined the 41 Club (ex-Round Tablers). A member says that at the Doctor's first attendance the chairman asked him, as the oldest member, to sit with him. "I found it difficult to hold a conversation, for his hobbies had been shooting, filming and cars, in which I had little interest".

John Porter, a local solicitor says, "Long after the trial I was in contact with Dr Adams in relation to the Estate of another client of mine who appointed me as her executor and gave her entire Estate to Dr Adams. This arrangement was perfectly justified as the lady had outlived all the people she wished to benefit, other than Dr Adams. He had been her doctor for a vast number of years and had shown great kindness to her, frequently sending his housekeeper to her with food from his table.

"After the death of this lady, it was necessary for Dr Adams to come to see me in connection with her Estate. I wondered what passed through his mind as he came into my office at 11 Hyde Gardens, as I have no doubt he would have remembered not only Hubert Sogno's part in his trial, but the fact that it was a client of ours he was alleged to have murdered.

"My firm belief is that he would not have turned a hair, since he had an absolute belief in himself and his motives, and could never believe that anyone in their right mind could see him as a murderer, or anything other than a medical man of the highest probity".

A local dental surgeon says that he sat next to him at a 41 Club meeting about 1982 and found him, "a benign, kindly person, although, of course, he was in the last year of his life".

With time the Doctor also experienced the usual restrictions and handicaps, including forgetfulness, of old age.

A local pharmacist says, "From the mid-1970s onwards he visited the shop almost daily with a 'Morning' to me and a bow to the lady in the dispensary. He would lean on my tall stool and begin, 'For Mrs er…' I would run through a list of his patients and eventually he would say, 'Ah yes. Give her some antibiotics. Er you know...' A favourite expression, and I would go through a list of antibiotics until eventually he would say, 'Ah yes, that's the one'. He would write a script, ask for delivery, bow again to dispensary lady, say 'Morning' to me, and leave.

"I could name at least five other Eastbourne doctors who had considerably more left to them in wills than Bodkin and I'm sure it was because they were good, friendly and attentive - *a la* JBA."

'The Doc' (with cap) and members of the Battle Gun Club, 1976.

One area where the Doctor did not admit to much change was in his careful handling of his finances. Mrs Sellens was paid £6 a week in 1967 and only £8 a week in 1983. She was given £11 a week for food. "He was a little tight in money matters. One day Mr White said that he couldn't live on his income and Dr Adams told him, 'Well, you're getting your old age pension'.

"What annoyed both of us", explains Mrs Sellens, "Was his way of dealing with the itinerant Irishmen who wouldn't work and spent their time drinking and begging outside Holy Trinity church. They also knocked at the Esperance Nursing Home and on doors around Trinity Trees, but if they came to the house, he would give them a pound because he wanted to be known as generous to the Irish. If he was out I sent them away with a flea in their ear.

"He would also give five pounds to the workmen at Caffyns so that they would give him priority the next time he took his car in for service. This also annoyed Mr White and myself. Mr White lived to be 90 and never said anything at any time."

Dr Valerie Gurney, however, confirms that into the 1970s Bodkin would pay for handicapped children from Chailey Heritage to have a day out at Drusilla's Zoo Park at Alfriston. And Margaret Kinman says that he used to lend his silver Rolls-Royce (the Hullett one) for Eastbourne's Carnival Queen procession.

A Hailsham resident said that, up to about 1971, Adams still attended meetings of the IAM at Battle, driving up in his Rolls-Royce. Mrs Sellens says, "He sold the Rolls in 1972 and bought a Maxi, to go with his Mini." Alan Caffyn observes, "The only man I know who had a chauffeur for a Mini".

Gordon Clark reported, "One day, his chauffeur said to me, 'I got it in the neck from the governor this morning, when I was three minutes late. He demanded to know why and I said I had cycled in and been held up by the traffic in Upperton Road. He said he didn't want it to happen again, and gave me a blank cheque adding, go out and buy a motor cycle and come here on time every morning'."

Dr Adams continued to run two or three cars, and doctors say, "If yours was being serviced he was always prepared to loan one out". When he passed the Maxi on to a friend, he transferred the JK1600 plate to a black Triumph Dolomite.

A GP says, "Even in old age, Bodkin acted promptly when a patient of his had the common bile duct cut by a junior surgeon at a routine gall bladder operation. [A classic mistake in this operation, rare, but potentially serious; allegedly it happened to Anthony Eden, Lord Avon.] Bodkin stormed into the ward and left the doctor in no doubt that he must send the man straight to Mr JL Dawson at King's College Hospital in London. The patient was referred and is alive and well today."

Mrs Sellens adds, "Mr Charles Aldous, an ex-nurse and member of the Plymouth Brethen, who lived in The Avenue, used to come to *Kent Lodge* and he invited the Doctor to the mayoral dinner when he was Mayor in 1981".

So Dr Adams kept up his professional work and interests, but especially shooting. In Jubilee Year, 1977, he presented a special trophy for the winner of a shoot at Westham. When Michael Hutchison, only 17, tied for first place and then lost the shoot - off 'The Doc' bought and presented him with a replica Jubilee Cup.

A member of Rotary declared, "I was grouse shooting with JBA in Scotland one year and I have to say he was a magnificent shot. He would just laugh when 'The Eastbourne Doctor' was mentioned".

John Hughes was chairman (1981-84) of Fairfield [later Westham] Clay Pigeon Shooting Club. He says, "The Fairfield committee meetings, which The Doc attended, were held at the *Smugglers Inn*, Pevensey. Still always known as The Doc at the club, he helped to organise shoots at other places such as Westfield, near Hastings. He wore a cap badge which read *Bisley 1951*, and I have a shooting bag that contains cleaning implements, which belonged to him.

"Dr Adams always attended the Club's Christmas Party, at the *Red Lion*. He often presented the cups at the party, and there was an annual 'Bodkin Adams Cup'. He supported the club and brought his girl friends to the parties."

Mr Deamer, "Towards the end he was tottery on his feet and used a stick for walking over the fields, but with a gun to his shoulder he was as good as anyone."

Mrs FM Hobden says that her son often shot with Dr Adams at the Battle Gun Club. "He was all for Dr Adams. The Doctor was a fine shot until the last year or two, when he used to ask jokingly, 'Am I pointing in the right direction?' His sight was also failing a little which was perhaps why he fell at the shooting meeting."

Tony Watkins, an Eastbourne dentist, said that Bodkin Adams was his patient, "although he hadn't many teeth. When he first rang for an appointment my secretary came to say, 'Oh, there is a gentleman on the phone with a wonderful Irish accent'. After any treatment he would shake hands and I would find a piece of paper in my palm about the size of a postage stamp, when unfolded it was a shilling wrapped in a £1 note - his way of giving me a guinea. Just before he died it went up to a £5 note so Bodkin recognised inflation sometimes."

The committee and winners after Dr Adams (centre) had presented the prizes at the Eastbourne Annual Table Tennis Tournament in May 1983 {D Wilkinson}

Mrs Sellens, his housekeeper, says, "There was a bracket clock in the hall, which he wound up every Saturday. In early 1983 he was standing on a chair to do this when he fell and knocked his head against the chair legs. His doctor, Dr Anthony Churcher, came and put five stitches in; he got over it".

Barbara Selby notes that he continued to support the table tennis events. "The very last time, in May 1983, he was in his eighties, very unsteady on his feet, had to be helped to his seat, and looked extremely frail."

Even so, on Wednesday, 29 June, he insisted on going upstairs at the house of a friend to see the new decorations.

Mrs Sellens reports, "Towards the end he was unsteady. On the evening of Thursday, 30 June 1983, he was at the *Battle Abbey Hotel* for a shooting meeting and slipped on some concrete steps on to his side, fracturing his left hip." Don Hutchison was about a yard behind him coming out of the meeting and always said that if only he'd been closer he could have saved him.

Mrs Sellens continues, "In the ambulance he asked where he was being taken, and when told Hastings he demanded, 'You turn round and take me to Eastbourne'. Mr Richards, Consultant Orthopaedic Surgeon, put a pin in on the Saturday and on the Sunday Miss O'Hara and I visited and he was bright. On the Monday he developed a bad chest, deteriorated and died about teatime of left ventricular failure. One of his sayings was, 'If I break my femur that'll be the end' and it was".

Derek Keay, who now worked in the Central Sterile Supply Department at the hospital, says, "The last time I saw him was when he was being wheeled into the operating theatre after he had broken his hip."

Dr Alistair Macleod tells how he had met Dr Adams at the Postgraduate Medical Centre, when he asked him to come for lunch at *The Court House,* then a restaurant in Moat Croft Road. In the course of the meal Dr Adams leant across and asked Dr Macleod, a Chapel Elder, if he would take his funeral service.

"I didn't know what to say, but agreed to help. When Ann my wife read of Bodkin's death in the paper, I rang his solicitor, who said he knew nothing of the arrangement and the ceremony had been arranged for Holy Trinity. I rang the Vicar of Holy Trinity and found a worried man concerned about the press coverage of the funeral, but we finally agreed that I would read a prayer."

The *Eastbourne Herald* reported, 'Around 180 friends and former patients gathered at Holy Trinity Church on Wednesday, 20 July 1983, to pay tribute to Dr John Bodkin Adams, the popular Eastbourne GP who was cleared of murder in a sensational Old Bailey trial in 1957.'

The Revd Kenneth Blyth described Dr Adams as a "quiet, sincere man who did much charitable work for individuals and organisations". Mr Blyth spoke of Dr Adams' trial, "We are all brought to a time of trial and sorrow. Most of us know what it is like to pass through the dark valley. He was accused of a major crime, tried by his peers and acquitted. Many Eastbournians would like to stand in his defence." He also spoke of Dr Adams' devout faith and belief in Christ.

Prayers were led by Dr Alistair Macleod, and in the course of a eulogy, Charles Aldous said of Dr Adams, "He became the victim of a vicious whispering campaign of rumour, engendered by those who had no knowledge of the man and his kindness".

Bodkin Adams had always said with a chortle, "They'll be round in swarms after my death", and the funeral did generate enormous publicity from Fleet Street, with reporters from national and foreign newspapers attending the service. Among the journalists present was Mr Geoff Nash, husband of well-known columnist Jean Rook, who was covering the occasion for the Press Association.

The ITN cameras were present at the church as mourners arrived for the service, and on ITV News at Ten there was an extensive report on the funeral.

After the service, the hearse, bearing 40 floral tributes from friends and former patients, moved on to Langney Crematorium for a private cremation service. Dr Adams' ashes were taken to his parents' grave in Coleraine, Northern Ireland.[1]

Mrs Sellens. "Mr White and me were very loyal to him and even though we were inundated with telephone calls after his death from local, national and international papers we didn't say anything and he knew we wouldn't."

An inauspicious *Daily Mail* review of 1 April 1995 stated that an unexpected claimant had stepped forward to hold up the will, but the *Daily Telegraph* of 9 September 1983 was able to announce that the Doctor left £402 970. He gave sums of between £500 and £5000 to relatives and 47 surviving friends, including 20 women who had stood by him at the time of the trial. 'In sincere appreciation of the loyal support given to me in my time of trouble'. The residue of the Estate was divided between the beneficiaries in proportion to their legacies, which could double the amounts they received.

His housekeeper for 16 years, Mrs Doris Sellens received £5000 and the choice of his furniture, Mr James W White, his chauffeur for 30 years, received £3000 and the Doctor's Triumph Dolomite car. There was also a bequest for his ex-fiancée Miss Norah K O'Hara, he left her the first choice of his possessions 'in gratitude and memories of our long-standing friendship'.

A friend of both said, "Bodkin and Norah were fond of each other and she was truly upset when he died. Whether, with their Irish temperaments, their marriage would have lasted I don't know."

Other bequests included £2000 to the Bisley Gun Club, and £1000 to Percy Hoskins, 'in recognition of the support he gave me at the time of my trial'. Mr Hoskins gave the legacy to a medical charity. There were also bequests of £2000 to his own doctor, and £1000 to his grocer. Dr Adams also left small bequests to various churches.

Dr Barkworth, the only partner to visit him in jail said, "I didn't receive anything in his will and didn't expect anything, we hadn't that sort of relationship".

The next year the *Eastbourne Herald* reported, 'Hundreds filled the auction galleries of Edgar Horn, in South Street on 28 February as items belonging to the late Dr Adams went under Anthony Harris' hammer, assisted by Lynn Weatherall. An old brass bound trunk went for £74, five leather suitcases bearing the initials JBA went for £210, and an oak bureau bookcase went for £215. Personal items including a top hat, spats, gloves and a travelling case went for £130.

'The next day 29 February the auction rooms were again packed and gun-cleaning equipment went for £50.' Many items he had been gifted were found stored away after his death, never used or displayed.

A local GP says, "I was amazed at the collection of trinkets on view for probate, there was a squirrel instinct. I took his rounded glasses, overcoat and instruments, with permission, rather than let them fall into other hands".

John Cheesborough says, "He had a couple of made-to-measure Purdeys, which were among the effects I had to deal with as joint executor of his Estate".

Anne Russell also went to the sale. "He had some nice bone china and I bought a couple of Wedgwood pieces". Members of the Eastbourne Round Table also bought several items at the auction.

John Porter says, "I was fortunate enough to secure the mirror which stood in his surgery, and which I cherish. I have often wondered what stories that looking glass might be able to tell".

The press soon forgot their grovelling apologies of 1961. In July 1983 the *Mail on Sunday* had published extracts from a book *Where there's a Will* by Rodney Hallworth & Mark Williams, under the headline *Did This Man Get Away With Mass Murder?* The solicitors acting for his executors claimed the paper would not have dared to publish this in the doctor's lifetime. The Press Council considered that the extracts constituted a serious attack on the reputation of Dr Bodkin Adams, but that there was an over-riding public interest which justified the publication.

Dr Ian Brown says, "At the time of Dr Adams' death, John Cheesborough, who must have been close to retirement, came into the limelight at the auctioning of the Doctor's home and contents." John Cheesborough finally retired in 1989 after 53 years with the firm of solicitors, Coles and James - now Wynne Baxter Godfree.

"After the death of Dr Adams", writes local solicitor John Porter, "I was interested in purchasing *Kent Lodge,* however, when I viewed the property I found it in a ruinous state and it was apparent that nothing had been done for many years. The only addition was a hideous shack-like structure at the rear in which he had installed a kitchen, in place of that originally in the basement. Beyond that there were no signs that any work or decorations had been carried out in the last 50 years. It was apparent that Dr Adams had more interest in shooting than his home."

According to the *Eastbourne Herald* of 22 September 1984, 'The auctioneer's hammer at the *Hydro Hotel* came down for the sale, at £95 000, of *Kent Lodge*, the Trinity Trees mansion of Dr Adams. Neil Cleverton of Stiles, Horton Ledger made the final bid for his client against three other main bidders at the auction conducted by Brian Kingston before an audience of 70.' Later it was disclosed that Mr Brian Valentine, a Consultant obstetrician, had bought it. He applied for planning permission to use the ground floor as consulting rooms and the other floors as accommodation for medical students. The basement was used as a dental surgery for a while, and later there was an application to convert *Kent Lodge* into flats.

Bodkin keeps in the news. In 1986 a BBC TV Sunday Premiere *The Good Doctor Bodkin Adams* written by Richard Gordon, had Timothy West as a look-alike Dr Adams. The Brighton *Evening Argus* of 6 November 1989 mentioned that Dr Adams' memorabilia had been on show at the Towner Art Gallery, Eastbourne, and Graham and Jan Upton of *How We Lived Then* in Cornfield Terrace, Eastbourne, have a permanent display of various Bodkin momentoes.

And every so often there appears in the national press the headline:-

"IS THIS ANOTHER BODKIN ADAMS?"

12. THE PERSON

In 1991 the Eastbourne District General Hospital requested names for its new private practice unit. Dr Tim Gietzen, a GP in Seaside, proposed that the ward be called *The John Bodkin Adams Wing* . "Not only is he Eastbourne's most famous doctor, but the name will encapsulate the spirit in which the NHS is now being managed". It was called *Michelham*.

The family home did not have much in the way of refinements; it was purposely simple. This meant that he developed little sense of style, fashion, colour, or the value of fine objects, but it made him admire and treasure possessions. It did mean, however, that his 'collections' would be described as those of the acquisitive rather than the discerning man.

For his mother, John Bodkin Adams, her only surviving son, was the repository of all her hopes for her husband and her other son.

Parents were honoured. Mrs Sellens, his housekeeper, said, "Dr Adams regularly sent money over to Ireland for the upkeep of his mother's grave."

The small town had been an ordered one, and everyone admired education and honest work well done. Sunday was devoted to God.

The person who talked with verve and humour was not considered the worth of the man who quietly got down to it. Those who bettered themselves by hard work were respected. The reliable tradesman, bank manager, the shopkeeper, doctor and the teacher were the means to betterment. Hard work was a way of life and equalled high esteem.

It was this inbuilt honour for the professions that came through when he said, "You can't arrest a doctor?" To him respect was total.

Until the 1920s many a doctor practised all his life what he had been taught when a student, without any comment. A visit and sympathetic word were worth more than most drugs. The doctor didn't always tell a patient if there was anything wrong, for he couldn't do much about it. Apart from, for example, insulin or sulpha drugs, to continue so into the 1940s wasn't dangerous, even if the doctor might be thought a stick-in-the-mud. Now if you practise too much of what was reasonable ten years previously you are in some danger of being accused of malpraxis.

More than most of us, Dr Adams was a man of his time – although even Sir Isaac Newton spent more time on alchemy than on gravity.

Dr Adams found the medical course a strain, and there was no question of becoming a Specialist. For one thing, in the 1920s you required private means because the training was unpaid, and he had no influence behind the scenes. Public Health did have a career structure so he worked hard, as he always had done, for his examination - and then up came this Eastbourne job.

It was a Christian practice and here he scored well, he was a worker, was teetotal, and over a short contact he could exert considerable charm, sufficient to convince the Eastbourne partners that he was their man.

They had indeed appointed a hard working, God-fearing assistant, but whether this gauche character who lacked many of the social graces was ideal to be let loose in prim Eastbourne was a different matter.

He thought himself fortunate [thanks be to God] to have landed on his feet. He was determined to provide a good service, and to achieve security to enable him to provide a decent establishment for himself and family.

He kept to simple routines. Mrs Sellens: "He had to have his cup of tea before 0700h - sometimes I only just made it – when he turned on the wireless, and all the watches and clocks in the house had to be put right by the pips. Went to bed about midnight. He prayed every night and morning." That he thought dancing doubtful and pubs immoral, and the countryside a work of God, didn't help his integration.

Did he gravitate towards the panel patients, the tiresome elderly and the dying or was he eased along those unpopular lines? Or was there some quirk of character that increased his isolation from his colleagues, never shown more gruesomely than in his weekend of striving to do his best for Mrs Hullett?

He noticed that one area did not change – the ways of the lonely elderly and their hopes and desires. He was not convivial, he did not make close friends easily, but he enjoyed listening to these patients, many with an interesting tale after a full life. He found that he could help many of their symptoms by reassurance and simple measures, and that what they liked best was a speedy visit. And a dose of what only he could provide – his time.

They were gentle people and treated him, a village boy, as an equal. He liked to think they were friends as much as patients. Thanks to them he would have some power, finance, and respect. He had the solace of his religion and would live it every day, and treat all his patients the same, and the rich would pay for his poorer patients. He satisfied himself which patients could afford it.

Both Dr Harris and Dr Barkworth stressed that Dr Adams kept his practice very much to himself and apart from covering his holidays, they hardly saw his patients. They agree that from what they saw he treated all his patients with equal assiduity. Lord Devlin also admitted, "Dr Adams was assiduous."

His family had not been wealthy, but they paid their bills promptly and expected their due. By working long hours over the years, he built up a flourishing practice. His most consistent quality was perseverance, always sneered at by the intelligentsia, and what he had created by his own efforts he wanted to keep. Such ways meant he was not fully accepted by his colleagues. He was an outsider, a prickly defender of what he considered his rights.

He tried with his charity work, in which every doctor had to be involved. Apart from the good image, you met potential patients, but apparent generosity of spirit was more important than hidden donations.

He was as much a magpie as a miser. Mr Deamer: "I worked at the Midland Bank where he was one of our leading customers, and he often donated anonymously to good causes, but he would only draw enough money for the week, say £20, and it had to be in new one pound notes. He would take each note in turn and fold it into a square and place the £1 notes in different pockets. He hated it when the one pound coins came in a few months before his death."

"Dr Adams poured money into activities for the youth of the town." according to YMCA members, "When it all happened any amount of people said he never charged them a penny and he only made money out of those who could afford it."

John Hughes: "We frequently went to *Kent Lodge* to collect clay pigeon traps which Dr Adams had donated to the shooting club. James White, his chauffeur, would show us to the basement to collect them, and we noticed that he turned off the lights as soon as we had finished; 'The Doc' was careful with money."

An amazingly fortunate aspect was his shooting ability, always a pleasure for him, and it provided companionship and also an entrée to different social strata. It was not much help towards better relations with his medical colleagues because few of them were involved, and when they did meet him they found a garrulous Irishman talking about guns and the county set or people they did not know, instead of interesting cases.

Dr John Bodkin Adams before the trial {Topham .Picturepoint}

He was childishly greedy. He craved for what he had not had as a child or a young man. It might be a special camera, a hand-made gun or a new car, and he could use the 'good eye' of his wealthy patients for a canteen of cutlery or a tie-pin, anything would be acceptable. He did not know what to do with these trophies of his success except to keep them for a rainy day. Just as he kept a pile of tyres for his cars in case they ran out of stock, although this might have been a harking back to wartime rationing and austerity.

The war saw all his rich private patients leave Eastbourne and he was in some financial straits, not helped by the attitude of his colleagues. Perhaps he made a resolution that he would not be poor again when his practice recovered. With his pugnacious tenacity and self-belief the addition of a cause made a powerful combination.

He was not a scientific doctor. He kept few records, apart from appointments for private patients. Otherwise he had his regular sessions; Thursday afternoons at the hospital, school or hotel doctor duties, daily surgeries and visits.

Dorothy Head, an Eastbourne laboratory technician in the 1950s, mentions that, "Dr Adams would stand in the doorway of the lab., waft a specimen about in his hand, and declare, 'I want a complete examination done'. Most doctors would say precisely what test they wanted, or a least a group of tests." Bob Elliston says, "I only saw Dr Adams on a few occasions, but he gave me the impression that he was a doctor of the old school who did not really understand the role of investigations."

In one way he was perhaps ahead of his time. He saw no danger in prescribing narcotic drugs for the elderly and, unlike many doctors in the 1950s, he felt that the danger of addiction was not a serious consideration at an advanced age.

An Eastbourne businessman, who knew him well, thought, "Once his mother had died and his engagement fell through, he may have become interested in acquiring things. I don't think, however, he was any different to most doctors with wealthy patients who want to leave valuable possessions to their doctor".

Dr Adams believed that he was entitled to a share of this world's riches; a Christian life and healing ways deserved recognition. The elderly did not always pay adequately, some forgot, others had a time warp as regards inflation, and after their death the families did not want to know.

He found legacies easier, they represented the deceased person's last wishes, to be respected, and were a personal matter between him and patient. Fruition took time, but over the years many patients left small bequests; by 1956 when he averaged £3000 a year, he could say to the police, "I accepted them in lieu of bills".

Did he believe he was providing a humane service as God's instrument? It could be that these friends and patients were prepared for death by prayer, and his other job was to see that they were untroubled by undue physical suffering.

Lord Devlin suggested that Dr Adams may have operated in that grey area between innocence and guilt, that he was a mercenary mercy-killer, perhaps a compassionate one, but at the same time avaricious.

Dr Adams would not see it like that. He found that a private practice of elderly, wealthy patients suited his style. They were demanding and could be slow to pay, but palliative care was not a popular option so there wasn't much competition.

Old people can be irritable, suspicious, difficult (like us all), and he made himself available at all times to soothe, discuss, sedate, or simply to hold hands. He stroked a hand as a nurse would mop a fevered brow - to comfort. A colleague explained away his manner with, "He didn't have a family to think of."

He also didn't have the satisfaction of alcoholic, drug, or sexual sociabilty. He had his family ethos, his hard work and his religion, all a great comfort.

Deeply religious, president of the local YMCA, a Sunday School teacher, the rotund doctor was at 57 the epitome of respectability, even if he didn't quite fit in.

He must have had something going for him, he was at ease with acquaintances from the Deputy Lord Lieutenant of the County to the bin men at Trinity Trees, who found him "a kindly and pleasant man". He could make an impression; Alan Kenyon says he only met him once, but hasn't forgotten the occasion.

Conversely, Jill Emslie comments, "Bodkin had big hands, and was a most unattractive person. I couldn't see what some women saw in him, but they did." Pearl Ayres: "I found him a huge man and intimidating. He made me shudder and I would not like to be treated by him, but he obviously had a way with him and I could see how people fell under his spell."

A partner, Dr Vincent Harris: "Dr Adams had a very kind and caring side to his nature – especially to his poorer patients."

Many patients were devoted to him. Mrs Betty Palmer said, "We knew people, when we lived in Hampden Park, who declared, 'My old Mum and Dad thought he was wonderful, and they never had a penny to their name. He would bicycle to them in the middle of the night and they were not likely to leave him anything'."

Eugenio Lopez: "I am Spanish, but he always cured my coughs and colds and never charged".

Mrs Maureen Devlin: "Much has been made of Dr Bodkin Adams' rich patients, we should not forget the work he did in the poorer communities."

Dr Adams did not forget old friends. He sent £10 every Christmas towards the election fund of local MP Ian Gow, and Mrs Sellens said, "He kept in touch with the prison warders from Brixton Prison up to his death. They had been impressed by his quiet approach, and in turn sent him Christmas cards". In April every year he sent a thank you note to Percy Hoskins.

His colleagues and other professional men were not so inclined towards him and Mrs Morrell's solicitor, Hubert Sogno, was one of those unimpressed.

Bodkin had always been a loner, perhaps the reason why he was so loquacious and talked about his financial gains, and after the trial he was a lonely man.

Christmas cards sent by 'Dr John' over the years – all country shooting scenes

A pharmacist: "Unfortunately for Bodkin he was not a likeable man. He could turn on the charm to people, but really he was withdrawn and taciturn. When I first knew him I was amazed at how he bullied the older staff in the pharmacy".

Mr Ray Ward: "Not an easy man to be with; he wouldn't stand any 'aggro'."

Dr Ian Brown: "I would say that he was not a sensible man; he was less intelligent than most doctors, obstinate and self righteous. He was also an indiscreet and incessant talker."

Sister Gladys Miller described the Bodkin Adams technique. No will form was produced, but she allegedly heard him say to Mr Downs, "Now look here Jimmy you promised me on the day Lily died that you would look after me and I see you haven't mentioned me in your will. Your nieces will get the lot and you don't want that, they haven't done anything for you, and I never charged you a fee."

There was no guile or subtlety about him, but an acquired deviousness perhaps. He had been scarred by the way he had been treated by colleagues during the war and just before the trial, and only his work, coupled with intense resolve and faith, kept him going.

John Porter, Eastbourne solicitor: "His absolute belief that everything would turn out right was a factor which made it extremely difficult for Geoffrey Lawrence to persuade Dr Adams not to go into the witness box. Lawrence quite rightly feared that the Doctor's disdain might well prove his undoing. It was the same over pleading guilty at the Lewes Assizes". Bodkin Adams would say, 'The Judge will understand', in his eyes he had the best support of all – that of the Almighty.

Dr Adams was similarly unconcerned about the gossip. 'Gossip the laughter of fools, the crackling of thorns under the pot' as he described it. He did not take the slightest notice, and he believed everyone thought the same way. He just could not comprehend that rumours might undermine a professional man.

Those who had raised themselves were not above the law, but they set the tone and their position did not warrant interference by blatherers. Petty restrictions were there for rogues, not for honest, hard working, God-fearing folk trying to do their best under difficult conditions. And if you didn't watch them rogues would use the regulations to their own advantage. Keeping the law was essential and lawyers were fellow professionals, but the mechanism was a necessary evil designed to deal with those who went astray.

In Lord Devlin's words, "He thought lightly of the law". Dr Barkworth perceptively explains, "In character he had a lot in common with Toad of Toad Hall … he was incapable of believing that anything he thought reasonable might possibly be outside the law". Similarly, he was also a fantasist and disaster prone.

In summary, he believed he was doing a kindness in easing the deaths of those who were dying, and he encouraged remuneration in gifts or bequests which maintained the patient's capital, and saved him from having to deal with uncertain, unedifying bills, and tax. His actions must have imparted a sense of power too.

He was no visionary, he hadn't a warm personality, he was not creative, there was an absence of artistic ability, and like many doctors, he was no mathematician. He could be a competent diagnostician and a careful anaesthetist. He was suited for a life of routine work, a most valuable contribution. Over 60 years he gave time to his patients, was always ready to go out at two in the morning, and had enough acumen to know when he should call in an expert for a consultation. Perhaps arrogance developed, in that he thought he knew what was for the best. Even so, not a bad epitaph, but it does not explain the world-wide notoriety. No, that was occasioned by the publicity, and the enigma of what happened when the nurses' backs were turned, and could you prove it?

He was foolish – he still acted as an executor into 1954, but in his words, "All I ever did was to make my patients as comfortable as possible towards the end."

13. TRIAL BY THE PRESS?

A local pharmacist: "In the course of the case I had my first meeting with members of the national press. Quelle horreur!"

Before the 1960s the press was under wraps: the abdication reporting is one example. Measures were effective because deference was a word more in use than it is today, and the press was not embroiled in circulation wars of such ferocity.

Yet the Bodkin Adams' case of 1956/57 was notorious for the publicity. As the Doctor's counsel stated at an appeal to the GMC, "Press speculation about what would happen to Dr Adams was a disgrace to the majority of national newspapers", and as mentioned, overseas copy was equally dramatic.

It is of interest to note that the *Daily Sketch* headline ***WAS THE £1000 CHEQUE WIDOW MURDERED?*** was a reasonable statement when published, although it must have emanated from a leak. Headlines in the *Daily Mirror* of ***WERE FOUR WIDOWS MURDERED?*** and the *Daily Mail's* ***ENQUIRY INTO 400 WILLS*** had no real basis, but the newspapers which have survived are the *Mail* and *Mirror*, while the *Sketch* has gone to the wall because its readership fell.

Many wills named Dr Adams as a beneficiary, and there were gifts from other patients, but proof that he killed these generous people is lacking. Yet it is '400 murders' that has stuck in people's minds.

The publicity went on and on. The conservative *Daily Telegraph* had a report about Eastbourne wills on 19 September 1956, and was still speculating ***An arrest is expected soon concerning wills forgery*** on 12 November.

Dr Ian Brown records, "Years after the trial I was introduced at a meeting in Germany as a doctor from Dr Bodkin Adams' town". Dr Brown adds that at a BMA Annual Meeting in Newcastle he was trying to find a seat at a crowded table when one representative, reading his label, said, "Eastbourne - we'll make room for you here, any friend of Bodkin Adams is a friend of ours".

An Eastbourne 41 Club member. "About 1982, 25 years after the trial, I was on holiday at a remote Black Forest hotel. I put my car away guided by a German porter who could not speak much English, but haltingly asked where I came from; when I mentioned Eastbourne the porter exclaimed, 'Ah! Bodkin Adams'."

The newspaper reports certainly influenced the average individual's perception of the case. Mr Wooller of Polegate states that at the time he was with a group of workmen who each day discussed the trial and read the accounts in the newspapers. "They didn't know him, but were convinced he was guilty, and when the Doctor got off some of my mates just couldn't believe it." Ann Whitehead describes how, "During the trial you couldn't wait to open the *Daily Mirror* and all the comments were read avidly. We thought he was for the high jump."

Why all the fuss over a decidedly ordinary, provincial practitioner who found himself the victim of snide, small town innuendoes in poor taste?

One reason given is that it was a classic Blue-beard case of Beauty and the Beast, guaranteed to rouse passions. The interest is heightened by the picture of a respectable family doctor, rotund and rosy-faced, up to no good in Eastbourne, that most select of Watering Places. Many folk had visited the town, if only for the day, and found it a bit snooty, and everyone knew it had an elderly population seeing out their days in wonderful surroundings. For some, their knowledge had come from a comedian's patter of, 'They don't have rows of deckchairs along the front, you know, they have commodes', but they had heard of its repute. Now these cosy assumptions were blown away. 'And how many more bodies are there?'

There are those who say it was Bodkin Adams' international fame as a sharpshooter which gave the world wide flavour. Others say that the publicity was really an attack on certain groups such as the Masons, the Irish, or homosexuals.

Another opinion is that it was a chance juxtaposition of Gossip, plus a 50-year-old's perhaps Unexpected Demise, combined with the Silly Season of the year with little else about for the news hounds when the story broke in August 1956.

The gossip had been building up for years and the scenario had most of the spicy elements required: money, sex, religion, race and murder – the only one missing was Royalty. Along comes Mrs Hullett's death. This was different; her relative youth and her powerful friends contrasted with Dr Adams' unpractised handling of a delicate situation. There was that element of 'Could it happen to me?'

Paul Harris suggests that the reason for the exceptional publicity, both local and international, was that, before package holidays, a chosen few seaside towns had a certain cachet and Eastbourne, in particular, had an international reputation for upper class respectability. Eastbourne was top of the league.

"It had an aura which is difficult to understand these days, when seaside towns have acquired a mediocrity where none stands much higher than the others. It had, since its original planning by the Dukes of Devonshire and subsequent Royal visits, been run by well-known figures who brought dignity to the place."

John Cheesborough agrees, "Eastbourne was a much more important town in 1956 than the small seaside Borough it has become since 1974. It was a County Borough with its own police force, and also responsible for its own education."

In 1950's Eastbourne there was still much snobbishness. It was not the done thing for a 'lady' to be seen with a shopping basket in the afternoon, and many 'ladies' would not venture east of the Queen's Hotel, along Seaside. Jill Emslie explains, "Eastbourne was prim in the 1950s, you went visiting, and the essential point was not who you were but where you lived. No one on the circuit lived in the east of the town, we were just about in at South Cliff. You only met the same people at dinners, all professionals, solicitors and doctors".

The press quickly recognised that Bodkin Adams was the fashionable doctor in this 'upmarket' town, with a lucrative private practice of the respectable and rich. He was well known in local social and Masonic circles, and was a top international clay pigeon shot. Even his name had a good ring to it.

The notion that both eminent town and doctor might be associated with the killing of hundreds of wealthy widows produced perfect newspaper copy.

Paul Harris: "The emotive subject of euthanasia was going through one of its phases as a topic of debate and the case seemed a natural to suggest this as a factor. When it became apparent that there might have been quite a number of his patients who'd had their lives terminated early, the concept of *Serial Killings for Gain* took off and the papers began to have a field day."

Mr D Deamer says, "I have no explanation for the headlines, but Eastbourne was a more cohesive place in those days, conducive to gossip."

John Cheesborough is one who thinks that a reason for the world-wide impact was that Bodkin Adams was an internationally-known clay pigeon shot.

Conversely, Richard James, another solicitor and a partner, thinks it unlikely that his skill in the shooting field was a reason for the publicity. "International yes, but such a small set". He proposes that the conjunction of select Eastbourne with lurid scandal, and inept early handling of the case, albeit with good intentions, might have contributed.

Correspondents have commented that Dr Adams was not popular with his medical colleagues and they were the source of the gossip; "they ganged up on him". A doctor exclaimed, "You could tell the type of person in his clientele - nervous persons, with nothing seriously wrong, who liked a good chat and good bedside manner in a Christian way. They didn't really need a doctor."

A partner at the *White House* practice in the 1950s, says, "Dr Philip Mathew and Mr Wilson Hall, of the *White House*, loathed Bodkin Adams". It was Dr Mathew who publicised the EC10 forgeries.

Michael Clark adds, "Apart from Anthony Churcher I don't know a GP in Eastbourne who had a good word for him".

He was an odd-ball in many ways. He didn't come from the same school or university as the other doctors, and many scoffed at his home-spun religion. "He didn't have any presence", "He was sure of himself, but he didn't invite confidence". He made few attempts to counteract these opinions, and he was not convivial with his colleagues. He would not credit it, but nothing feeds conjecture more than silence and absence, "You can't be too rude about someone on whom you'd spilt beer the week before".

A few actively disliked him – perhaps he had pinched a patient, or had treated a patient in what they considered an unethical manner. Dr Norman Carlson, of Pevensey, thought that he was a disgrace to the profession, but doctors are not adept at co-operating in any campaign of hate (or affection). There were also those who coveted his wealth when they thought him such a poor doctor. Could such steaming sentiments keep the pot of rumour running over?

And why him? Yes, he did have an enviable private practice of elderly wealthy patients. Since, however, a quarter of Eastbourne's population was over 65 years of age there was no shortage, and such old people do tend to die.

A GP: "He wasn't popular with his colleagues. I put it down to jealousy. GPs thought that he was getting more than he warranted."

A local pharmacist: "Some professional people seemed pleased to see him fall; a few were quite vitriolic and came in the shop daily, avid for the latest news".

An Eastbourne doctor: "Every week at medical meetings around 1950 you would see a doctor nudge another and say, 'I see Bodkin's at it again', referring to news of more bequests, and colleagues and nurses repeated the adage that he kept will forms in a pocket. In my opinion some half-a-dozen other Eastbourne doctors received similar amounts in bequests, and two received twice as much, but no one talked about it. Definitely not in Ronnie MacQueen's case for while he was another bachelor with a large private practice, he was a gentle and respected surgeon, and as he might be called upon to treat the GP's family he was sacrosanct".

It was also put about that Dr Adams had more newspaper reports of bequests than others, even if they were for small amounts, and you were looking for them.

The widow of a press photographer who was involved with the case said that every week there were reports in the Eastbourne newspapers of bequests and most of the doctors benefited. "I didn't notice Dr Adams particularly, but Dr Jack, my doctor, seemed to have a regular mention, usually only small amounts".

A crucial point was that other doctors kept quiet about their rewards. Dr Adams made no secret of his bequests and seemed to think that patients' generosity was deserved recognition for his work, a merit award which warranted a broadcast.

Lord Devlin wrote, "Dr Adams was a legacy hunter, but he was not secretive about it, and it may have been his talk which originated the rumours".

Nat Barnardiston adds, "There are allusions in Hoskins' book to a vendetta between the Northcliffe Press (*Daily Mail*) and The Doc. This observation must be taken with a grain of salt as the author was associated with the *Daily Express*. However, to draw attention to the Crippin/Himmler appearance of his metal-framed glasses and to question his motives in organising boys' clubs seem too personal not to rule out some bias involving an individual in the Northcliffe Press. The Northcliffe Press had contacts with foreign press offices so papers in other countries could easily be involved."

Ron Parsons admitted that he had no idea why there was so much publicity. "I can well believe that other doctors received as much in legacies so the amounts were not the reason. A factor could be that Bodkin wasn't an attractive personality, he didn't look impressive and he had fat ugly hands."

His trait of seeing the patient alone lent itself to conjecture in the press. "You never accompanied Dr Adams to a patient", said a Nursing Home nurse, "He would say 'I'll find my own way'." Dr Adams didn't have a sense of occasion, and in specific cases, such as Mrs Morrell, it is quite definite that the patient told the nurses to stay out of her room. 'Autocratic', the nurses called her, in turn she described them as 'common' and for her the doctor was the only person with whom you could speak on anything like equal terms. Dr Adams, of course, might have encouraged this understanding to cover any nefarious ways. As usual, with the Doctor, you can interpret his actions as you will.

Another purported cause of the publicity, the influence of certain groups, has no real evidence to support it. They were the usual butts of social chit-chat.

There was about as much anti-Irish feeling in the town as there is anti-British feeling in Skibbereen, but there is always some bigot who will point the finger in that direction, and the same goes for the Freemasons, and homosexuals.

A businessman said that the gossip was about a high Eastbourne policeman, a Mason with Dr Adams, who had lost documents which were vital to the case.

Ralph Hall, who was Eastbourne Cemetery Superintendent, was another who believed that it was a Freemason conspiracy and that a senior Eastbourne policeman lost the evidence. Reading through the inquest and trial, there seems to be no evidence that being 'on the square' had any influence on the result.

Mr Deamer, "I think Dr Adams' actions were misinterpreted. He wasn't an evil man, but you can understand how, in his soft Irish brogue, the words. 'I'll just give you something to help', could be given sinister implications."

Nat Barnardiston says that the theories included resentment in certain quarters at the large numbers of Irish doctors coming to practise in the UK.

It is alleged that 'old Mrs Hemsley' of Hemsley Garages, Beach Road, always complained of, "That terrible Irish doctor".

The homosexual gossip concerned a group that had allegedly spread throughout Sussex. It is possible that some of his acquaintances were homosexuals, but there is no evidence that Bodkin Adams was involved. It could well be that he had little idea of their activities, but they had motoring, or photographic, or shooting interests in common.

A local pharmacist: "There were rumours about Bodkin and his associates playing trains, but I have great doubts about Bodkin's involvement. He might have been in the company of some, but I don't think he was a practising homosexual".

Peter Smith, who was a Consultant Surgeon at the Eastbourne hospitals, said, "These days anyone unmarried is considered homosexual, and if there is no evidence of such behaviour, then the tendency is supposedly occult. Bodkin Adams just had a low sex drive." And did his 'lady friends' realise this?

Michael Clark says, "The story was that JBA was protected by a member of the Police Force", and Dr Michael Emslie thinks, "A policeman was involved".

A Willlingdon resident said that her family lived on the Folkington estate and there was talk about Roland Gwynne putting his car into a ditch during the magistrates' hearing and the police keeping it quiet. "It was said he was distraught because he was afraid about what information might come out."

It so happens that the car crash of Lt Col Gwynne was reported on the front page of the local paper. He had been to a dinner at the *White Hart Hotel* in Lewes with Lord Chief Justice Goddard, Sir Hartley Shawcross QC and other notables; he was teetotal so he was not drunk, and he was an abysmal driver at the best of times.

Paul Harris confirms, "Roland Gwynne was in my opinion one of the worst drivers around Eastbourne. If I ever saw a car being driven on the wrong side of the road, or weaving about, as likely as not it would be R Gwynne."

Yet another gossip theory has it that Mrs Morrell's chauffeur started the stories. A correspondent who worked in one of Eastbourne's pharmacies says, "My personal view is that gossip was rife in the town, and was it begun by Mrs Morrell's chauffeur? He was peeved at not receiving her Rolls and having to suffer the indignity of being told to drive it round to Dr Adams."

On reflection, the Doctor had his eye on the car since before the war, and the Morrell family believed that it had been promised to Dr Adams for years.

It does not seem reasonable to postulate that one person could initiate and orchestrate the gossip of a town of 58 000, although he might have augmented the buzz about a doctor who killed for legacies. John Underhill, in the town at the time confirms, "There was a tremendous amount of gossip about him in the 1950s". The

Doctor himself said that it was the prattling of the bridge-playing ladies of Meads which started off the rumours.

Supt Hannam encouraged both the gossips and the press to greater heights, partly by his very presence, but also by planting stories of Dr Adams as a mass murderer. It was Hannam's flamboyant ways that aroused the indignation of Percy Hoskins, who considered Hannam to be an unreliable and ambitious man.

Michael Foot said, "The papers would not have run those stories unless there was encouragement by someone in the police".

Lord Devlin proposes that Hannam cultivated the press for his own glorification. True, he was flashy, and looking to go out on a high, but it is to be assumed that the Superintendent's plan was that by hounding the Doctor under the glare of publicity he would crack and either confess or cut and run. Hannam could hardly have miscalculated more comprehensively. Until his arrest Dr Adams was naïve enough to believe that Hannam was in Eastbourne to prove that the rumours were baseless; he was far more convinced of his own innocence than ever the Superintendent could be of his guilt. Dr Adams considered the whole rigmarole was a test set by God, and he was not likely to fail that examination. He was quite convinced that somehow he would be delivered even if the verdict was guilty.

With all the factors for gossip, and so many reasons to keep it going, it is safe to assume that once the Bodkin bandwagon rolled it would pick up momentum.

A barrister says, "The Bodkin Adams case was followed with great interest in the profession, not just because it was a case of *Doctor Murdering Patients for Money*, but because of the personalities involved. The giants of the law were there; Geoffrey Lawrence, the greatest advocate of his time, Patrick Devlin probably the cleverest and ablest judge of the century, and there was also the Attorney-General there by tradition. You don't often get all those together".

Whatever the causes, the gossip was there to be acquired by the resident journalists and fastened on avidly by the national press.

Percy Hoskins, the *Daily Express* reporter said, "People ask me why I made my stand against the publicity. For many reasons: I thought Bodkin was being trussed up by scurrilous reports ready for a monstrous miscarriage of justice. Second, I didn't think he would murder for a few hundred pounds. Thirdly, I didn't trust Hannam, and another factor was that when I talked to his solicitor, Herbert James, he pointed out that it all came down to 'They say' – in other words gossip".

With the exception of the *Daily Express*, the press published highly defamatory material, for which a vindicated Dr Adams later sued them. He also took action against foreign publications sold in the UK, although some escaped. Perhaps the most barefaced example was the American magazine *Newsweek* which came out in the middle of the trial containing photographs of the defendant (400 victims) and the Judge, with text linking Haigh (nine victims) and Christie (seven victims) to the case and mentioning the Hulletts. This led the Judge to enjoin the jury to "avoid such publications and to read only the well-known daily press".

Genuine concern, wagging tongues and jealousy, push-started the slide towards the Old Bailey by forcing the Chief Constable to call in Scotland Yard. Injudicious remarks at the inquest, and the reaction of the national press, greased the slope to produce the furore that rendered the magistrates unable to reject the charges.

All in vain would Geoffrey Lawrence argue at the committal proceedings that, since publication could prejudice any eventual trial, the evidence should be heard in camera, at least that relating to other patients . Mr Justice Devlin was to remark that it would have been wiser if the preliminary hearing had been held in private.

Lord Devlin said, "I don't read newspaper reports. Normally they exaggerate - *Family Doctor Poisons Patients.* It goes against all a reporter's instincts to scotch a good story". Public interest is all and the public buy the papers.

Daily Mail

MORNING SPECIAL

NO. 10,769 TWOPENCE FOR QUEEN AND COMMONWEALTH WEDNESDAY, AUGUST 22, 1956

YARD PROBE MASS POISONING

25 deaths in the great mystery of Eastbourne

Comment

WEDNESDAY, AUG. 22, 1956.

THE LOST LEADERS

AT the end of the 278 page Report of the General Council of the Trades Union Congress

INQUIRY INTO 400 WILLS

RICH WOMEN BELIEVED TO BE VICTIMS

By RODNEY HALLWORTH

SCOTLAND YARD Murder Squad is to investigate the suspected mass poisoning

THE MAIL DOES IT AGAIN

The Log of The Lost One

EXCLUSIVE

LATE on Monday afternoon three men aboard the raft L'Egare (The Lost One) saw an aeroplane approaching from the direction of the Cornish coast.

Daily Mail reporter Keith McDowall chartered a motor boat and boarded the raft for the last few miles as she was towed by lifeboat into Falmouth.

Natio[n] rally to Britai[n]

By WALTER FA

Daily Mail Foreign

FOUR Eastern which had be garded as waverer denly rallied at London Conferenc night to Britain's p international cont the Suez Canal.

This, coupled with sion by Spain to "acc form of international

It was certainly to the benefit of a newspaper to print the stories. Nationally the story led to a circulation war, and the circulation of the local papers rocketed whenever a Bodkin Adams' item appeared. The reason why the *Daily Express* proprietor was worried when the paper didn't join in the fray was that he was afraid the *Express* was being scooped. "Lord Beaverbrook rang to ask why we weren't carrying the story", says Sir Edward Pickering, the editor, "I explained the reasons, and he said, 'Well, you'd better be right'."

For the Magistrates' Court reports the local papers started with most of the front page and three inside pages. This increased for the Old Bailey trial to a display on the front page and a detailed report on five inside pages. *The Times* started with part of an inside column and soon extended to four full columns.

Richard Addis, a former editor of the *Daily Express*, believes that newspaper competition in Britain can reach absurdity at times. "Sometimes a story is pumped up, with ferocious energy, simply because it had appeared in a rival paper. When other papers have ignored an exclusive it has faded away."

Has the case made much difference? The politicians remain afeared of the press, the Press Complaints Commission is not censorious, and despite the media's occasional hand wringing after misjudging the public mood, trials are still being prejudiced. During a multiple murders trial of a few years ago no fewer than six newspapers published background information on the case, and other trials have had to be aborted because of pre-trial publicity.

As early as April 1957, Ronald Bell MP sought leave to introduce a Private Member's bill to control the reporting of preliminary hearings, and one result of Dr Adams' trial, the Criminal Justice Act of 1967 which restricted reporting at the committal stage, has proved its worth. Why should any innocent man (which we all are until proved guilty) have unproven charges publicised?

The dilemma is that the public have a right to know what goes on in our courts, but once the press runs a campaign against an alleged villain, it colours the picture and it needs courage to resist.

There is seldom need for mention in the press of any trial before the verdict, and only anonymous reference if the accused is acquitted, unless the defence agrees. Hence, English Law should continue to be modified.

Over the ensuing years the Bodkin Adams' libel actions have hardly influenced journalism, nor has there been frequent emulation of Percy Hoskins' actions. Good reporters can maintain justice, bad reporters always go with the hue and cry, although you have to admit that it was only Hoskins' repute that saved him. Those involved are all intelligent, basically reasonable people, but they have mortgages and schooling to pay, and so long as the public is prepared to pay for digging the dirt so the reporters have to comply.

Michael Foot asked, "Why did people believe the stories? Some still think he was guilty, but he was tried by headlines which can have a powerful effect. If stories of cruel murders are repeated day after day it imprints itself powerfully on the mind. You can imagine what it was like over a period of months".

Lynch rule is another description. Lord Devlin wrote, "The public is swept by waves of emotion which it doesn't reason about. No one wanted to hear about the possible innocence of Dr Adams, long before he was tried".

Perhaps the earliest example was Elizabeth, Empress of Austria, whose public image tragically ended her life. In 1914 the propaganda of the day manufactured tales about the 'terrible Boche' hurting Belgium children, of which no evidence was found when investigated. Not much has changed. This effect was seen to its greatest extent after the death of Diana, Princess of Wales, in 1997. The inevitable and worthy distress for the death of a youngish personality engenders the press to promote a Camelot image of perfection and innocence cut short, whether it be a 'Lady Di' or a 'Bobbie Hullett'.

No one wanted to know about the tortured mind of Diana, or consider what troubles were in store. The public would round on anyone who observed, 'Sad, but perhaps all for the best', or they would select an object on which to vent their pent-up scorn. So in 1956, when any comment on Bobbie Hullett along the lines of, 'Her mind was distraught, she had contemplated suicide on many occasions, isn't it more than likely that she succeeded in her purpose', would be countered by the image of an evil, cunning, ingratiating presence, cutting her off in her prime, and 'what more objective evidence do you want than speeding up the £1000 cheque?'

At a Parliamentary debate in May 1957 Mr Chuter Ede, a former Home Secretary, made reference to the press, "which was becoming Americanised and must be carefully watched".

It could be that where it mattered, in the court, the press campaign rebounded somewhat. Auberon Waugh wrote, "Liberal England decided that Dr Adams was a compassionate man anxious only to relieve suffering, and that all rumours to the contrary had been got up by the press".

Yet there were many areas of public interest which, if the press had brought them into the light, would have been of general benefit.

Parts of the Police investigation were not made public. An example of one-sided publicity. With fanfares Hannam applied for two exhumations, implying that examination would provide the final evidence he needed. In both cases the conclusion of the pathologists was natural causes. This finding was not trumpeted, it was hardly whispered in the press. The doctor was not given any favours.

The conduct of the Attorney - General was glossed over. Not done homework, not prepared witnesses adequately, must do better. He didn't, however, depend on his law practice for either his bread and butter or his advancement.

The right of a defendant to remain silent. Latterly there have been suggestions that more questioning should take place in the dock rather than at the police station, but in 1957 the right of an accused to remain silent was paramount.

The possible prejudice to a fair trial of earlier publicity. Undoubtedly, the press should not have reported details of the Hullett deaths, or termed Dr Adams a mass-murderer, when he was only charged with the murder of Mrs Morrell.

Whether the Crown should have pursued other charges of murder against Dr Adams. To put aside the Hullett case by *nolle prosequi* was an unusual line to take and only possible if the Attorney-General was leading, after all he is the Law. The Attorney-General said it was in the interest of a fair trial, but the chances of him obtaining a conviction on the evidence of prescriptions and with Dr Douthwaite as his main witness were slim. Politically he survived the Morrell acquittal, survival would be less likely if Dr Adams got off the Hullett murder charge.

The propriety of doctors advising patients on the making of wills and benefiting from wills. It could be said that they are as entitled as anyone else to benefit and patients should be allowed to disperse their belongings as they wish, but there is a sense that doctors might have too much influence over the decision. Doctors would be wise not to be executors and beneficiaries. Where do you stop? Do you say that solicitors should not be allowed to buy items in the Estate of a client?

To sum up, the affair had most of the ingredients for scandalous gossip. Such disreputable happenings were simply not supposed to occur in ultra respectable places like Eastbourne, and there was little else of dramatic interest happening in the country. Once the story warmed up, the circulation war ensured it bubbled.

It was perhaps the first international post-war scandal. The world was coming out of the war, economically and conceptually. Starving and slaying were less often on the news menu, with sport and scandal taking their place. With extra leisure for readers more magazines were being published which needed copy, and tittle-tattle was in fashion. The public were coming to realise that the newspaper was there to entertain as much as inform, and the world press was ready to be of service if the circulation and number of advertisers went up.

With hindsight there is a sense of disbelief that Dr Adams could be placed in danger of the scaffold on the basis of such a flimsy case, amplified by the press.

But as Richard Gordon puts it. "Gossip! So delightfully irresponsible, so imaginative, which once burnt women as witches. How uplifting to see it routed."

14. "MURDER? CAN YOU PROVE IT?"

It's the mortuary chapel
If they touch an Adam's apple
After parting with a Bentley as a fee.
So to liquidate your old kin
By the needle or the bodkin,
Bring them down to sunny Eastbourne-by-the-sea.

Gordon Clark, a mechanic who worked on Dr Adams' Rolls: "Did he murder those old ladies? Well he was a funny chap, personally I think he did kill them, not in a deliberate way, but he helped them."

Philip Cheal, who worked at Brewer's where the Doctor shopped, summarizes his impressions. "Greedy, self-opinionated and often difficult, but murderer I doubt."

A pharmacist at Eastbourne's Boots the Chemist: "He was as guilty as hell."

Apart from such divergences of opinion, those with views as to Dr Adams' guilt or innocence are imprecise about what they mean by murder. What is certain is that if you ask people who knew him whether he was a murderer or not, you will finish up more confused than after a re-read of the average political manifesto. Some are convinced that he caused the deaths of over 400 widows, others that he was not only innocent of such deeds, but was a kindly, caring doctor.

People have asked, did the number of deaths of old ladies in Eastbourne go down when he was struck off, and when he was allowed back did they increase? It is not as simple as that. For example, the natural variations in deaths, depending on the weather and influenza epidemics, could obscure any effect. Presumably, he would be more careful afterwards. What can be said is that although his practice recovered, it was less than before 1956, and there were no more comments.

Even if he killed them, it was not necessarily murder. As Richard Gordon expresses it, "Bodkin Adams was a terrible doctor, but that is not a capital offence. Perhaps it should be?"

The act of 'Murder' occurs only when the perpetrator acted with the intention of killing the victim or inflicting grievous bodily harm. If there was intent to kill, it is no excuse to say death would have occurred anyway; the law regards any intended acceleration of death as homicide. On the other hand, if a doctor inadvertently kills a patient in the course of treating symptoms that is not murder.[1]

Where the accused has caused death without such intention, the killing may be treated as 'Manslaughter', a less serious offence, but to obtain a manslaughter verdict against a doctor he would have to commit a gross negligence which caused a patient's death.[2] If a surgeon forgot to do something in the course of an operation, or did something that he should not have done, such actions may lead to a charge of negligence, but not manslaughter. It would have to be that the surgeon was, say, so drunk that the patient's life was sacrificed.[3] Whether any particular act is sufficiently heinous is for a jury to decide, but the implication is that the breach of duty has to be an offence against society.[4]

Other factors may influence the verdict. In 1995 a junior doctor injected penicillin into a patient's brain instead of into a vein. He was acquitted because the mistake came about partly through overwork and lack of resources.

The Law next asks, was death due to negligence? The court bears in mind that a doctor will not be negligent if what was done would be thought proper by a responsible body of medical opinion.[5] The final question is to decide whether the negligence is gross enough to justify a criminal sanction?[6, 7]

Doctor Adams, however, was charged with murder.

Gordon Clark may have the answer. Yes, Dr Adams killed patients, but if his aim was to help the symptoms and the patient happened to die it wasn't murder.

Mrs Jessie Leybourne, ex-nurse at St Mary's Hospital: "He was a rogue, but I don't think he went out to murder patients. His patients were the sort who were elderly and he cultivated them." Lord Devlin was another who thought Dr Adams a rogue, but was not certain that he was a murderer. 'He may well have blurred the distinction between helping symptoms and helping to die.' Could it be that certain of his elderly patients were attracted to his practice for that reason?

A GP: "I think he killed patients, but not intentionally. He started terminal care too soon. As Sir Max Rosenheim put it, 'Don't let the patient die twice'." Presumably, in certain conditions there is a moment to increase the drugs to ease the patient's symptoms, whatever the result. Perhaps he was impatient.

Pharmacist Tom Searle: "He used morphia and heroin more than other doctors of the day, and some of his patients might have become dependent upon it. I am also in no doubt that he 'eased the passing' of some of his patients, although you have to say they were very elderly and ill, and here you are in very muddy waters". He adds, "There was a lot of suspicion, but impossible to prove."

The assumption is that it is hardly feasible to lay down guidelines to cover every situation. Each patient is a law unto himself.

The BNF states that opioids (e.g. morphia) 'may cause dependence and tolerance, but this is no deterrent in the control of pain in terminal illness'. Dr Adams was free in his use of such drugs for all conditions. A retired nurse said that he prescribed pethidine [an opioid pain-killer] for young women with period pains.

Margaret Kinman, whose parents knew him. "I have little doubt that he killed his ladies for the money, he wanted to be secure."

Mrs Babs Morris: "He helped his patients as and when they wanted."

Lily Corbett and other members of the Eastbourne Ulster Society say he often came to their meetings. "He was always most polite and a real gentleman, if anything he was perhaps naïve."

Dr Adams was naïve. He was the sort who believed that insurance salesmen sold policies to help him. How otherwise would he have telephoned the coroner, waking him up early on a Sunday morning, to ask for a post-mortem before the patient was dead? Or proclaim to Supt Hannam, "Don't hurry. Please be thorough".

Not the doctor if you were ill, but just the mentor if you were feeling low.

Pharmacist Michael Clark: "I think he was foolishly greedy, in many respects naïve, but not a murderer. I feel sure that he was a Faith Healer to a suitably receptive neurotic patient who was imagining her maladies." Others have described him as the alternative therapist of the day.

Nurse Doris Cruttenden: "I don't think he was guilty of all the things they said. There were a lot of elderly people who were not given the same attention as today; he was kind to them and he talked to them. So often isolation worsens conditions such as Alzheimer's. He did his best. I doubt if there was any coercion."

Richard Gordon was convinced of his innocence. "He was lazy, greedy and a bad doctor, but no murderer. The trial evidence states that Mrs Morrell was coughing and breathing rapidly before she died, those aren't the symptoms of morphine poisoning." By lazy it is assumed he meant the Doctor did not keep notes or up-date his medical knowledge, for all accept that Dr Adams worked long hours.

Mrs V Cooper: "He was always ready to stop and talk, both before and after the trial. I wrote to him when he was in prison, sympathising with him, and had a reply. We certainly didn't believe all that was said of him. He always said there was no need for patients to suffer, and I'm sure other doctors believe the same." Yet another example of a patient understanding that he helped dying patients.

Mr DW Lander worked at the main Terminus Road branch of the Midland Bank from 1950. "One of my first customers was Dr Adams, a miserable looking man who wanted to cash two privately crossed cheques for £50 and £60. I explained that this was against the rules, the idea of a crossed cheque was to stop it being cashed by a third party, whereupon he got difficult, so I referred to the manager. To my embarrassment he said, 'That's all right, we do it for Dr Adams'.

"If I had been on the jury at his trial I would have found him guilty. I would not have him making a house call to any of my family. He must have been a Jekyll and Hyde to change from an awkward person at the counter to one with a bedside manner capable of obtaining cheques and being included in women's wills."

Mr Lander makes a point about the Doctor's many sides. There is no doubt he could be brusque and cussed, and he could be kind and caring, and with those he knew well he displayed a lighter touch. Just like all of us. After the trial, naturally, he was more uncertain and withdrawn. His housekeeper said he would keep his head down in the street to avoid people.

Mr Charles Aldous, ex-Mayor, knew Dr Adams from 1964. "In my opinion Dr Adams suffered a terrible injustice, and was scarred by it. He was a charming, quiet gentleman as you could see from the way his patients went back to him after he was restored to the Register". It could be argued that Mr Aldous was of a similar religious background and he would understand him; it could be added that he did not know him before the trial.

Paul Harris says, "Subsequent to the trial I felt that here was a man who had convinced himself of two areas in which he could do no wrong. First that by advancing the death of terminally-ill patients, he was performing a humane service, and second that payment for this service by goods in kind rather than cash, when he was not short of the latter, was more acceptable, whether during the patient's lifetime or as a bequest.

"He felt there was nothing wrong in receiving gifts, which the patient could well afford, especially if they related to his interests in cars, shooting and fishing, when it was in return for what he considered was, 'Doing them a kindness'."

Mrs Barbara Selby: "I've never been quite sure in my mind just how guilty he was. It was well known that his ladies adored him. If they had no friends or relations living, it would be natural for him to be left money in gratitude for his concern and attention; he was the only one in their lives who they felt cared."

An elderly woman declared, "If a professional man would chat with me about events and happenings in the world for two afternoons a week, I'd leave him £1000 in my will tomorrow. And people want to talk about their minor ailments".

Michael Clark: "My feeling about JBA is that in one respect he was a Robin Hood. He was undoubtedly kind to poor people. In one instance, I know from the patient, the washing up had not been done in the house and JBA did it."

Mrs Hutchison said that, "The Doc never mentioned the trial until we visited him in hospital a few days before he died when he was rambling on about it and saying that he was not guilty of the charge. Knowing the kind of man he was, I know for certain that was the truth."

Mrs HJ Wells (née de Pinto) ex-Matron of the Princess Alice Hospital: "Of course, he was never a murderer, but a friendly man who acted in a naïve way".

Dr Basil Barkworth, junior partner: "John Adams was a fool and a greedy fool, but never a murderer. He made mistakes and he paid for them, but he was incapable of murdering anyone".

A correspondent who worked in one of the local pharmacies: "At no time did I consider Bodkin guilty of murder. Having had a visit from Scotland Yard at home it amazed me how set they were on proving something."

Michael Clark was also concerned. "The police over confidence worried me. Whilst in my opinion Dr Adams' lesser offences were deserving of him being struck off the Medical Register, I was concerned that he would be sent to the gallows when he was innocent of murder. I went to see the Chief Constable to say I was worried about Bodkin's fate because I did not want to say anything when hanging was the penalty for murder. He said if I was straight, they would be straight and if I gave factual evidence I could not be responsible for the outcome."

A senior police officer, now retired: "Many police and solicitors in the town believed he was guilty".

Long after the trial an Eastbourne resident found a wallet. There was no address inside, but he did notice a number of prescriptions signed by Dr Adams. He took it to the Police Station where he pointed out the prescriptions to a policeman, who commented, "Sadly, I don't think we'll be able to get him on these".

Whether jokingly or not, most of the 1950s Eastbourne police considered the Doctor was up to no good, although Inspector Pugh was one of the few senior officers who felt certain that he was guilty of murder.

A senior Eastbourne doctor: "In my estimation he was a careless Christian, justifying in his mind the way he conducted his practice, for instance he felt it was wrong that private patients were denied NHS prescriptions. He continued to pray in the depths of his suffering, and believed that his prayers led to the unfolding of evidence in his favour. He claimed that his eventual restitution appeared in the words of *Psalm 37:24 Though he fall he shall not be utterly cast down: for the Lord upholdeth him with his hand'*."

Percy Hoskins wrote, "Dr Adams was avaricious, but not a murderer. If he'd kept them alive he would have made more from their fees. Most left only a few hundred pounds, the nurses got more in the Morrell case."

Barry StJ Nevill concludes, "Looking back, it seems that he relieved the pain and suffering of patients who had, for whatever reason, lost the will to live. One wonders whether there would have been any case had not the women in question left him legacies which annoyed the families."

Apart from the many views, there are outstanding questions. Was the Morrell case mishandled? Was the wrong case selected? If so, which one should have been chosen? Would there have been a better chance of a conviction in the Hullett case?

As to the conduct of the Morrell case, a correspondent writes, "The trial at the Old Bailey was ineptly handled. Some considered Bodkin Adams was a greater mass-murderer than Haigh or Christie combined. He was an affable man with an apparently pleasing personality, and incidentally, he was a good shot."

A London solicitor: "For the Bodkin Adams' trial Reggie Manningham-Buller was incompetent, he should have asked questions which could only be answered by Bodkin Adams in the witness box".

Lord Devlin's belief was that 'Reggie' never grasped the possibility that Dr Adams finished off Mrs Morrell with the last prescription of heroin, describing it as paraldehyde - the final injection. He suggests that Dr Adams' reason for calling it paraldehyde was to stop the nurse questioning the amount? Perhaps, he says, Adams and Hannam were at cross-purposes? It was true when the Doctor said he gave all the heroin; it was in the last dose which he called 'paraldehyde'.

From parts of Manningham-Buller's cross-questioning the possibility had crossed his mind, but he dismissed it. It is doubtful if Dr Adams would concoct such a scheme, for in 1950 no nurse would dream of questioning a senior doctor's treatment so the deceit would be superfluous. And if it were given with the aim of easing Mrs Morrell's "terrible agony", it would not be murder.

Even legally the prosecution could not have it all its own way. As Lord Devlin pointed out, the sentence, 'Poor soul she was in terrible agony, it was all used, I used them myself' could not be split into, 'she was in terrible agony', untrue, while, 'I used up all the drugs' was considered true. Again, if Dr Adams believed she was in agony it would not be murder.

Manningham-Buller was hardly the man to pick to save your neck. The defence choice of Geoffrey Lawrence gave it a massive advantage. He was a barrister who had court ability and yet no medical point escaped him.

A local businessman sums it up, "The defence lawyer was heading for the top of his profession and Manningham-Buller had a mixed reputation for competence, whilst I guess Roland Gwynne did his best to bend his ear."

At the least everyone in the prosecution team should have been sure of the dose of paraldehyde, but did the Attorney-General know himself? Rodney Hallworth has

Sgt Charlie Hewitt saying, "The hallmark of the prosecution case was no anticipation and a lack of attention to detail".

It has not been stressed that in 1948 Mrs Morrell presented Dr Adams with a therapeutic dilemma. She was on morphia, started in Cheshire; did he stop it with the risk of collapse, or continue it to help her to sleep, to relieve her arthritic pains, and 'buck her up', but at the risk of addiction? In fact he delayed for four days. Doctors have commented that while in the 1950s the morphine-type drugs were mostly prescribed in doses such as $^1/_6$gr (10mg) eight-hourly, it was accepted that more was needed for certain patients. Doses of 50gr a day have been mentioned, and Dr Adams prescribed 70-80gr a day for Mrs Morrell.

Was Mrs Morrell given all the drugs prescribed? Probably not, the prosecution merely had the lists of prescriptions, not the precise dose given to each patient – not required in 1950. Yet the Attorney-General doggedly quoted the lists, even though once the notebooks appeared, they were hardly valid. Mrs Morrell could, however, have tolerated even the prescribed doses if gradually built up.

In 1950 with only a requirement for the dispensing chemist to keep a Sale of Poisons' Register, a doctor could have saved up and hoarded morphine for an overdose, and if planned could still have a perfect "Poisons Book". Dr Adams did not keep any notes at all, even after 1953 when he should have kept a drug register, which he surely would have done if he had been planning murder.

Dr Barkworth points out, "If Dr Adams meant to murder, he would never have been caught without a Dangerous Drugs Register. It would be easy for him to balance a register, while accumulating drugs on the side. He wasn't stupid".

Manningham-Buller tried too hard for a murder conviction. It has to be said that, once the prosecution case was hand-bagged by the nurses' notebooks, murder would not be easy to prove without a body - an obvious handicap for a poisoning case - and facing a well-marshalled defence. The Crown did not adapt to the changes, Sir Reginald was heavy-handed in his attempts to introduce details of other patients, and he should have obtained the nursing notes from Cheshire.

Michael Clark: "The police were convinced they had JBA, and perhaps this led Hannam to slackness in not chasing up the treatment given in Cheshire."

Richard Gordon: "Lawrence's mastery (when you remember he was not a criminal barrister), and Manningham-Buller's ineptitude, convinced the jury."

The adversarial system, which does not lend itself to a proper evaluation of scientific evidence in court, did not help. Both parties should share the technical details with all relevant data and its interpretation agreed before the trial.

There was considerable public unease about the conduct of the case at the time, mainly politically inspired. In April 1957 Mr George Wigg, a Labour MP, asked the Attorney-General whether he would institute an independent inquiry into the prosecution's case against Dr Adams. This was refused.

What about the demands that another case should have been chosen for trial?

Michael Shera, son of Dr AG Shera: "My father was convinced that Dr Adams was a murderer and would say that the wrong victim was chosen for the trial."

Dr Shera's view was probably based on Dr Adams' cavalier approach to signing prescriptions. He did have a chance to insist that Mrs Hullett was sent into hospital when Dr Adams asked for his advice, and might have had more to say if the Hullett case had come to trial.

John Stevens, on the Town Hall staff for many years: "The opinion of many professional legal people in Eastbourne following Dr Adams' acquittal, was that the prosecution took the wrong case."

Dr Michael Emslie: "When the case blew up the envelope with the forged prescription was discovered and that was one of the original charges. There is no question in my mind that he killed patients. There are far too many stories of him opening bedroom windows on cold nights to help finish them off and of him saying, 'There is no charge, but you might like to think of me in your will'. I think the prosecution chose the wrong case and he was helped by people behind the scenes. How otherwise would they have lost the £1000 cheque?"

On the other hand Lord Devlin's opinion was definite, "I should put the Morrell case as the least weak. Certainly the Hullett cases were decidedly weaker."

If you ask 'Which other case should have been taken?' no consistent answer is forthcoming. The one usually mentioned is the Hulletts, with many arguing that it was a mistake not to adjourn the Hullett inquest until any criminal charges had been heard, but this is from hindsight.

The Hulletts murder charge was a case of 'system'. Jack died in the March after an injection, leaving £500 to Dr Adams; Bobbie died in the July after injections, leaving him £100 and a Rolls. As far as the police were concerned this sequence needed an explanation.

Jack had a heart attack and was given the correct treatment of the day (although our dear Doctor certified him as a stroke). For Bobbie, there is an abundance of evidence that she wanted to commit suicide, and no evidence exists to show he was there or assisted her, but did he help her to hoard the tablets? He said he doled them out each day, apart from the holiday - so he was wary of a suicide attempt.

Should he have considered the likelihood of barbiturate poisoning earlier? He said he couldn't believe it. Was he such a naïve doctor, or was it part of a tacit conspiracy between them? Did he genuinely not know about *Megimide*? Very likely. That his housekeeper says he took the *Lancet* and *Practitioner* journals to his dying day does not mean he read them. His state of mind can be gauged by his antics in telephoning the coroner. It is on the cards that one motive for him to continue labelling Mrs Morrell as a "stroke" (apart from self preservation) was to avoid her being stigmatised 'a suicide' – still a crime in 1956.

And then there was the will. What did he know of that? He had been asked to be an executor, but turned it down, and was said not to know the content.

All in all, even his vapid responses at an anxious time could attract sympathy, but not if he encouraged her to suicide in order to obtain the cheque and a Rolls.

The rushing through of the £1000 cheque is a bizarre episode. Peter Palmer: "Dr Adams was aware that when a bank is notified of a customer's death, all outstanding cheques are returned by them, marked "Drawer Deceased" and this was why he asked for special clearance of Mrs Hullett's £1000 cheque. For me it is very significant that he told the bank cashier, 'She's not long for this world', before Mrs Hullett had taken the fatal dose."

The 'not long for this world' is a Bodkinism. He was one of those who believed death to be a friend, a release from the strife of existence into a better life, and his conversation was sprinkled with 'Her time has come', and 'Poor dear, she'll soon be released from her suffering'. All implying how fortunate they were soon to be eased from their earthly trials. It might be that he was an instrument in that release, but that was not an essential component of the phrase.

Why did he rush through the £1000 cheque? A possible explanation is that while Dr Adams didn't kill Mrs Hullett he was in collusion with her about suicide. The cheque was unexpected and he naïvely thought that expediting it would prevent it being cleared suspiciously close to her death. Or was it just that she was obviously suicidal and he realised she could commit suicide at any moment, so if he delayed cashing the cheque he might lose it? Whatever, it was another example of being keen to get his money, but surely, if he had planned her murder he must have been extremely naïve to think his action would not attract attention.

In 1956 it was 'wilful murder' if a medical practitioner prescribed drugs for a patient with the purpose of attempting suicide, or if the doctor deliberately prevented resuscitation when a patient had taken a drug overdose. The actions would have to be extremely wilful, and if there were extenuating circumstances, the judge might direct the jury towards a verdict of manslaughter. Lord Devlin said he "could be convinced that Dr Adams had helped to end Mrs Hullett's life".

A manslaughter, or a negligence, charge against Dr Adams for the Hullett case stood a chance of success. Only a few months had gone by and if he had not gone into the witness box to answer whether he assisted her suicide, and what part the £1000 cheque played, the jury would draw their own conclusions. On the other hand, she undoubtedly committed suicide and the only material the prosecution had were the prescriptions and Dr Douthwaite; not much help in Mrs Morrell's case.

Another discussion point of Mrs Hullett's coma was Dr Adams' failure to send her to hospital. Dr Adams always said he had promised he would never send her into hospital, and we know that was her wish. As far as he was concerned that was a professional promise which you kept because the other half was no longer able to have her say. The other view is that he desisted from sending her into hospital to ensure she would not wake up. Nowadays, a doctor would always send such a patient to hospital, mainly because more can be done for overdoses, and partly because he would be crucified if the patient died at home. Mrs Hullett would have died wherever she was taken.

He knew her well, 'She was a dear friend', and collusion was possible, but blatantly against his beliefs and he appeared genuinely surprised at her coma. Quite likely he was naïve enough (yet again) to believe she wouldn't do it.

Devious though he might be, he was not crafty, and there must be disbelief that he was capable of all this scheming. In his book murder and suicide were sins, whatever the definition, and Dr Ian Brown says that his pharmacological knowledge was limited. It is more likely that he just did not know what to do.

This wasn't everyone's opinion. The Police had thought that any association with the Doctor was worth scrutiny, and the reputation persisted.

An Eastbourne Consultant says that, about 1980, Dr Adams asked him to visit one of his patients in *La Ronde Court*, Trinity Trees, just by *Kent Lodge*. "She'd had a breast cancer removed some years before, but wasn't seriously ill, a little bronchitis, hence I was surprised to hear that the patient died a week later. If it had been any other doctor I would have thought, 'How sad, she must have fallen downstairs or developed a sudden pneumonia – perhaps she had some cancer not showing on the X-ray', but with it being Bodkin I asked myself, 'Have I been set up as the fall guy here? Was I brought in just before she was knocked off to add a veneer of respectability to his practice?' which I'm sure wasn't the case at all."

That was the paradox with Bodkin Adams. If it is said he was assiduous in visiting, this is countered with, he was just ingratiating himself. If it is said he went to America in 1935 to learn at the Mayo Clinic, the retort is that he really went there to have special lenses made for his glasses to improve his shooting. And if it is said he was the first hospice doctor, who eased pain at the patient's request, others will say he was just making them addicted, to have them in lien to him.

John Seath, a pharmacist, asks, "I wondered whether his aim was to make patients dependent on him."

As he was impervious to any idea that he was guilty, being so labelled did not cross his mind. If anything, he thought that he brought serenity to terminal suffering. In law if he was easing the suffering he was innocent, if his purpose was to finish the life he was guilty. A narrow distinction as Lord Devlin puts it.

Dr Keith Simpson: "It is lawful to ease the process of dying. That is not euthanasia, but a humane service. Drugs which can help can also kill and there is no sharp definition between painless sleep and death".

In practice it is almost unknown for a jury to convict for a mercy killing. If, however, a doctor used his position for personal gain that would go against him.

Lord Devlin: "For some of his acts Dr Adams would win … sympathy, if not approval. If he sold death for money, he dishonoured a great profession".

The Police investigations into the deaths of Dr Adams' patients turned on six aspects, *Death Certificates, Cremations, Embalming, Statements from relatives or witnesses, EC 10s and Drug Prescriptions.*None were of much help.

Over half of the *death certificates* signed by Dr Adams stated that the cause of death was a stroke. Was this likely, or were they overdoses and the Doctor was just too lazy to think up alternative diagnoses for his poisonings? It is conceivable that most were strokes, it was a common cause of death in the elderly in the first half of the century when there was no effective treatment for high blood pressure, and the only exhumed body to be examined satisfactorily was confirmed as a stroke.

The Police noted that most of his patients had been *cremated*, halting any further examination, but the majority of Eastbourne's bodies were cremated. Where it could be checked, the patient had expressed a preference for cremation before Dr Adams came on the scene, hence there is no question of him exerting undue influence in order to remove the evidence. These checks did disclose that Dr Adams benefited when he wrote *Of this I do not know* on the cremation forms.

Another point the Police raised was that most of Dr Adams' patients had been *embalmed* by the undertakers; was this another ploy by the Doctor to interfere with any future post-mortem examination? We can be sure that Dr Adams had nothing to do with this practice. Over the years Eastbourne doctors complained to the undertakers about routine embalming – in case further investigation was required – but the reply was always that it was desirable if the deceased was to be viewed. With the funeral parlours in the centre of the town, it was also a hygienic measure.

The *statements* were nearly all by relatives or friends of the deceased who had been cut out of wills, or had some other grudge, and would not stand up in court. The nurses' statements also fell apart, but only because of the notebooks.

There was, however, another possible line. Was the Doctor angling not primarily for small bequests and gifts, but to have *drugs* left over to sell?

SIGNATURE OF PURCHASER (Or where a signed order is permitted by the Poisons Rules, the date of the signed order).	[illegible]
DATE OF SALE	31-1-51
NAME AND QUANTITY OF POISON SUPPLIED	Omnopon Oral tabs 50 | Sod. Phenobarbit. gr 1/4 100 tabs. | Barbitone et Amid 50 tabs.
PURCHASER'S NAME	Dr JB. Adams
PURCHASER'S ADDRESS	Kent Lodge. Eastbourne
PURCHASER'S BUSINESS, TRADE OR OCCUPATION	Medical Practitioner
PURPOSE FOR WHICH STATED TO BE REQUIRED	Professional
DATE OF CERTIFICATE (IF ANY)	
NAME AND ADDRESS OF PERSON GIVING CERTIFICATE (IF ANY)	
SIGNATURE OF PURCHASER (Or where a signed order is permitted by the Poisons Rules, the date of the	John B. Adams M.D.

A sample of Dr Adams' poison book prescriptions for Omnopon and barbiturates

The differences between the amounts prescribed and what the notebooks showed had been given, provoked some Police and lawyers to think that Dr Adams was selling drugs on the black market. As Lord Devlin writes, "I suspected – wrongly as I now know – that dealings on the black market might account for the [drug] discrepancies."

There is no evidence for these suspicions. If he had been trading, it is most unlikely that something would not have surfaced, even if it could not be proved.

Usually he didn't handle the drugs. He ordered from the pharmacist, the drugs were sent to the patient's house or the nursing home, where they were (un)locked in the drug cupboard. Dr Adams either prescribed for a nurse to administer the dose, or she prepared it for him. Only occasionally would he take a drug out of his bag, and then it appears to have been a vitamin injection or similar "pick-me-up". It was, of course, two of the nurses who lied about drug matters at the trial.

Dr Adams' records were sparse to say the least. He ordered drugs, probably in more than adequate quantities to ensure he never ran out, charged them up to the last patient he had seen or had on his mind, and administered them to the next patient he saw. He would have thought it most pedantic and wasteful to spend time and effort recording precisely which patient had $^{1}/4$gr morphia and how often, and who had $^{1}/6$gr, and who gave it. 'Is the patient pain-free?' was the only question.

In his book, doctors did not go round bothering with statistics, they went on rounds helping patients.

There was also no market for drugs. Until the 1980s Eastbourne had no drug problem of note, and in 1956 you would have been lucky to find half-a-dozen registered addicts in the town.

Doctors, in general, were horrified at the prospect of inducing addiction. Patients were grudgingly prescribed morphine $^{1}/6$gr [10mg] administered eight hourly, on occasions even when in pain and with not long to live. This was a fine way to keep a tight check of stocks and to ensure no addiction, but if the patient's pain came back after four hours he or she had to suffer another four hours of pain.

Compared with the average doctor of 1950, Dr Adams did use large doses of morphine-like drugs, amounts which if given in one initial bolus were capable of killing. Patients with long-term discomfort, however, become tolerant of pain-relievers and to ease their symptoms completely they need many measures, which may include large doses of narcotics, administered whenever, or before, the pain recurs. Most hospices, including St Christopher's, Sydenham, used heroin.

A Guy's doctor records that in the mid-1950s he worked in Nuffield House, the private wing at Guy's Hospital. "I inherited a man in his sixties who had a cancer of the prostate which had spread to the spine and he was in great pain. Understandably, he was given heroin, pethidine, and morphine with the thought that his days were strictly numbered. Over the months he developed a tolerance to the drugs and the doctors found that the only way to give him some comfort was to give large doses of morphia. I conformed to the established routine and gave him regular injections of, as I recall, 2gr of morphia several times a day. These doses were, in terms of the usual doses those days, enormous, and yet he was so tolerant that any comfort was only temporary.

"Dr Keith Simpson appeared on the ward one day, and asked if I would agree to have the pharmacy book photographed with my signature showing that I was authorising the dispensing of large doses of morphia. I was a junior doctor and in those days you obeyed your senior's instruction, so I bowed and agreed. As I recall this was just after Douthwaite had said in court '2gr of morphia would kill'."

Similar tales of 50gr doses unfold at other hospitals. "Among our responses to the Bodkin trial details in the papers were guffaws when it was suggested that paraldehyde was a dangerous drug."

While there may be some merit in Dr Adams' drug regimes, he was nonchalant in his approach to drugs. He admitted it himself, "Yes, I was lax over the drugs register and cremation certificates, but so were most other doctors in 1956". There is something in this. After the case there was a crackdown on drug registers and at least a couple of Eastbourne doctors were found wanting.

In the 1950s this was not asking for trouble quite so much as it would be today; however, Bodkin not only used narcotic drugs in doses far more than was the custom at the time, but he freely boasted that he received many bequests. Surely a combination with the potential for disaster in any age?

The Bodkin Adams' case answered some questions, but the medical press highlighted other aspects. 'Many a patient has been kept under to save agony. Now a doctor will be looking over his shoulder for the *smiler*, somebody making notes to use against him later.' The result being that some doctors would be scared to give adequate pain relief. There will always be those who believe that life should be prolonged whatever its quality, and those who are not averse to reducing distress in death whatever the effect. Just as one patient is entitled to declare 'I do not want that to happen to me', so another patient can decide to be helped, and it is not for either patient to determine the other's treatment.

Most doctors do not wish to be involved with euthanasia, a recipe for losing the trust of patients, but a patient who believes that not enough is being done to ease their distress should feel free to ask their doctor for unbiased advice and assistance. Patients want a good night's sleep regardless, not the step of the executioner.

With an ageing population the situation will recur. *The Times* of 12 May 1999 reported that GP, Dr David Moor, was cleared of murdering a patient, to cheers in the court. "I don't believe in euthanasia," he said, "but I am prepared to give potentially fatal drugs to ease suffering." The trial lasted 18 days, and the jury was out 65 minutes. The patient, an 85-year-old man, was deaf, incontinent, had bowel cancer, and had suffered a stroke and a heart attack. Mr Justice Hooper announced, "Dr Moor was of excellent character, but was silly making comments to the press".

Dr Bodkin Adams was certainly unwise in his remarks, but did his 'little problem' start with his original partners believing that he didn't fit into Eastbourne? Not expecting him to get his MD, did they cocoon him away and confine him to unfashionable sectors (where he would be expected to start as the junior) such as anaesthetics, panel patients, and looking after the dying? He lived his religion, treated the patients equally, and steadily over the years he found friends among the patients, and his associates in sporting activities, until he was distancing himself from medical colleagues. Security and professional satisfaction followed when he found he could make more money than his colleagues.

In the *Daily Express* Dr Adams wrote that he made the choice. 'Being of a shy disposition and unable to give dinner parties, I built up my practice by being available rather than gaining introductions through a social life.' Whether by chance or design he did have many elderly patients, who needed comforting, wanted the minimum of invasive procedures, and after all that could be done had been done, wished to be eased through death. He would say he helped patients who were in distress to a better life. He would think, 'She's suffered enough, poor soul'. It is unlikely that he set out to break the law in pursuit of a higher imperative. That would mean he was a judge in his own cause, foreign for someone to whom religion was a companion to be consulted and satisfied and thanked every day.

We will never know if more could have been done, or whether anyone else could have done better. Doctors cannot bestow immortality.

With medical attendants of integrity, like Dr Moor, who are doing their professional best for the good of the patient, it is advisable not to enquire too intently, but there is always the danger that someone will abuse the trust.

Most people would support Dr Adams for easing the passing, silly though he was in talking about it, the sticking point was his interest in the money.

Dr Adams was not the first professional man to be interested in money, but he was seldom gracious where money was concerned. He had always wanted to be secure, partly his upbringing and partly his experience of life. He discovered that while his extra cash payments went on income tax, his wealthy patients avoided tax quite legally, and he was introduced to the benefits of bequests. They weren't keen to touch their capital while alive, but if the dear Doctor took part of their Estate otherwise earmarked for that horrid nephew in Yorkshire, so what? Well, it meant no tax for the Doctor.

Whatever the truth, but for the discovery of the nurses' notebooks, Dr Bodkin Adams' life story could have been 26 years shorter.

Percy Hoskins agrees, "Dr Adams put the nurses' files on a cabinet in a store. He nearly threw them away, before forgetting about them. It was a good job he did forget, they saved his life".

Dr Adams' loquacious version: "After the patient died her son sent me a parcel which I thought contained some small effects and I put it away at the back of the files in the old air-raid shelter, and was going to throw it away one or two times, but – and here was a sign that I was not forgotten – I didn't, and it fell behind. It contained the books of the doses given over the years, and when at the Old Bailey my counsel said to the nurses, 'And you know all the injections given?' and they said, 'You can take our word for it' he produced the books which showed I'd only given the same doses over three years and had not gone on to give any more".

Such a verbose style does make one wonder what would have happened if Manningham-Buller had got at him without the notebooks? And if Bodkin Adams had hanged, would he now be forgotten?

On the centenary of the Doctor's birth, perhaps we can say that while it is unlikely that Lord Devlin, or Lord Dilhorne, or Sir Geoffrey Lawrence will be remembered in 100 years' time, Mrs Morrell and the enigmatic Dr John Bodkin Adams will be staggering on?

So there you have the strange case of Dr Adams. Did he murder for legacies, or was he a maligned comforter of the lonely and dying?

What do you think?

What happened to the rest of the cast?

Mr Geoffrey Lawrence QC was the "hero" of the trial. Edward Fursdon comments, "A performance to put Marshall Hall in the shade". Albeit, in a different style; a dialectic approach and always with an awesome sense of responsibility, heightened in the Bodkin Adams case by the threat of the rope which hung over his client. John Cheesborough adds, "Geoffrey was probably the most intelligent man at the Bar and went on to be a Judge". He became world famous, and was knighted in 1963. He died in 1967 at the age of 64.

Sir Reginald Manningham-BullerQC MP. Attorney-General 1954-62. He was 52 at the time of the trial. Did Sir Reginald see the Bodkin Adams' murder prosecution as an open and shut case which would be another step along his road to political advancement? While the Bodkin Adams' result did not help his legal career, his political climb continued unchecked. He went on to become 1st Viscount Dilhorne of Greens Norton and Lord High Chancellor of England. He died in September 1980.

Supt **Hannam** left the CID in 1960 to act as a security adviser, and died a few months before the Doctor. Michael Clark's belief was that, "Hannam was a pompous person, but I found Charlie **Hewitt** a nice man. He came into the shop to say 'Hello' after the trial, and ended up as a Chief Superintendent." Michael Harding relates, "I remember Inspector **Pugh** exclaiming, 'I've got that bugger banged up for rights'. It was almost a crusade for him and a disaster when Dr Adams wasn't found guilty."

Supt Evans recalls that Inspector Pugh was a fit, healthy man who, when he came on duty, always vaulted over the desk counter at the Police Station, instead of using the desk flap. "Strangely, he died before Hannam who looked far more unhealthy." Inspector Pugh fell victim to Alzheimer's Disease and died, age 69, in a Sussex hospital on 10 March 1977.

Dr Arthur Douthwaite. If any of the protagonists is to be called the "villain" it must be Dr Douthwaite. As Percy Hoskins put it, "When he replied 'Yes' to Geoffrey Lawrence's suggestion that according to him the Cheshire doctors should be charged with murder too, he lost the Presidency of the Royal College of Physicians". Dr Peter Cook agrees, "Douthwaite was made to look foolish by Lawrence. He was an over-confident, over-dogmatic witness and his arrogance tripped him up. My recollection is that he was very much in line as the next PRCP but his reputation never recovered."

A doctor who was on the staff of Guy's Hospital at the time says, "Arthur Douthwaite's statements and actions in court were so out of character that I thought there must be an emotional drive motivating his campaign. Rumour had it that, like many in those times, he had been a general practitioner for a short while and he might have met 'another Bodkin Adams' and developed a fierce antipathy".

When the nurses' evidence was discredited he realised that something more was needed to nail Bodkin, and hastily and foolishly produced his witness box theory that Bodkin reduced the morphine tolerance so that a final sudden increase in the dose would kill the patient.

That he cared for his patients is shown in BMJ articles.[1,2] He was perhaps unlucky, for example, a few weeks before the devastating effects of thalidomide [*Distaval*] on the unborn child burst on the public, he wrote, "Not only is this preparation apparently free from untoward side-effects, but, astonishingly, it seems to be completely non-toxic both to animals and man." [3]

He was also extremely gracious. After Geoffrey Lawrence had effectively destroyed his reputation, Dr Douthwaite wrote to thank him for his 'unfailing courtesy'. He died on 24 September 1974.

Herbert Victor James. He never recovered from his stroke at the Old Bailey, and remained in the Esperance Nursing Home, Eastbourne, until his death on 17 November 1959. His son, Richard James adds, "My father did speak at the hospital to ask me whether the Crown had entered a *nolle prosequi* for the other indictment. I recall Bodkin visited my father in the Esperance".

David Saunders confirmed that Herbert James was a personal friend of Dr Adams as well as his solicitor. "He was not a young man, but did a lot of the spade work for the Bodkin Adams case."

Percy Hoskins (1904-1989) was the crime correspondent of Beaverbrook newspapers 1924-1986. He wrote, "My head would have been on the block if he'd been found guilty. Lord Beaverbrook, the proprietor of the newspaper, phoned and declared, 'Two men have been acquitted today'."

Patrick Devlin. Became a life peer in 1961. Was a Lord of Appeal, Chairman of the Press Council and a Judge of the Administrative Tribunal of the ILO. A man of high intelligence and wit, he was a Privy Councillor and High Steward of Cambridge University. He died on 9 August 1992.

He wrote, 28 years after the trial, the first full-length book that any British judge has ever written about a trial over which he presided. Written to explain his actions, it is of help in understanding the complicated issues, and notable for a devastating attack on Manningham-Buller.

Dr Adams' practice. His partners need not have worried, for the practice flourished without him ; only 50 or so patients left in the wake of the trial. Mr Laurence Snowball died in 1979 aged 74. Dr Vincent Harris, who naturally found the case a great strain and always said it took ten years off his life, managed to survive to 86 before his death in 1996. Dr Basil Barkworth, who retired in 1982, is the last surviving partner of the Bodkin Adams' practice.

1. Abrahams A, *The importance of communication* BMJ 1996; **312**: 1264.
2. Dixon WM, *Learning from the past* BMJ 1997; **314**: 1511.
3. *Drugs in the Treatment of Disease* Ed Clegg H p34 BMA London 1961.

Notes and References

Chapter 2

1. Plymouth Brethren, a Protestant sect started in 1830 with a Calvinistic approach and no ministry.
2. The Crusaders' Union ran Bible classes and holidays for schoolboys. In 1949 there were some 250 classes over the country attended by 11 000 members.
3. M&B 693 was a sulphonamide, forerunner of antibiotics. *Prontosil* was the first sulpha drug, 1935.

Chapter 4

1. Many antisera were prepared from horses. Patients allergic to horse proteins developed a rash ten days after the injection. Tetanus toxoid, introduced in the 1930s, was made in the laboratory, gave long-term protection, and obviated the need for a routine antiserum injection after an injury.
2. Sir Ivan Magill qualified at Belfast, 1913. A leading anaesthetist, he was in the team treating the soldiers requiring plastic surgery after the 1914-18 war. Introduced dry bobbin flowmeters (instead of Boyle's bubbles) in 1928, and was a proponent of rectal *Avertin* and paraldehyde from the same year. Introduced intravenous *Nembutal* in 1933. He was a strong advocate of professional examinations for anaesthetists and was involved in the inception of the DA in 1935 and the FFARCS in 1954.

Chapter 5

1. To 'Smoke' was the term used when a shot hit the centre of the clay and it disintegrated.
2. The international recommended name for phenobarbitone is now phenobarbital.

Chapter 6

1. One grain (gr) was an Imperial measurement of weight equivalent to about 65 milligrams (mg).
2. *Megimide* was usually delivered by injection of the 0.5% solution into an intravenous dextrous or saline infusion, hence it was more suitable for hospital administration. The dose was 30-40ml "for patients in a light coma, but doses up to 300ml have been used". Data Sheet Compendium 1974; 465. "Bemegride (BP 1968) *Megimide* ... In the treatment of barbiturate poisoning bemegride has been given intravenously in doses of 50mg repeated at intervals of 3 to 10 minutes up to a total dose of 1g." *Martindales Extra Pharmacopoeia.* Dr IM Brown states that it was first used in Eastbourne in 1955.
3. The pons, part of the brain. Pontine haemorrhage is said to be associated with a raised temperature.

Chapter 9

1. *Sedormid* was an hypnotic similar to barbiturates.
2. In 1956 many doctors used cc as a unit of volume. For practical purposes 1cc equals 1ml.
3. Paraldehyde was a safe drug, with a usual dose of 5-10 ml; its main disadvantage was that it had a horrible smell and the patient smelt it for hours afterwards. Heroin was about twice as effective as morphine, dose for dose, and said to cause less nausea, but the main advantage was that it could be given in a smaller volume – a boon for thin patients. *Omnopon* consisted of opium alkaloids and could be given by mouth. Long-acting barbiturates often give a hangover and are misguided in insomnia.
4. Persistent pain after stroke is commoner than most doctors think. *Jl Neurology Neurosurgery & Psychiatry* 1996; **61:** 560-64.

Chapter 11

1. The family mourners were Dr Louise Garfitt-Clowes and Mrs Daphne Henry, second cousins. Among the mourners were Percy Hoskins, Roy Bedford, Allen Howarth, Bernard Morley (Eastbourne 41 Club), Peter Page (director Clay Pigeon Shooting Association), Roy Greatorex & Mrs Connie Greatorex, Ray Ward (Association chairman), Mrs Betty Ward and Mrs Betty Elms (members), George Digweed and Chris Barnes (East Sussex Gun Club and Wildfowlers' Association), Derek Penfold and Mike Hearn (Brighton Group Institution of Advanced Motorists). Others were Mr H Kirkland (Ulster Society), Mr EG Turner (chairman Eastbourne YMCA), Mr F Mepham (Sussex County Youth FA), Mr Charles Short (Marine Hall), Mrs Jacklyn Agar (Hospital League of Friends),

Mr Kenneth Stevenson (London branch of the Coleraine School OB Association), Mr & Mrs John Cheesborough (represented Mr Harry Price, his accountant), Mrs Peter Deane (rep. the Robinson and Simmons families). Mrs Gillian Warner, and Mr Edward Clarke (rep. Mrs Ashworth).

Chapter 14

1. R v Adams [1957] Crim LR 365. Any acceleration of death is homicide, but if a doctor inadvertently shortens life when treating symptoms that is not murder.
2. R v Williamson [1807] 3 C & P 635. Male midwife did not realise he had ruptured uterus, acquitted.
3. R v Doherty [1887] 16 Cox CC 306. Sets out some examples of negligence.
4. R v Bateman [1925] 19 Cr App R8. Uterus torn, jury convicted, verdict overturned on appeal.
5. Bolam v Friern HMC [1957] 2 All ER 118.
6. R v Prentice and another [1993] 4 All ER 935. Two junior doctors injected drug into spine. Death due to combination of errors many beyond defendants' control. Convicted, but overturned on appeal.
7. R v Adomako [1994] 3 All ER 79. House of Lords considered scope of manslaughter.

Selected Bibliography

Bedford S, *The Best We Can Do* Black Cat/Collins 1958.
Bedford S, *The Trial of Dr Adams* Grove Press New York 1958.
The Bookseller 22/6/1985; 2556.
Briffett D, *Sussex Murders* Ensign Southampton 1990.
Brown Ian M, *A Doctor's Visits* Ashford Gosport 1987.
Claremont JVC, *A History of the Eastbourne Law Society* Eastbourne 1998.
Devlin P *Easing the Passing* Bodley Head London 1985.
Eastbourne Hospitals Management Committee, Annual Reports.
Eastbourne Medical Gazette 1986; **3**: 106-9. 1992; **3**: 134-5.
Finch J, *Pulse* 20/2/1982: 19.
Fovargue HW, *Municipal Eastbourne* 1933.
Furneaux R, *Famous Criminal Cases IV* Wingate London 1957.
Gordon Richard, *Where there's a will. The Good Doctor Bodkin Adams* Radio Times 11-17 /10/1986 p4-5.
Gray TC, *JMDU* Summer 1985: 11.
Hallworth R, Williams M, *Where there's a Will* Capstan Jersey 1983.
Hoskins P, *Two Men were Acquitted* Seeker & Warburg London 1984.
Real-Life Crimes 1994, 13, 288-91.
Simpson K, *Forty Years of Murder* Harrap London 1978.
Surtees John, *Barracks workhouse and hospital St Mary's Eastbourne 1794-1990* ELHS 1992.
Surtees John, *The Princess Alice and other Eastbourne hospitals* ELHS 1994.
True Detective April 1984.
Unsolved 1984, 1; 13: 249-68.
Unsolved Murders & Mysteries J Canning Ed. Michael O'Hara London 1987.

Abbreviations used

BAO Bachelor of the Art of Obstetrics
BMA(J) British Medical Association (Journal)
BNF British National Formulary
DA Diploma in Anaesthetics
DL Deputy Lieutenant (of the county)
DPH Diploma in Public Health
EC10 a GP prescription form
EMS Emergency (wartime) Medical Scheme
ENT Ear, Nose & Throat
FFARCS Fellow Faculty of Anaesthetists RCS
FRCP Fellow of the Royal College of Physicians
FRCS Fellow of the Royal College of Surgeons
GMC General Medical Council
GP general practitioner
IAM Institution of Advanced Motorists
ILO International Labour Organisation
MB Bachelor of Medicine
MD Doctor of Medicine
MDU Medical Defence Union
NHS National Health Service
PA Princess Alice Memorial Hospital
RPS Royal Pharmaceutical Society
TA Territorial Association
WRNS Women's Royal Naval Service
YMCA/YWCA Young Men's/Women's Christian Association

INDEX